LIVERPOOL DOCKS
THROUGH TIME

Ian Collard

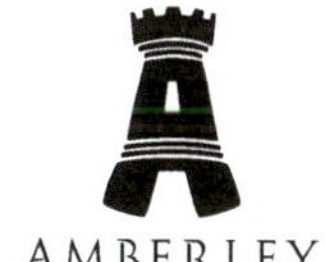

AMBERLEY

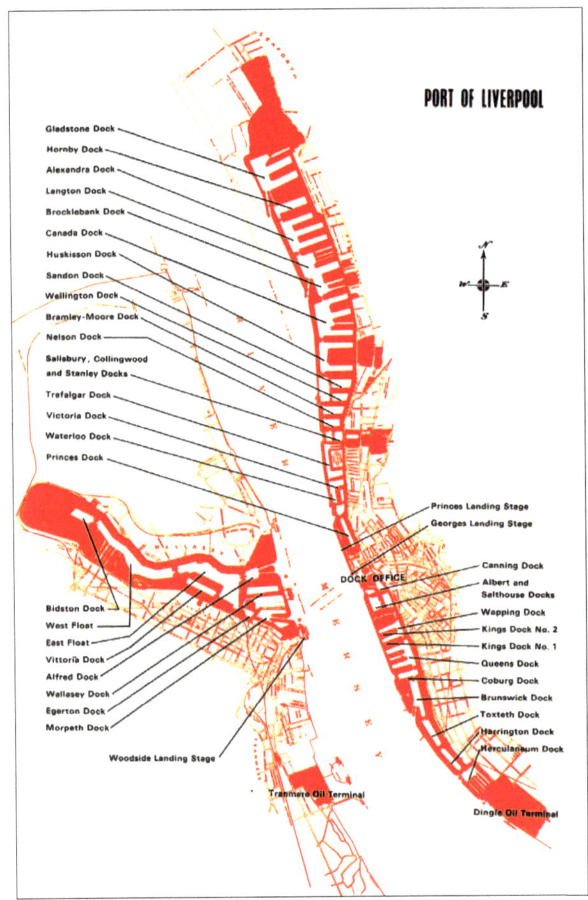

A. Map of the Mersey docks system.

First published 2012

Amberley Publishing
The Hill, Stroud
Gloucestershire, GL5 4EP

www.amberley-books.com

Copyright © Ian Collard, 2011

The right of Ian Collard to be identified as the Author of this work has been asserted in accordance with the Copyrights, Designs and Patents Act 1988.

ISBN 978 1 4456 0414 5

British Library Cataloguing in Publication Data.
A catalogue record for this book is available from the British Library.

Typeset in 9.5pt on 12pt Celeste.
Typesetting by Amberley Publishing.
Printed in the UK.

Appointed GPSR EU Representative: Easy Access System Europe Oü, 16879218
Address: Mustamäe tee 50, 10621, Tallinn, Estonia
Contact Details: gpsr.requests@easproject.com, +358 40 500 3575

Introduction

The River Mersey is mentioned in a deed dated 1002, in the reign of Ethelred. The deeds later passed to Edward the Confessor and gave the district between the Mersey and the Ribble, including 'the borough of Leuerepul with all its liberties' to Ranulf de Blundeville, Earl of Chester. King John granted Liverpool borough status in 1207. Ranulf de Blundeville died in 1232 and the South Lancashire fief was passed to his brother-in-law, William de Ferrers, Earl of Derby, who constructed a castle in Liverpool following royal approval for the plan in 1235. Robert de Ferrers forfeited his lands for treason in 1266, and the king brought together the area between the Ribble and the Mersey with the Honour of Lancashire, which was given to his youngest son Edmund Crouchback, who was created the Earl of Lancaster.

By 1295 the town was returning members of Parliament as a borough and royal charters of confirmation were granted by Edward III in 1333, and by Richard II in 1382. A mayor was appointed in 1352 and the Bodleian map of Britain in 1355–66 described Liverpool as a small town in comparison with Chester. The port developed trade routes to Ireland and corn, iron, wine and other goods were shipped through Liverpool in the fourteenth century. However, in 1565 Liverpool had only twelve ships, with an aggregate of 223 tons, navigated by seventy-five men. Over twenty years later, in one quarter of 1586 sixteen vessels arrived at Liverpool from Ireland with cargoes of yarn and hides and seventeen ships sailed to Ireland with cutlery, soap, textiles and saddles.

However, near the end of the Tudor period a bitter rivalry developed between Chester and Liverpool, with Chester insisting that the port was a mere dependency and claiming the right to control its trade. The dispute was not settled until 1658, when the Surveyor General of Customs decided in favour of Liverpool. At the end of the seventeenth century the trade between Britain and America began to expand. West Indian sugar and Virginia tobacco were imported and Lancashire textiles were loaded onto ships at the port bound for countries around the globe. Coalfields were being developed across Lancashire, and the coal was exported from Liverpool. Sugar refineries, salt and glass works, metal crafts and potteries were established in the town and Cheshire salt was exported through the port.

Trade with the British colonies was increasing in this period and London merchants preferred to ship goods from America to Liverpool and then transport them by land to the south of England. Liverpool ship-owners also carried goods to Africa, slaves to the southern ports of

America and sugar, rum and tobacco back to Britain. However, the original harbour was a small creek, fed by a stream which was exposed to the winds and strong currents of the river. Local merchants were discussing enlarging the Pool inwards or building a canal along the line of Paradise Street. In 1708 a resolution was passed by the town council:

> Ordered, that Sir Thos. Johnson and Richard Norris Esq. the representatives of the corporation in Parliament, be desired and empowered to treat with, and agree for a person to come to the town and view the ground and plan of the intended dock.

In 1709, Thomas Steers began construction of the first wet dock to be built in the town and it was opened in 1715. Paradise Street and Whitechapel were built on the sections of the Pool that were drained following construction of the new dock. The road network was being improved in this period by the development of Turnpike Trusts. The roads from Liverpool to Preston and Birkenhead to Chester were improved at the end of the century, and a stagecoach service between London and Liverpool began in 1761. An Act of Parliament had been passed in 1720 for making the rivers Mersey and Irwell navigable from Liverpool to Manchester. Further acts were also passed to make the River Douglas navigable between the Ribble and Wigan in 1719, and the River Weaver between the Mersey and Northwich the following year. The Sankey Canal was used to bring coal to Liverpool from St Helens, and the Bridgewater Canal, Grand Trunk Canal and the Leeds to Liverpool Canal were all completed.

The trade in slaves contributed to the prosperity of the town. Cargo was shipped from the Mersey to Guinea and slaves were taken to the West Indies, where they were sold, and the ships returned to Britain with sugar, molasses, rum and cotton. In 1750, fifteen ships were involved in this trade and by 1770 there were over one hundred. The last British ship involved in this trade left Liverpool in 1807, shortly before it was abolished.

As the trade through the port was gradually increasing, the first wet dock proved insufficient and a resolution was passed in 1737, stating that it was necessary to build a new dock and basin and this dock, to the south of the original, was opened in 1753. It was named South Dock, becoming Salthouse Dock in 1784, and further development took place when George's Dock was completed in 1771. Dock trustees were appointed by the Town Council to control, and be responsible for, lighthouses and dues levied on all vessels and cargo passing through the port. The Liverpool & Manchester Railway was founded in 1823 to transport goods between the port of Liverpool and Manchester. Thirty-five miles of track were opened in 1830 to enable imported raw materials to be carried from Liverpool and manufactured goods to be sent to the port by rail and exported by sea.

At the beginning of the nineteenth century trade with the United States was increasing and the American Chamber of Commerce was founded in Liverpool in 1805. Commercial traffic had increased dramatically during the American War of Independence and King's, Queen's, Prince's and Coburg docks were built. A new Custom House was completed in 1839 and Brunswick Dock was opened in 1832 for the timber trade. Waterloo, Clarence and Victoria docks were built for the coastal trade and the Albert Dock and warehouses were opened in 1846 by Prince Albert.

It was at this time that the Corporation faced competition from the Harrington Dock Company and a group led by Sir John Tobin and William Laird in Birkenhead. The Birkenhead Docks Company was formed in 1847 and Egerton and Morpeth docks were opened. However, the Dock Board took over the Harrington Dock Company in 1843 at a cost of £253,000 and Liverpool Corporation purchased the Birkenhead Dock Company in 1855. The Great Float was completed in 1866 and new entrances were built at Alfred Dock, Birkenhead, and were opened by His Royal Highness the Duke of Edinburgh on 21 June that year. The Vittoria Dock was built at Birkenhead at the beginning of the twentieth century and graving docks were provided at the West Float. Bidston Dock was completed in 1933.

Merchants using the port began to get dissatisfied as they felt that the dues which they paid were being used to improve the town and were not being reinvested on improving facilities in the port. A Royal Commission was appointed in 1853 and it recommended that a new body be formed to take over the management of the docks. A Bill was introduced in 1857 which created the Mersey Docks & Harbour Board, which would be responsible for all the port accommodation and controlled by twenty-eight trustees. The first work it undertook was to build Canning Dock for the timber trade and to construct the Herculaneum Graving Docks. In 1873, an Act of Parliament was passed to enable the Board to spend £4 million to construct Langton, Alexandra and Hornby docks. Another £3 million was spent on deep-water berths at Langton and Canada docks, and a new graving dock at Canada Dock. Three thousand workers were employed in the building of both schemes.

For the year ending 1 July 1874, the number of ships entering the Port of Liverpool was 19,186, with a total tonnage of 6,710,093 tons. The gross revenue derived from the ships was £380,588; the amount from goods was £562,910; and from other sources £233,731, including rents of property and revenue from dock traffic, dock line of railway, weighing materials and dock warehouses. The total gross revenue amounted to £1,177,230 and the surplus (after setting aside £80,000 for taxes) was £173,994. The bond debt, authorised by Parliament, on 1 July 1874 was £14,297,982.

The Liverpool Overhead Railway was opened in 1893. It was an elevated passenger transport system which operated initially between Herculaneum Dock and Alexandra Dock. It was known as the 'docker's umbrella' and was extended to Seaforth, Waterloo and Dingle in 1894. It ran along the Dock Road and gave passengers a view of vessels moored in the dock system.

A further Act of Parliament in 1906 allowed the Board to construct Gladstone Dock and Gladstone Graving Dock, which were opened by King George V on 11 July 1913. A cotton exchange had been in operation in Liverpool since 1808 and this was replaced by a new building in 1906. Liverpool was able to take advantage of its geographic position by providing the Lancashire cotton industry with a convenient way of importing their raw material and shipping the finished goods around the world.

The water had been run out of George's Dock in 1900 to enable the Mersey Docks & Harbour Company to build their new headquarters accommodation, which was designed by Sir Arnold Thornley and F. B. Hobbs; work commenced in 1904. The structure was built with a reinforced concrete frame, clad in Portland stone and designed in Edwardian Baroque style, with a large dome on top. The building was completed in 1907 at a cost of £350,000. The foundation for the

Royal Liver Building was laid on 11 May 1908 and it was officially opened by Lord Sheffield on 19 July 1911 as the headquarters of the Royal Liver Group. The Cunard Building is the third building constructed at the Pier Head and this was built between 1914 and 1917. It was designed by William Edward Willink and Philip Coldwell Thicknesse and is a mixture of Italian Renaissance and Greek Revival in style, inspired by the grand palaces of Renaissance Italy. It was built as the headquarters of the Cunard Line, which became Cunard White Star in 1934.

In 1925 the electrification of the dock system was completed and electrical energy was supplied at high pressure and distributed for power and lighting. Eighty-one miles of mains cable were laid and the Clarence Dock Power Station, which also generated power for parts of Lancashire and Cheshire, supplied the power.

Liverpool docks suffered extensive damage from German bombers during the Second World War. In 1941 the Pier Head offices of the Mersey Docks & Harbour Board took a direct hit. The Brocklebank Line cargo vessel *Malakand*, berthed in Huskisson Dock with a cargo of explosives, caught fire and exploded several days later. The ship and the dock were severely damaged in the action. The headquarters of the Battle of the Atlantic was based in Liverpool city centre and was responsible for coordinating action against the U-boat threat to convoys passing through the Western Approaches. During the war a total of ninety-one ships were sunk by bombing in the port, 1,285 convoys arrived, 75 million tons of cargo and approximately 4¾ million troops passed through.

At the end of the war a decision was made to embark on a massive rebuilding and reconstruction programme to enable the port to compete with others being rebuilt around Europe. The world's first port radar station for controlling the shipping traffic within a twenty-mile range of the port was opened in 1948. The Liverpool Overhead Railway was assessed by engineers, who found that it required substantial investment and rebuilding to continue and consequently it was closed down in 1956 and later demolished. In 1962 new berths and a new dock entrance were built at Langton Dock at a cost of £23 million. It was the largest major dock programme carried out in the country since the Second World War and included warehouses and the provision of 3,600 feet of berth space, 60,000 square yards of transit sheds, rail and road access and other ancillary services. A special iron ore facility was also opened at Bidston Dock, Birkenhead, for John Summers Steelworks. An oil jetty had been constructed at the south end of the Liverpool dock system and storage tanks were built to the rear of the site. The increase in this traffic after the war gave the Mersey Docks & Harbour Company the opportunity to build two large jetties at Tranmere, on the Birkenhead side of the river, and these were operational in 1960.

The changing pattern of trade and the development of cargo carried in containers gave the Mersey Docks Company the impetus to look at building a new dock to provide container and other cargo handling facilities. A feasibility report was commissioned in 1964 and a survey into the economic factors involved in providing a new dock was authorised by the company the following year. The plans were sanctioned by the Government in 1965 and the contract for the building of the new docks at Seaforth was awarded to John Howard & Company.

However, following a dramatic loss of trade and a series of labour disputes, the company was forced into liquidation and assistance to help the port to operate was obtained from the Government. The Mersey Docks & Harbour Company was formed in 1971, freeing the old

Board of many of its responsibilities and obligations. The Seaforth project enabled the new company to provide deeper docks and longer berths, supported by extensive land areas for larger ships and container services. It also provided specialised accommodation for packaged timber, bulk grain and installations for the mechanical discharge and handling of meat and other perishable cargoes.

Vessels entered the new Royal Seaforth Dock through a passage 1,070 feet long and 130 feet wide that was cut through the north wall of Gladstone Dock. The dock enabled the port to enter a new phase in its history, allowing the company to provide modern facilities for larger vessels and specialised container ships. The Grain Terminal was designed to accommodate vessels of up to 75,000 tons deadweight and incorporated provision for feeding grain directly to mills on adjacent sites. There is also an inlet dock capable of accepting barges and vessels up to 10,000 tons. While the new container berths were under construction, temporary facilities were provided at Gladstone Graving Dock, which was converted to a wet dock, and another at Hornby Dock for vessels trading to Spain, Italy and Portugal. A new fruit-handling berth was built at King's Dock for the Aznar Line, enabling perishable goods to be unloaded by conveyor belts directly to vehicles.

The Prince's and George's Landing Stages formed a continuous structure, 2,534 feet long by 80 feet wide, which was carried on approximately 200 pontoons. There were ten bridges connecting with the shore and a floating roadway which gave access to private and commercial vehicles. By 1972 the number of passenger liners using the Port of Liverpool had declined to two and the Mersey Docks Company planned to scrap the structure. However, this would have meant that there would be no berths for the local and Isle of Man ferry services. Discussions were held between the Merseyside Passenger Executive and the Isle of Man Government and a smaller stage was built on the site to accommodate the ferries and vessels of the Isle of Man Steam Packet.

New berths were built for the Belfast Steamship Company in West Prince's Dock, and the British & Irish Line in Trafalgar Dock, to provide facilities for the new roll on/roll off car and passenger ferries being introduced on the Belfast and Dublin services. With the opening of the new facilities at Seaforth, a decision was made to close the South Docks system in 1972–73 and many of the facilities provided at Birkenhead were transferred to Liverpool. By 1982 the amount of cargo passing through the port had fallen to 9.3 million tonnes because of a very bad industrial relations record, and also as a consequence of Britain's entry into the European Common Market. The Mersey Docks & Harbour Company embarked on a major reorganisation and implemented drastic changes in working practices. In 1984 there were signs of improvement to their financial situation and a profit of £800,000 was made on a turnover of 9 million tonnes of cargo. In 1999, containers shipped through the port rose to a new record of 515,000, compared to 487,000 the previous year, placing Liverpool in the top ten North European ports. PowerGen have developed a £40 million environmentally sensitive bulk terminal at Gladstone Dock that has the capacity to handle up to 6 million tonnes of coal a year, mainly for outward shipment by rail to Fiddlers Ferry power station.

The Mersey Docks & Harbour Company owns 2,000 acres (809 hectares) of dockland in Liverpool and Birkenhead. It is responsible for maintaining the channel and approaches to the Mersey. A £2 million development at Canada Dock provides a 65,000 cubic metre bulk terminal and store for animal feed. The Dock Road at Bootle was closed, creating an expansion to the Freeport to provide warehousing and industrial space. In 2000, the Port of Liverpool was ranked fourth among United Kingdom container ports serving the North Atlantic routes.

The Port of Liverpool handles more container trade with the United States of America than any other port in the country and now serves more than 100 none-European Union destinations, from China to India, Africa, Australia, the Middle East and South America. It is the United Kingdom's leading gateway for imports of grain and animal feed, for the export of recycled metal and the shipment of freight between Britain and Ireland. The Royal Seaforth Grain Terminal is the country's largest import facility, with a total capacity of 168,000 tonnes, and the Seaforth Container Terminal handles nearly 700,000 teus (20ft Equivalent Units) a year. Approval for a new river berth has been granted and this should be operational by 2014, allowing the new generation of post-Panamax large container vessels to be handled outside the dock system. This new facility will add another 600,000 teus of capacity to the port's existing container operations and will help to ensure that the Port of Liverpool remains one of Britain's major deep-sea ports for many years in the future.

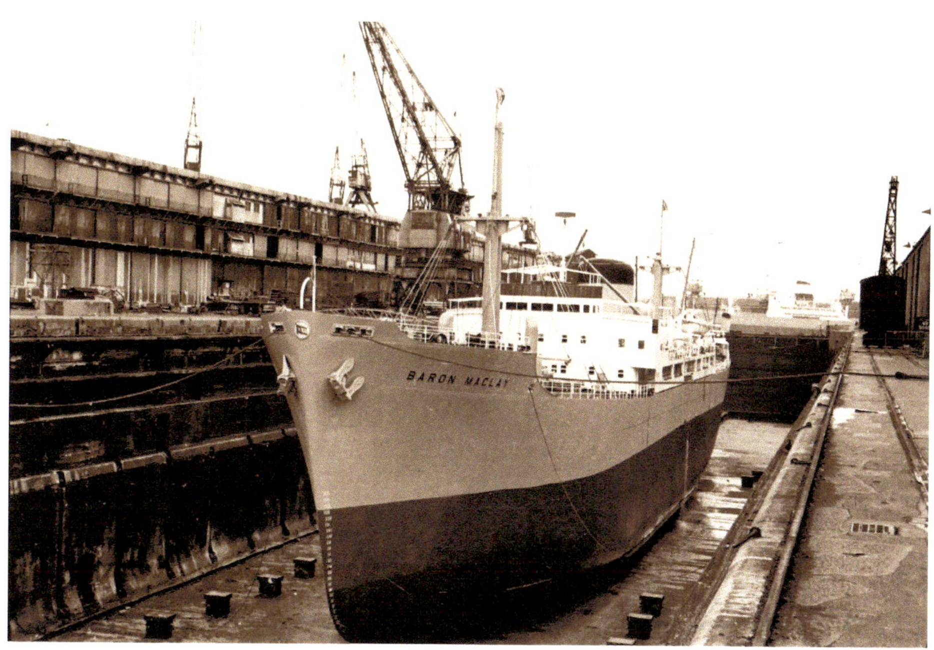

Above: Baron Line's *Baron Maclay* in Gladstone Graving Dock. She was built in 1959 and was sold to Liberian interests after nine years of service, becoming *Artagan* and *Sea Power* and *Skyrian Hope* in 1980. She sank in the Atlantic later that year. The graving dock was completed in 1913, before the rest of the Gladstone dock system, and was 1,050 feet long and 120 feet wide.

Below: The dry dock is now a wet dock, used by P&O for their service to Dublin; this photo shows the P&O berth in 2011.

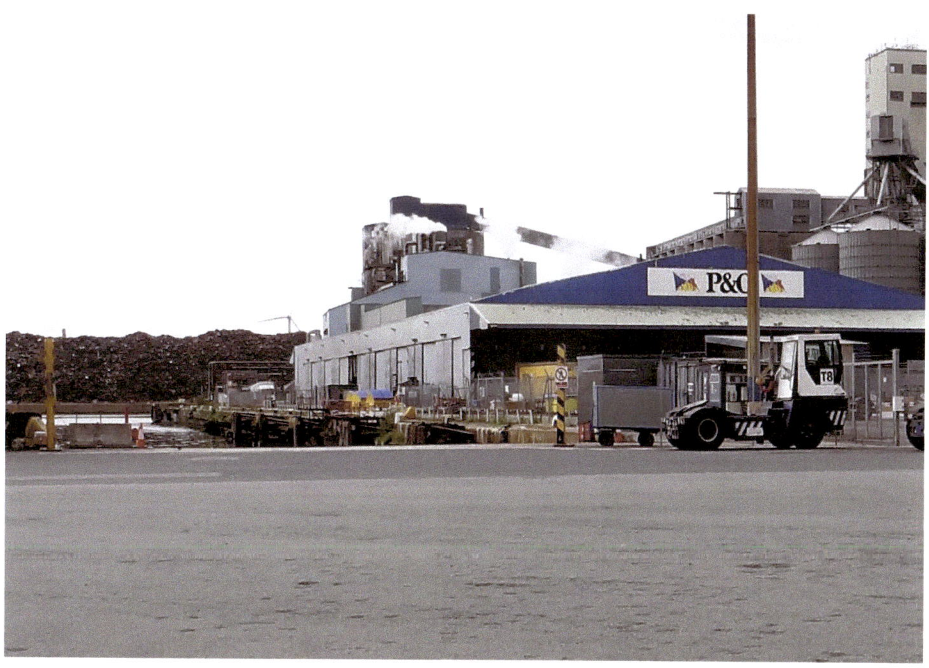

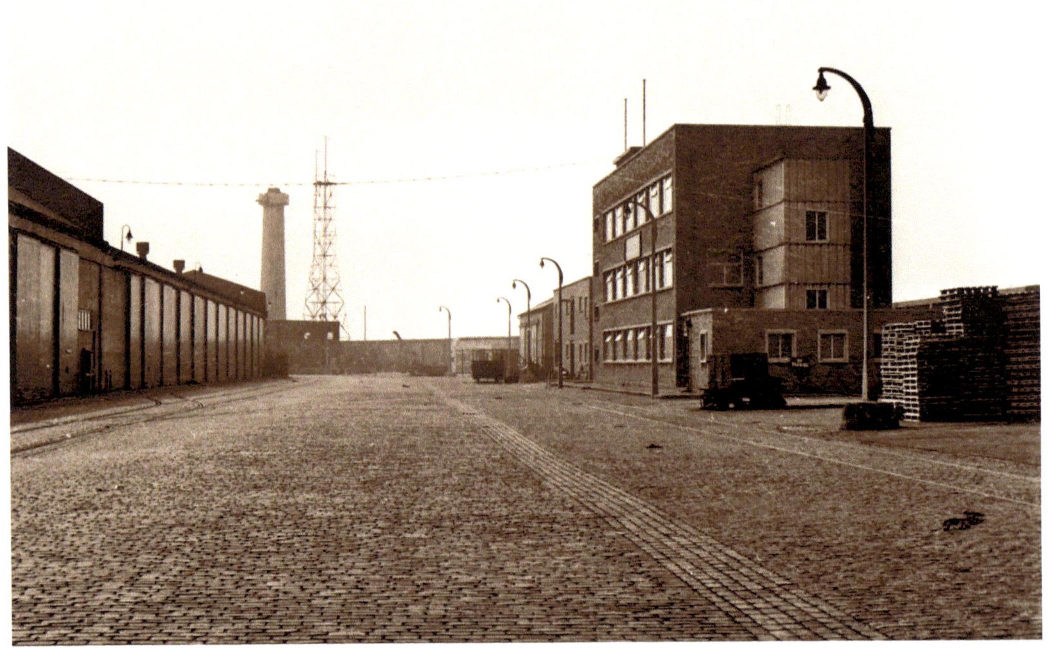

Warehouses and offices and radar tower on the north side of Gladstone Branch No. 2 in 1966 (*above*). The same view in 2011 shows Cargill's Seaforth Mill and refinery. The soyabean crush and refinery has been operating since 1986 and produces high-protein soyabean meal, soya hulls, crude soya oil and crude lecithin.

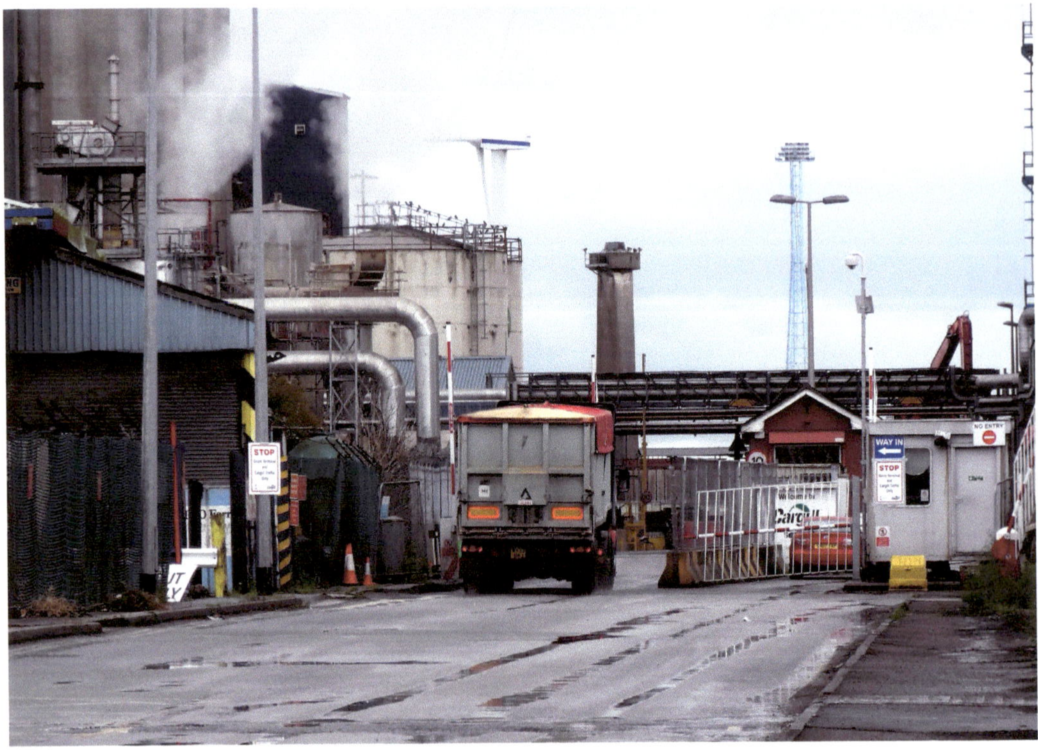

New Zealand and Federal Line
vessels loading at Gladstone
Branch No.2 berth. *Hinakura*
(*right*) was built in 1949 for the
New Zealand Shipping Company
and was given Federal Line
colours in 1966 and the P&O
colour scheme in 1973. She was
broken up the following year.
Sussex (*below*) sailed on her
maiden voyage from Glasgow to
Brisbane on 23 April 1949. She
was transferred to P&O ownership
in 1973, and was broken up at
Hong Kong in 1977.

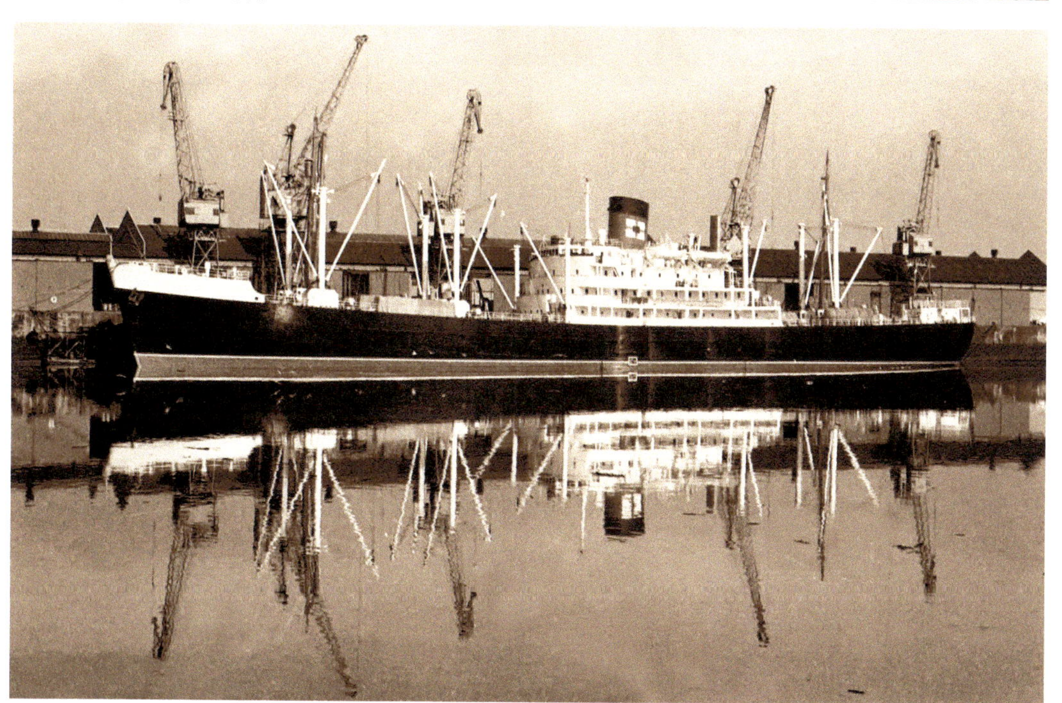

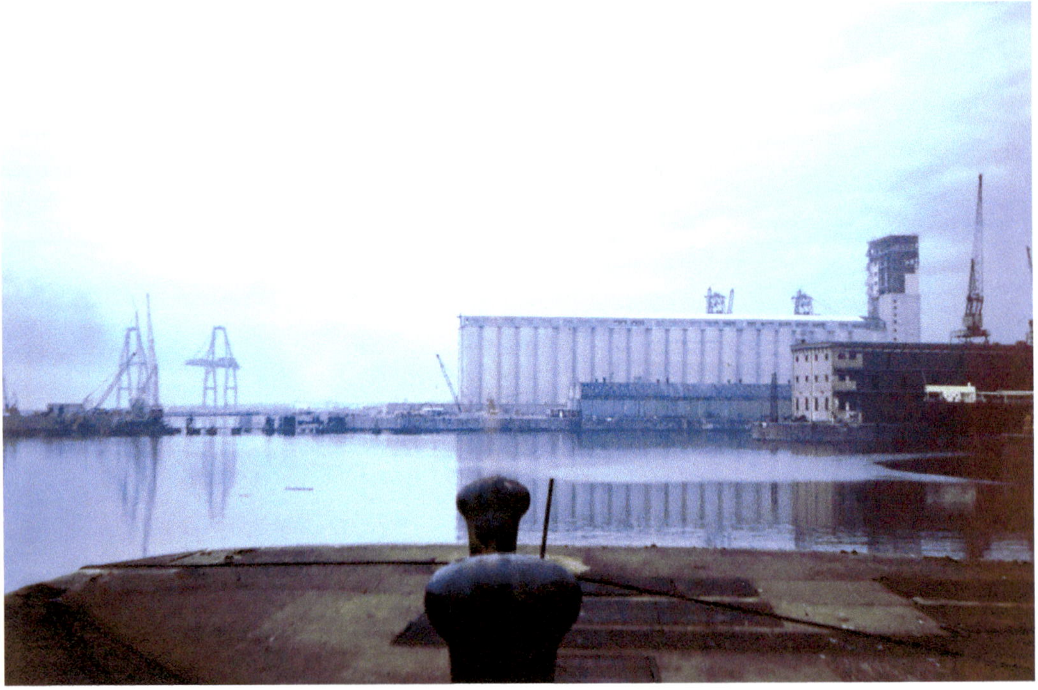

Above: Construction of the Royal Seaforth Dock in the 1970s.

Below: The Ramsey Steamship Company vessel *Ben Varrey* in Gladstone Dock in 2011.

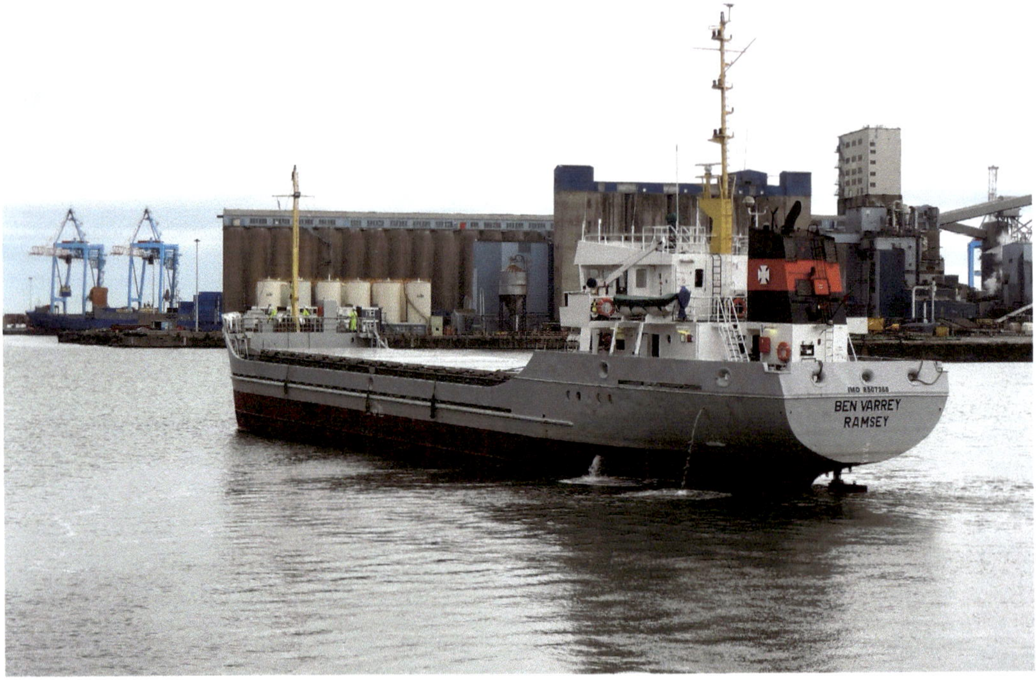

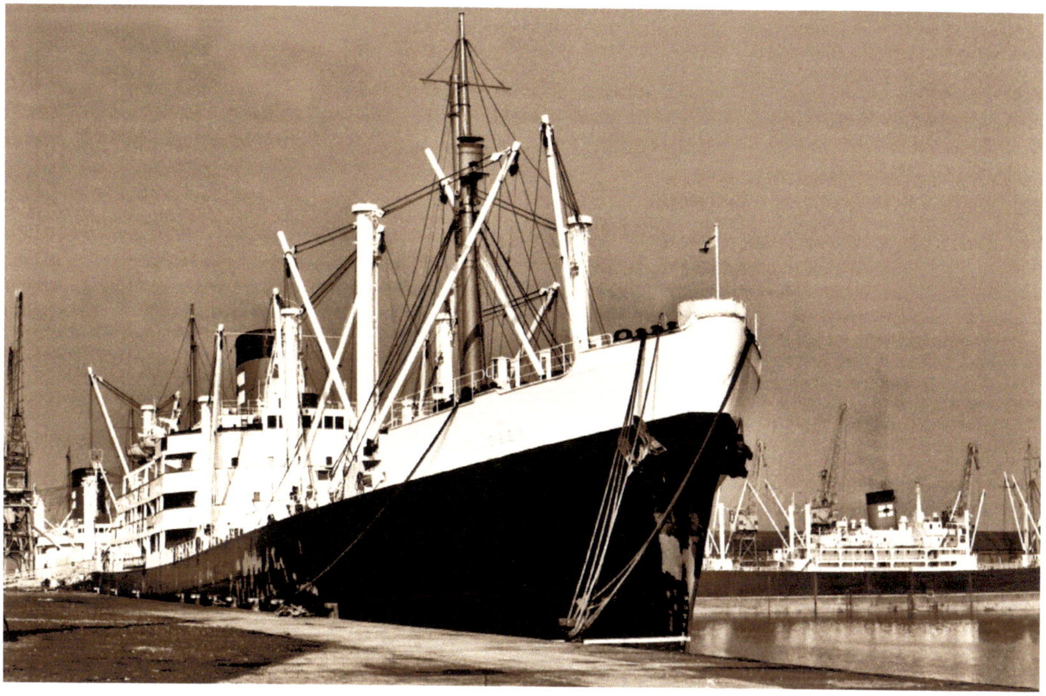

Above: Federal Line vessels loading in Gladstone Dock.

Below: The berth is now used to load scrap metal.

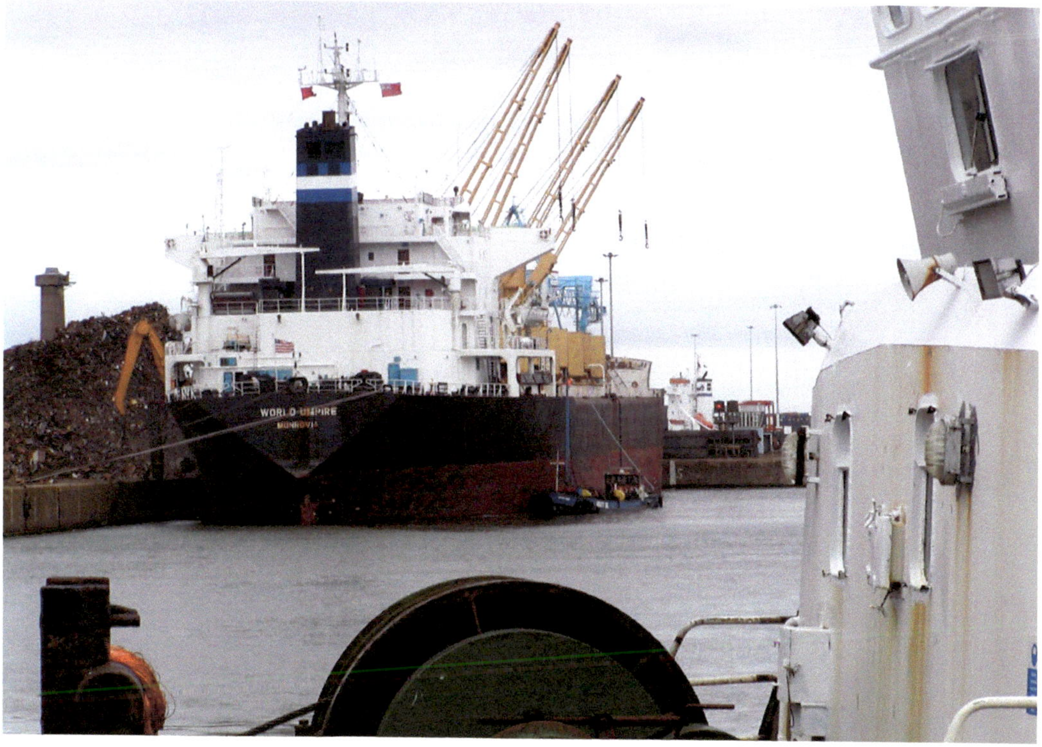

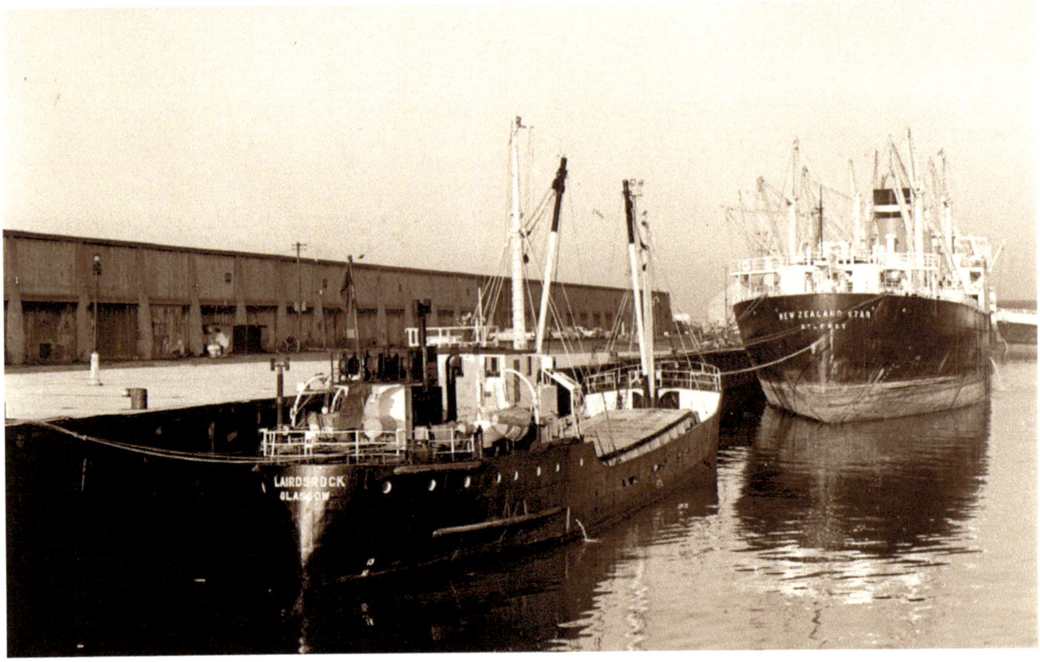

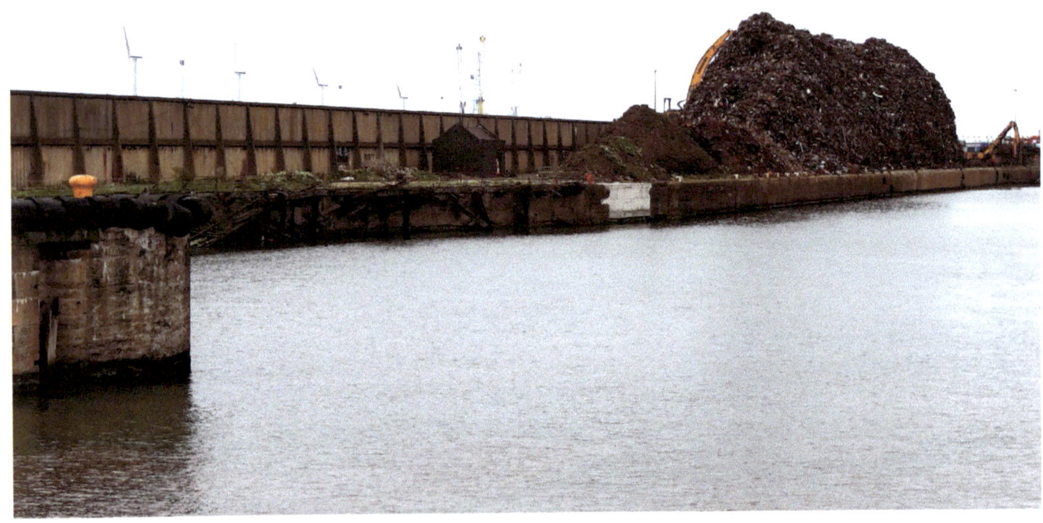

Above: The Burns & Laird coastal vessel *Lairdsrock* berthed aft of the Blue Star cargo vessel *New Zealand Star* in Gladstone Dock. *Lairdsrock* was built as *Glen* in 1935, becoming *Belgium Coast* in 1946, *Lairdsrock* in 1947 and *Giorgis* in 1966. She was renamed *Lefteris D* in 1979, *Tenaron S* the following year, and was stranded and sank off Karpathos island on 10 December 1980. *New Zealand Star* was built in 1934 by Harland & Wolff at Belfast and was transferred to the Lamport & Holt Line in 1950 and to the Booth Line in 1953, retaining the same name. She was broken up in Japan in 1967.

Below: A mountain of scrap metal awaits shipment on the quay at Gladstone Dock.

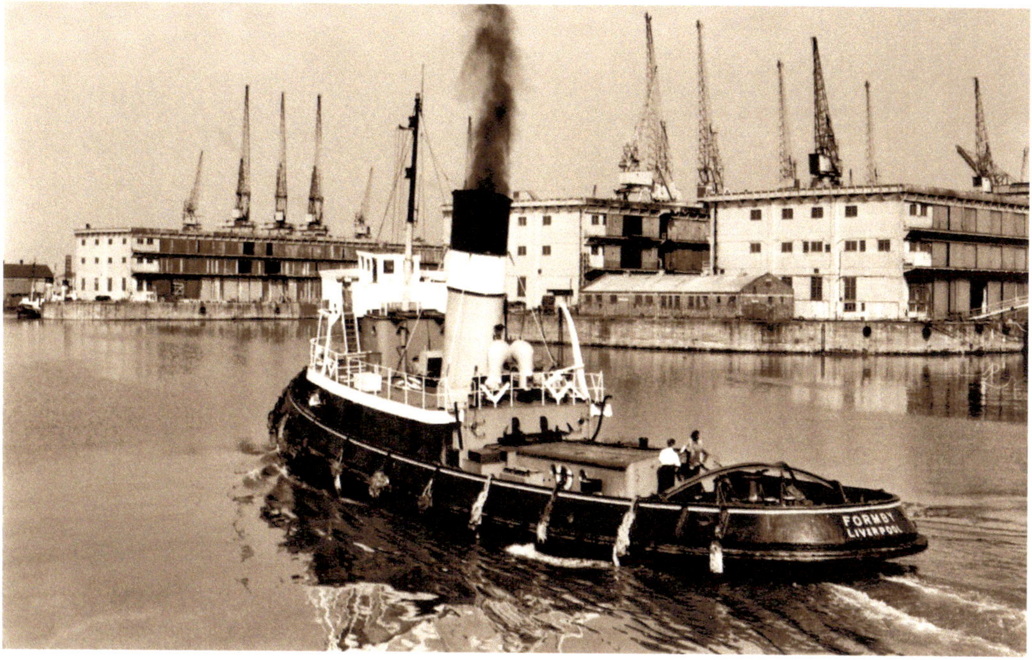

Above: The Alexandra Towing Company tug *Formby* was built in 1951 and is shown here in Gladstone Dock.

Below: The Smit tug *Smit Barbados* in Gladstone Dock.

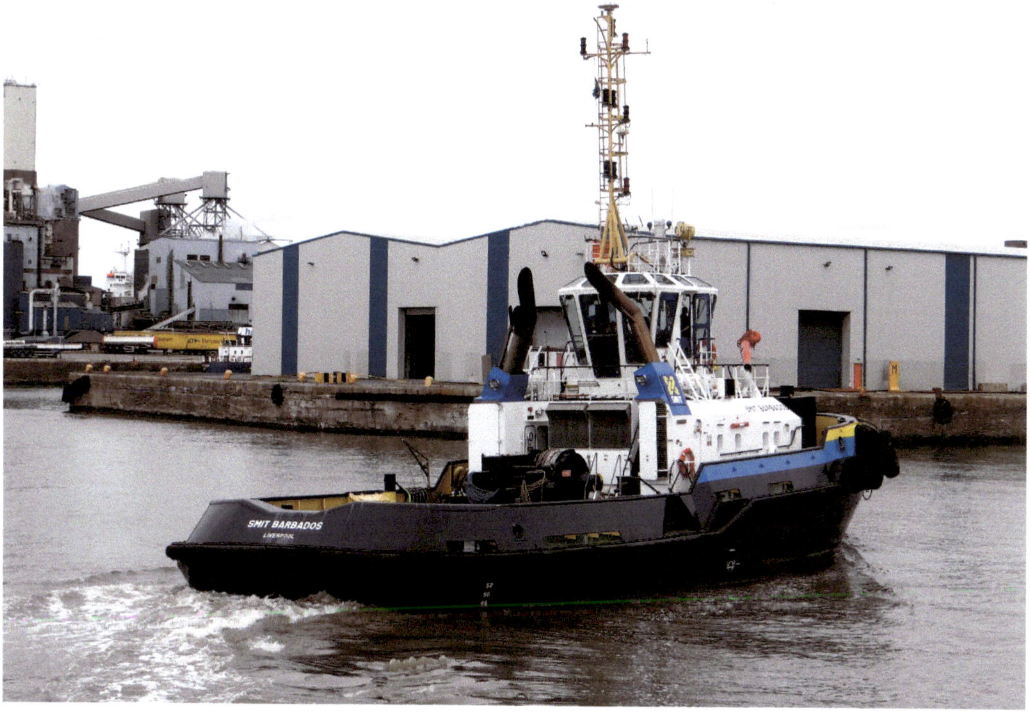

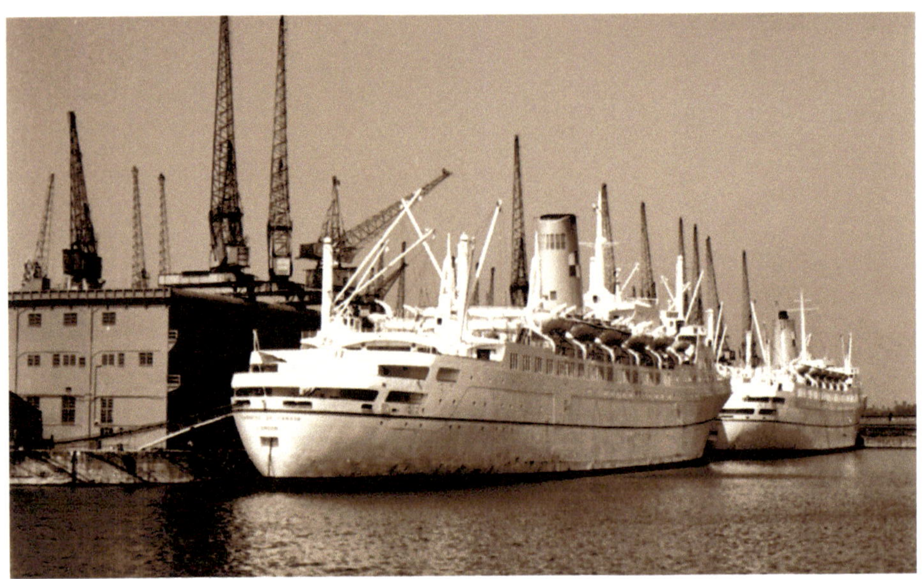

Above: The Canadian Pacific Railway Company's passenger vessels *Empress of Britain* and *Empress of Canada* at their berth in Gladstone Dock. *Empress of Britain* was built by the Fairfield Ship Building & Engineering Company in 1956 for the Canadian service from Liverpool, and for cruising during the winter months. She was chartered to the Travel Savings Association in 1963 and sold to the Greek Line the following year, becoming *Queen Anna Maria*. She was employed on their transatlantic service until 1975, when she was laid up at Piraeus. She was then sold to the Carnival Cruise Line and renamed *Carnivale*, *Fiesta Marina* and *Olympic* in 1994, *Topaz* in 1997 and then chartered as the peace boat until 2008. Following a period laid up at Singapore, she was broken up at Alang later that year. *Empress of Canada* operated for Canadian Pacific until 1972, when she was sold to Carnival Cruise Line and renamed *Mardi Gras*, *Olympic* in 1993, *Star of Texas* in 1994 and *Apollon* in 1996. She was broken up in 2003.

Below: Safe Hand passes through Gladstone Dock.

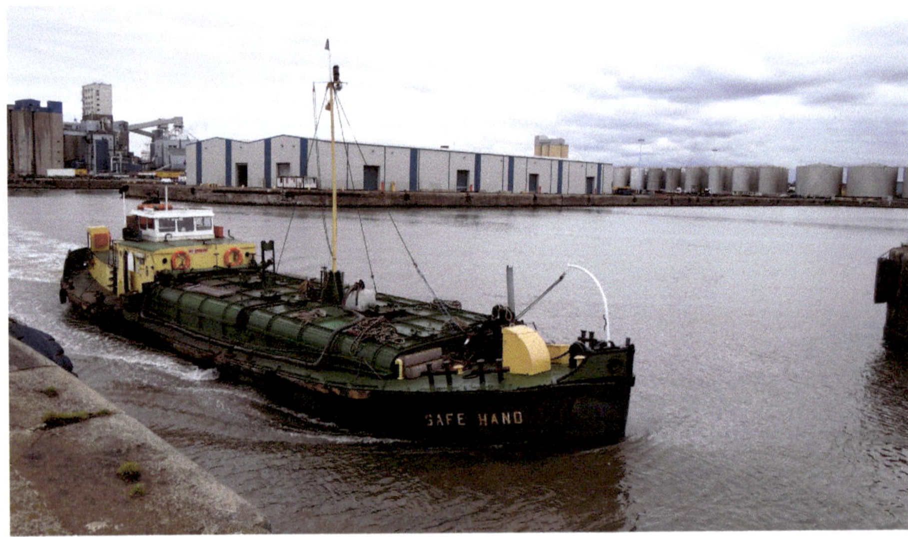

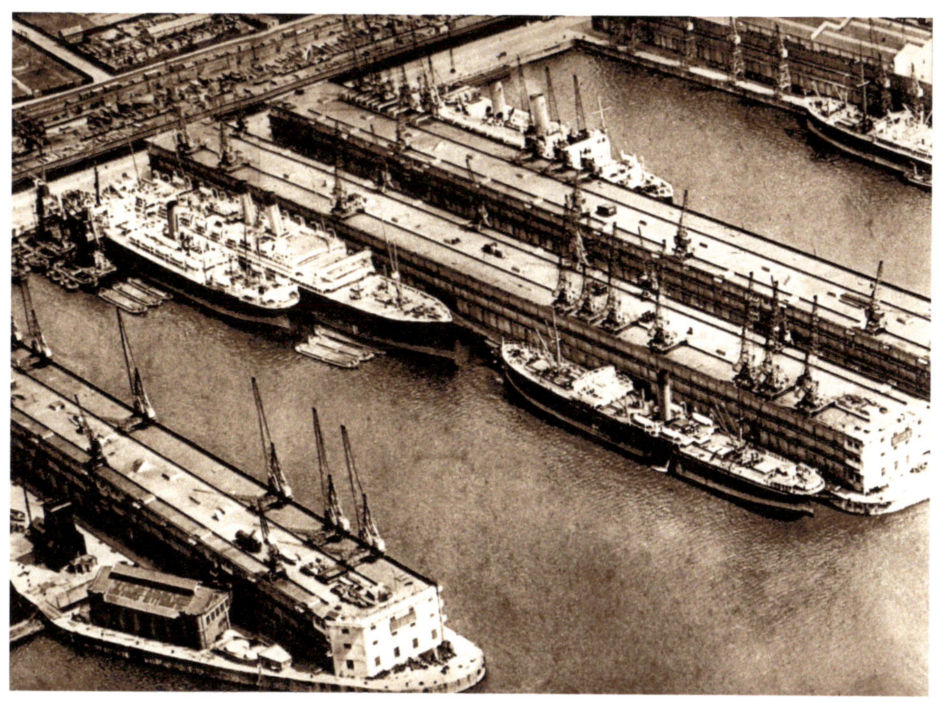

Above: The White Star liners *Adriatic, Megantic* and *Delphic* berthed in Gladstone Dock in 1927.

Below: Vessels unload their cargo at Gladstone Dock in 2011.

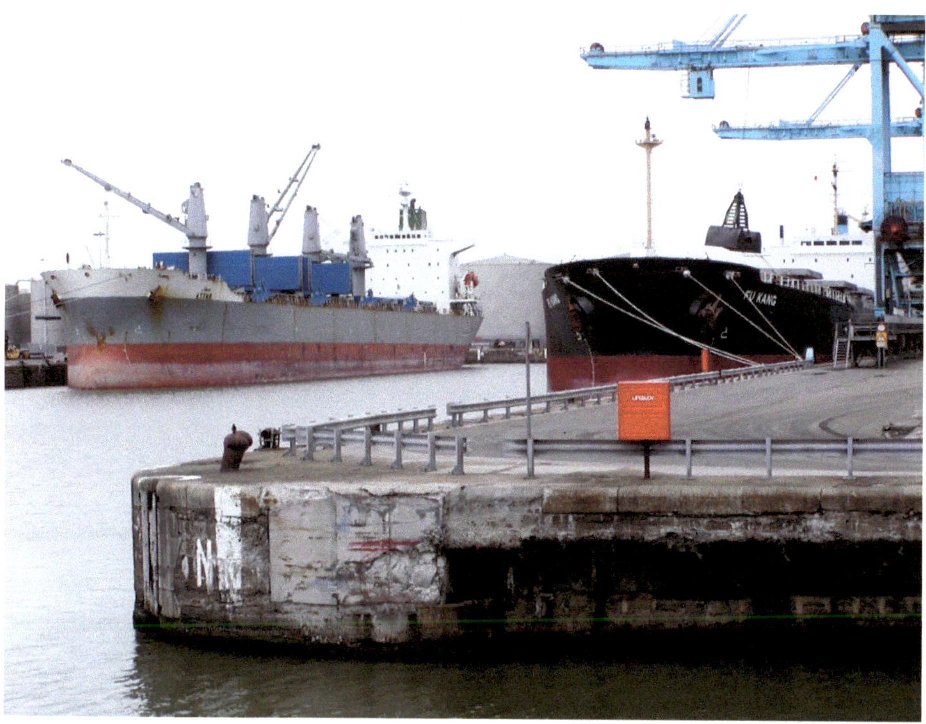

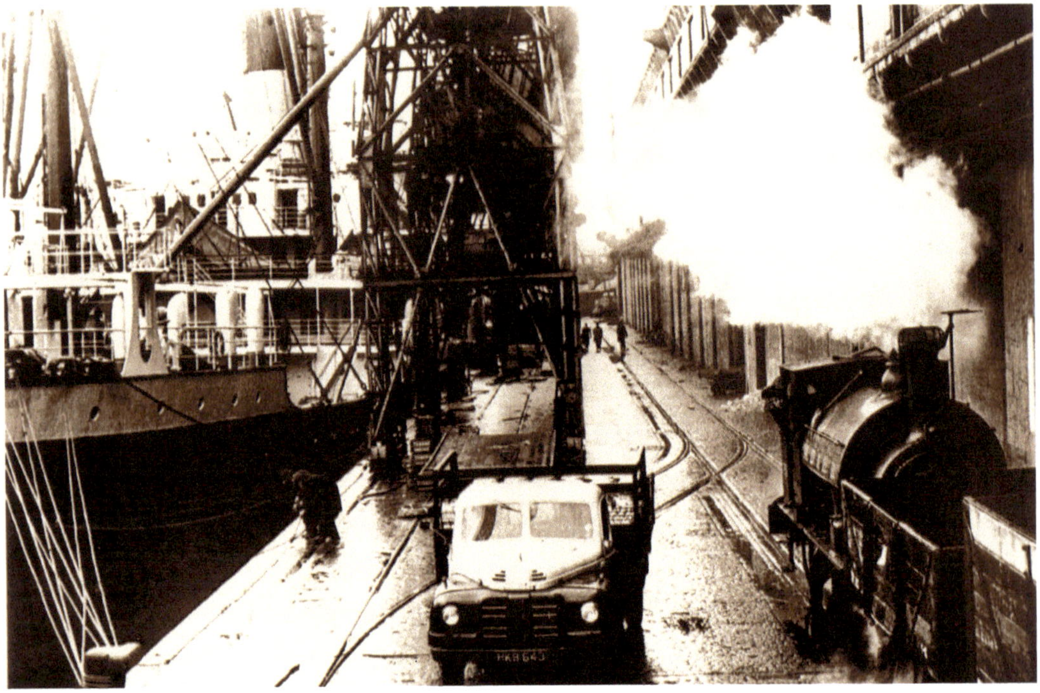

Above: The Blue Funnel berth at Gladstone Branch No. 1, south side berth.

Below: The PowerGen coal berth at Gladstone Branch No. 1, south side.

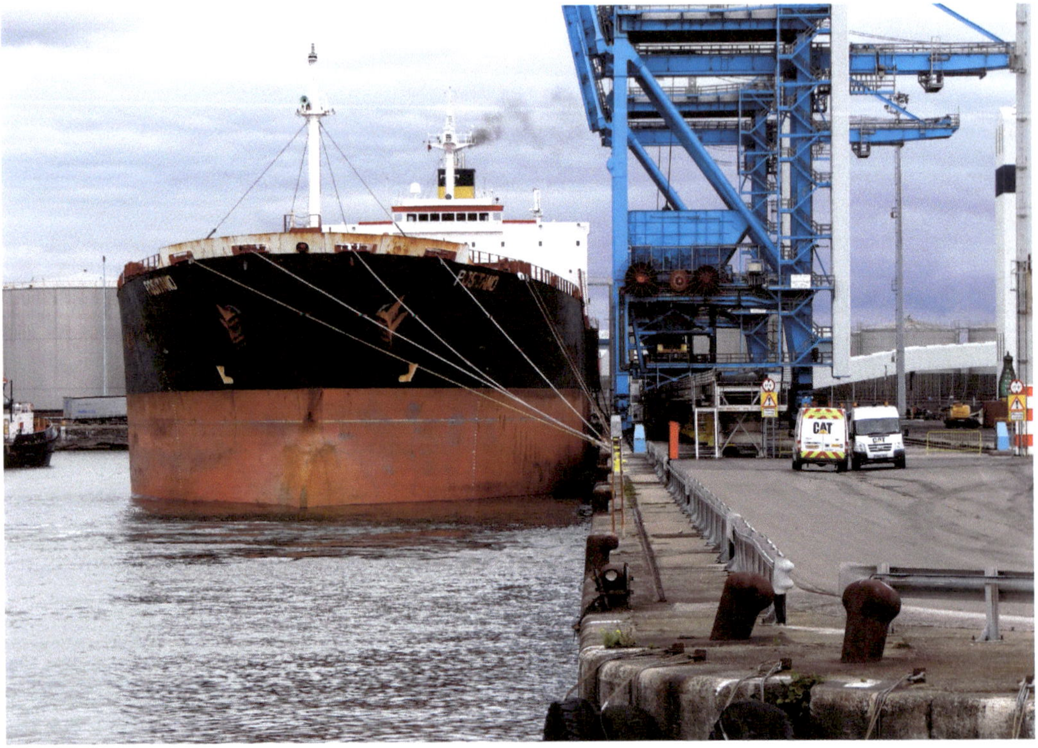

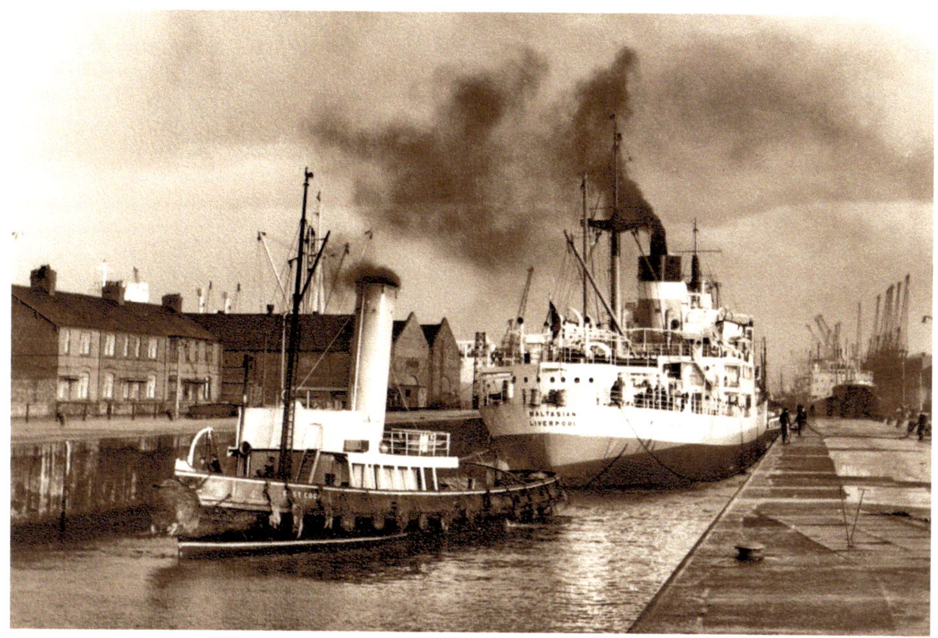

Above: The Ellerman & Papayanni cargo vessel *Maltasian* being assisted by tugs between Gladstone Dock and Alexandra Dock. She was built for Westcott & Laurence in 1950, becoming *City of Norwich* in 1962, reverting to *Maltasian* two years later, and was sold to Panamanian interests in 1967, becoming *Capetan Christos P.* She was sold to a Greek company in 1975, and renamed *Aias* for her delivery voyage to the shipbreakers. This was the site of Hornby Dock, which was used by the timber trade and was named after Thomas Dyson Hornby, chairman of the Mersey Docks & Harbour Company between 1876 and 1889. The dock was in-filled to provide space for the coal terminal at Gladstone Dock.

Below: Safe Hand moves from Gladstone Dock to Alexandra Dock in 2011.

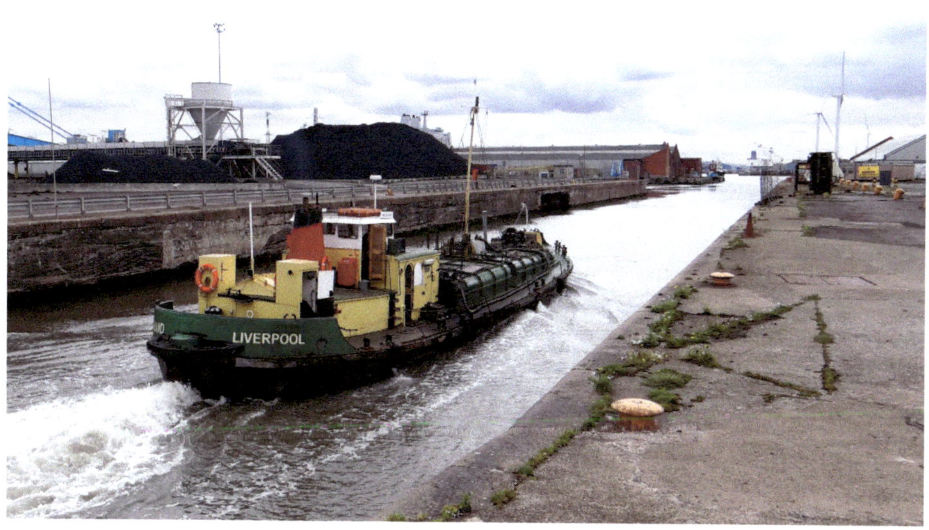

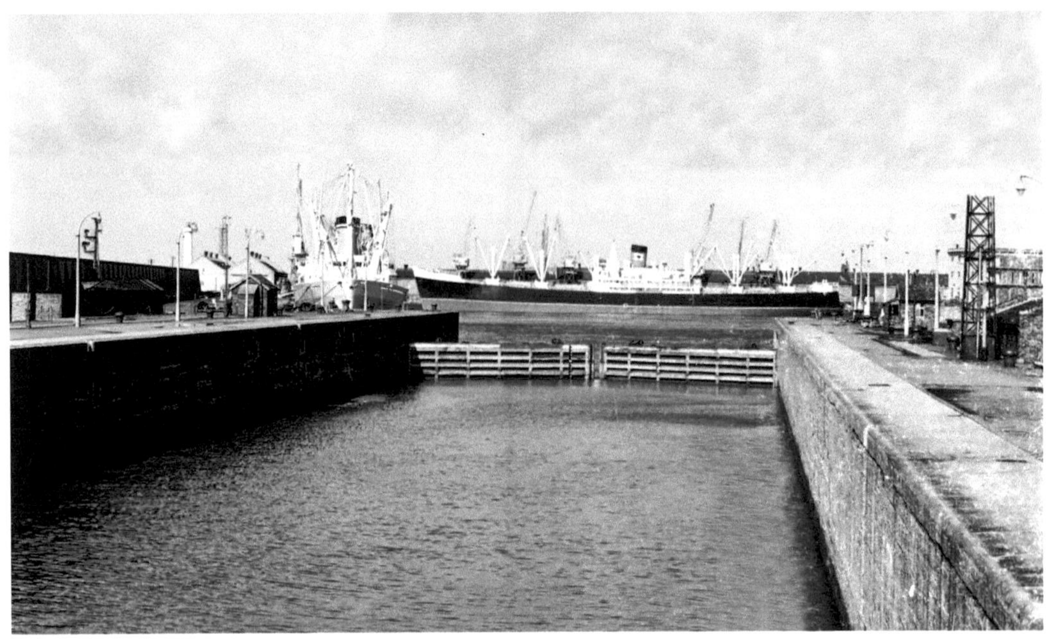

Above: Gladstone Lock looking northwards.

Below: Gladstone Dock in the 1960s.

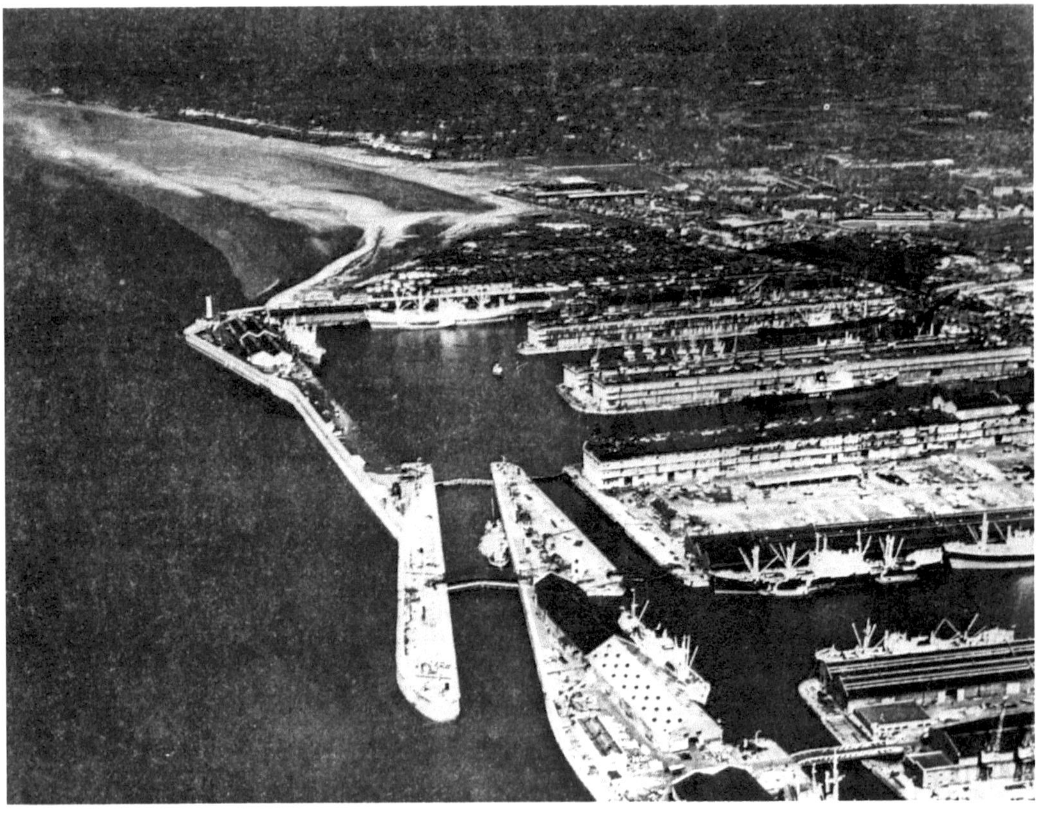

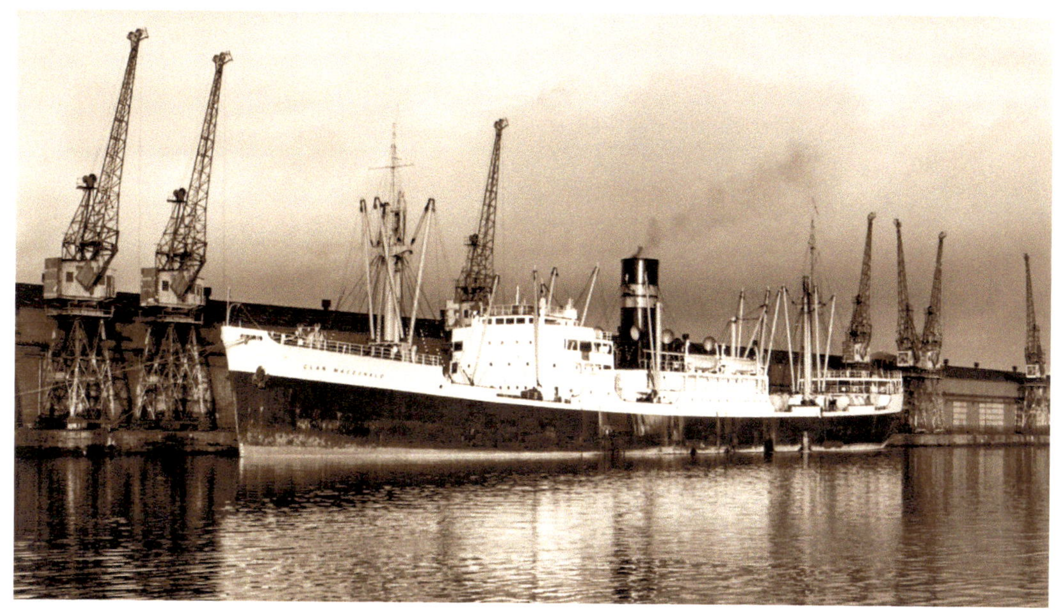

Above: The Clan Line vessel *Clan MacDonald* is seen unloading cargo at Alexandra Dock. She was built by the Greenock Dockyard on the Clyde in 1939, and acted as the main vessel in an ammunition convoy sailing from Britain to Piraeus in January 1941. She was attacked several times and later moved to Alexandria, sailing from there to Brisbane to load a cargo of meat, which was brought back to Britain. In 1960 she was transferred to the Houston Line, and on 14 March 1966 she picked up survivors following a collision between the tankers *World Liberty* and *Mosli* in the Red Sea. She was broken up in 1970 at Shanghai.

Below: Alexandra Dock consisted of three branch docks which were located off the main basin and was opened in 1880. It is connected to Hornby Dock to the north and Langton Dock to the south and was involved in the grain trade and the importation of frozen meat. It now contains scrap metal berths for exportation.

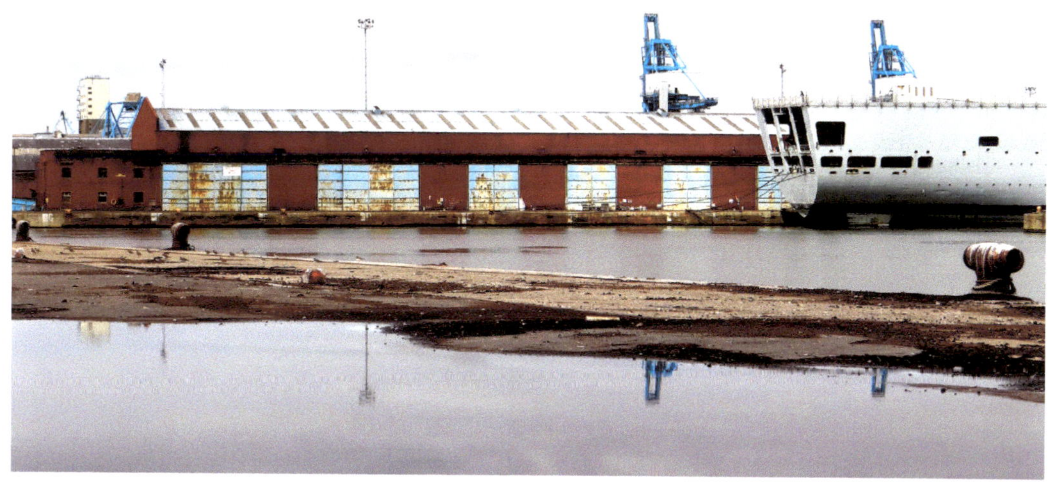

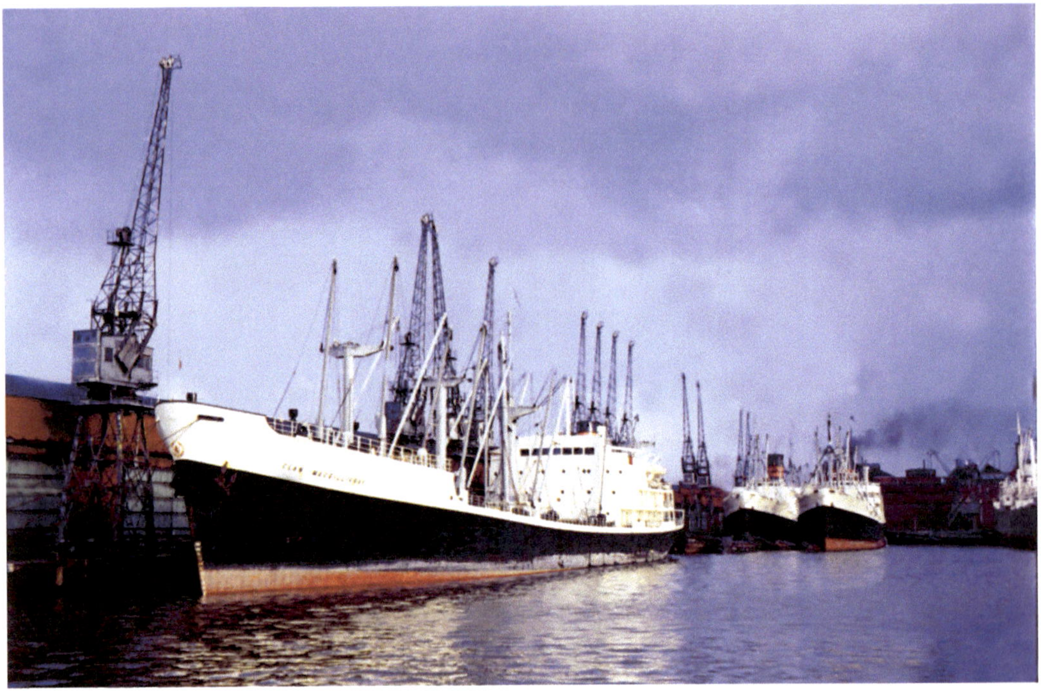

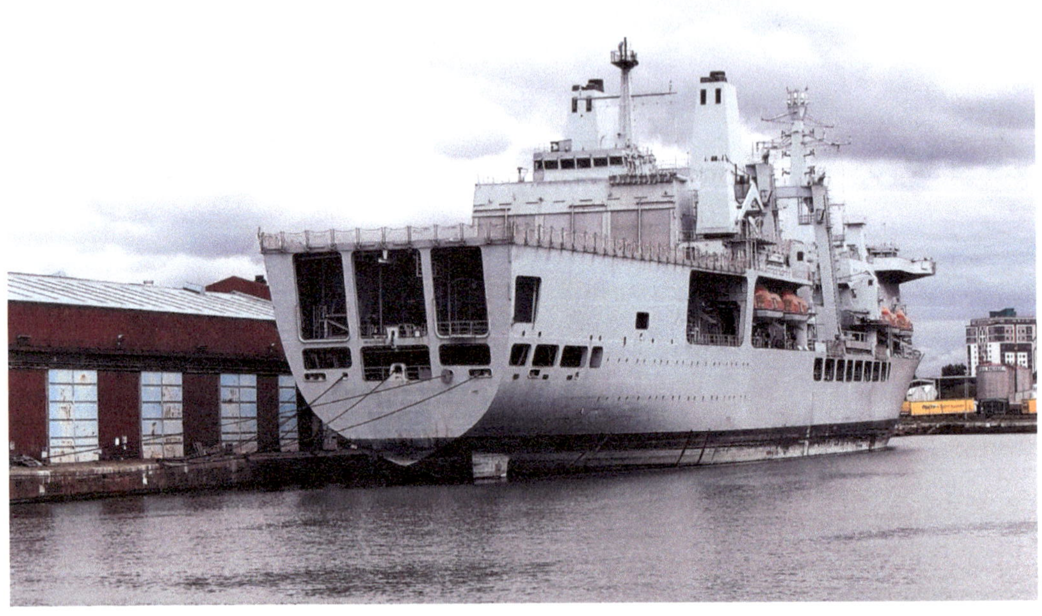

Above: Clan Line vessels unload cargo at Alexandra Branch No. 3, north berth. *Clan Macgillivray* was built in 1962 and was transferred to King Line ownership in 1969. She was sold by the company in 1981 at Hong Kong and renamed *Clan Macboyd.* On 17 September 1984 she left Singapore for Shanghai, where she was broken up.

Below: The Royal Fleet Auxiliary *Fort George*, laid up in Alexandra Branch No. 3 north in 2011.

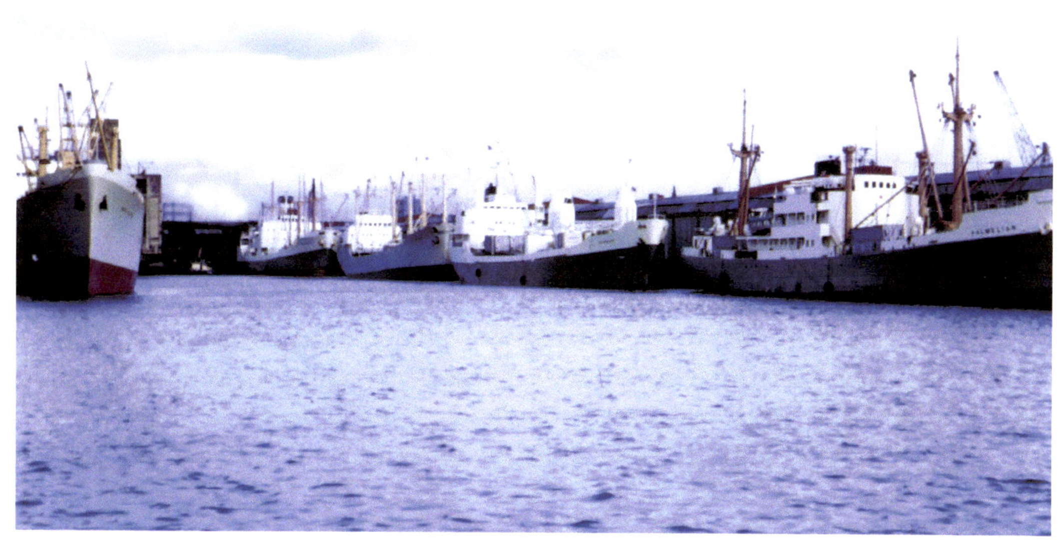

Above: Alexandra Dock in the mid-1960s with vessels of Ellerman & Papayanni loading cargo opposite Furness Withy's *Newfoundland.*

Below: The same dock and berths in 2011.

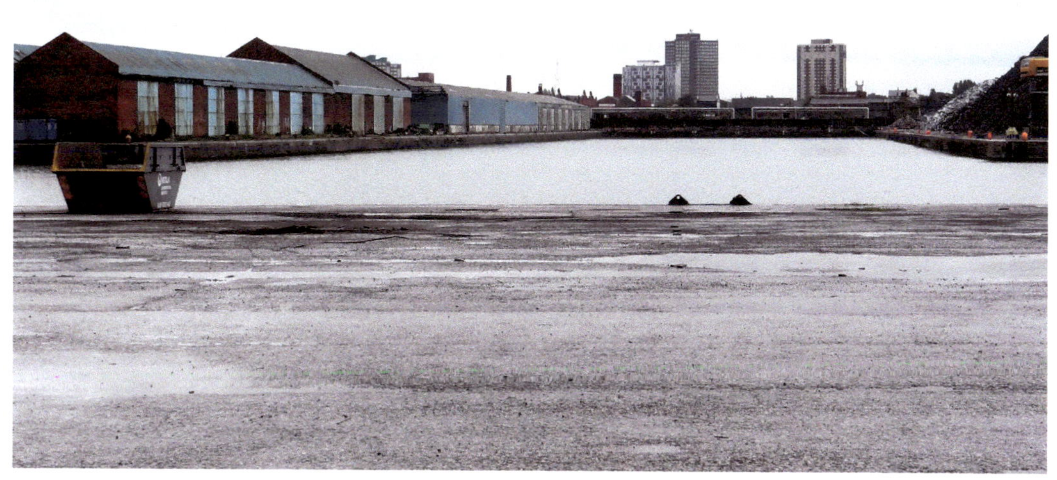

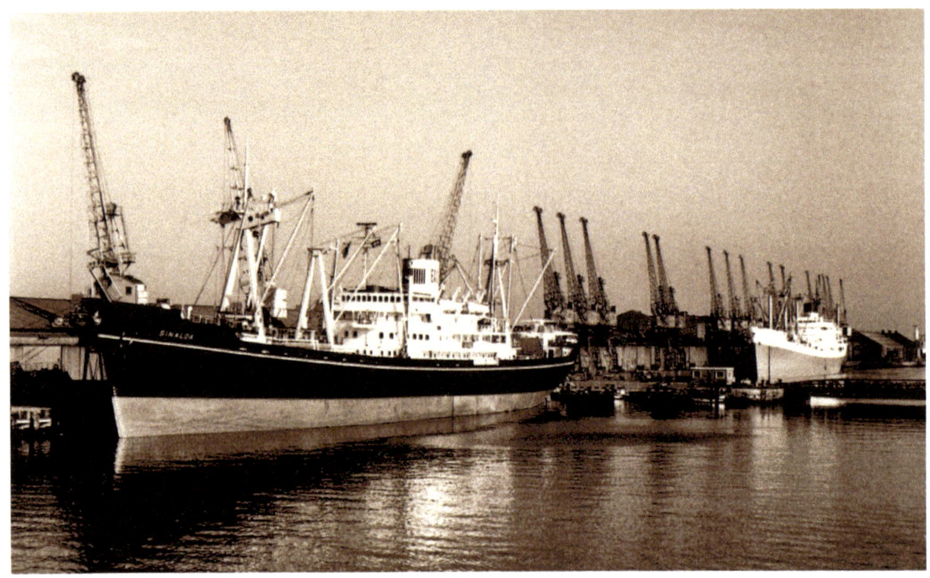

Langton Dock in 1967, with the Danish East Asiatic Company's *Sinaloa* unloading cargo at the riverside berth (*above*). An Ellerman 'City' liner is loading in Alexandra Dock. *Sinaloa* was built in 1956 by Nakskov Skibsvaerft, Nakskov in Denmark and was sold in 1978 to Panamanian interests, renamed *Yuen Chau* and was broken up in 1983. Langton Dock was named after William Langton, a member of the dock committee and a former chairman of the Bank of Liverpool. As built, it consisted of a basin adjoining the river wall, with a branch dock and two graving docks, with access to the River Mersey through Canada Dock. Various modifications were made to the dock in the twentieth century, with the new Langton river entrance opening on 14 December 1962.

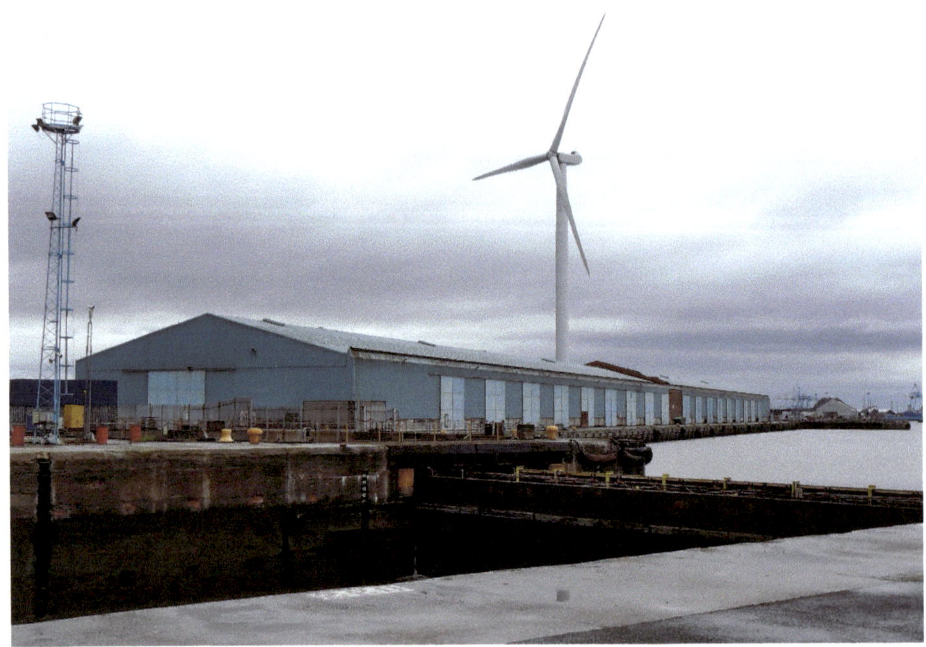

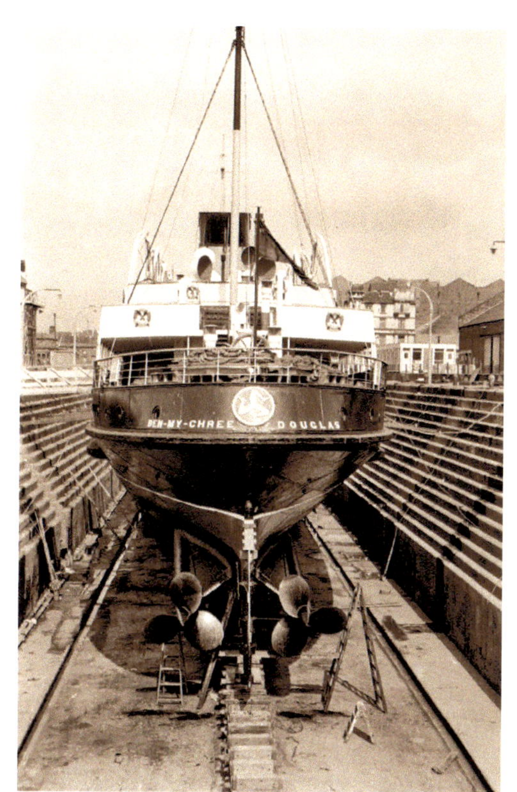

An Isle of Man steamer in Langton dry-dock (*right*). The dry docks were filled in to provide car parking space for the car ferries which were operating services to Ireland in the 1980s (*below*).

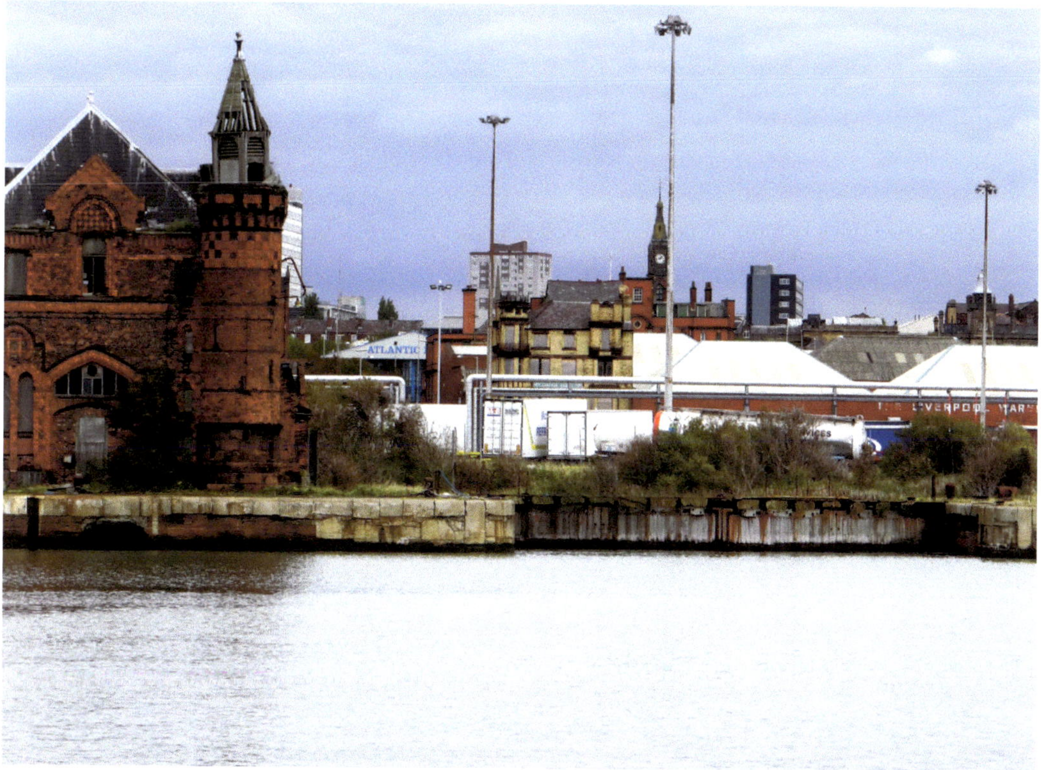

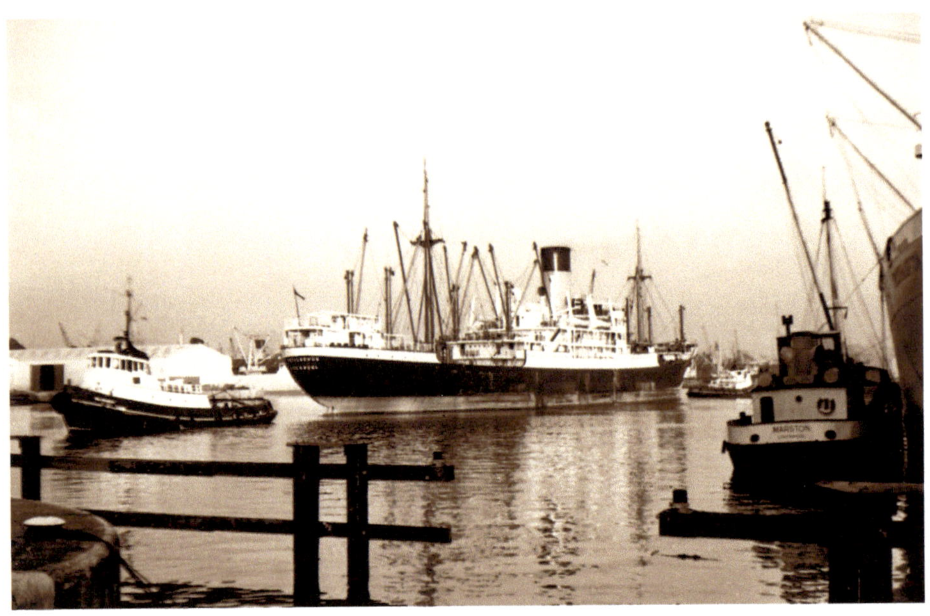

Above: Langton Dock looking south towards Langton lock entrance. The Blue Funnel Line cargo vessel *Antilochus* is assisted through the dock system by two Rea tugs. *Antilochus* was a member of the Calchas class and was built in 1949 for the Ocean Steam Ship Company. She was transferred to Elder Dempster ownership in 1975 and sold to Gulf (Shipowners) Limited of London two years later, becoming *Gulf Orient*. She arrived at Gadani Beach to be broken up on 9 May 1978.

Below: Langton Dock in 2011.

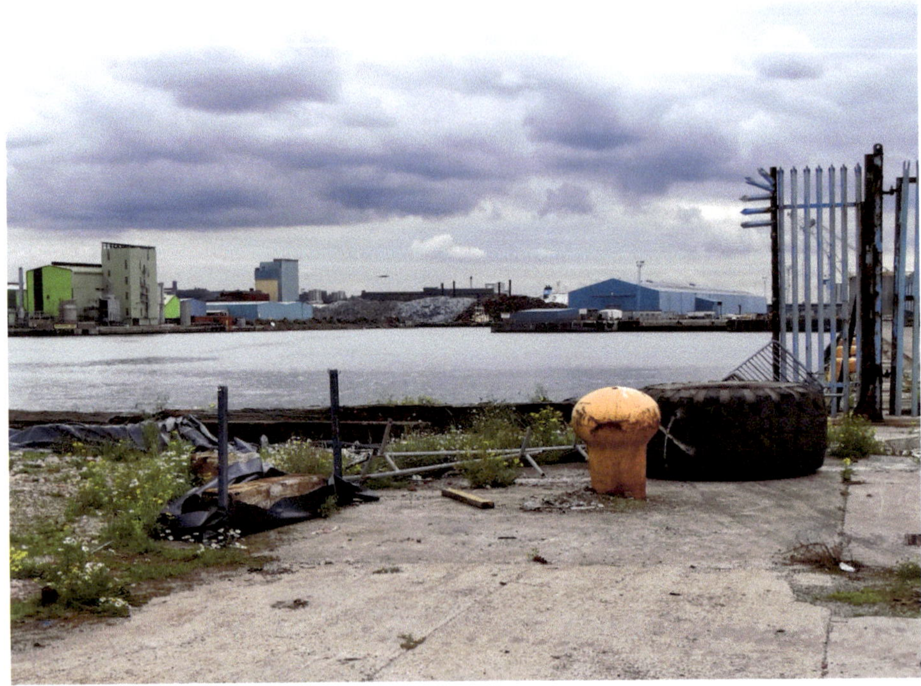

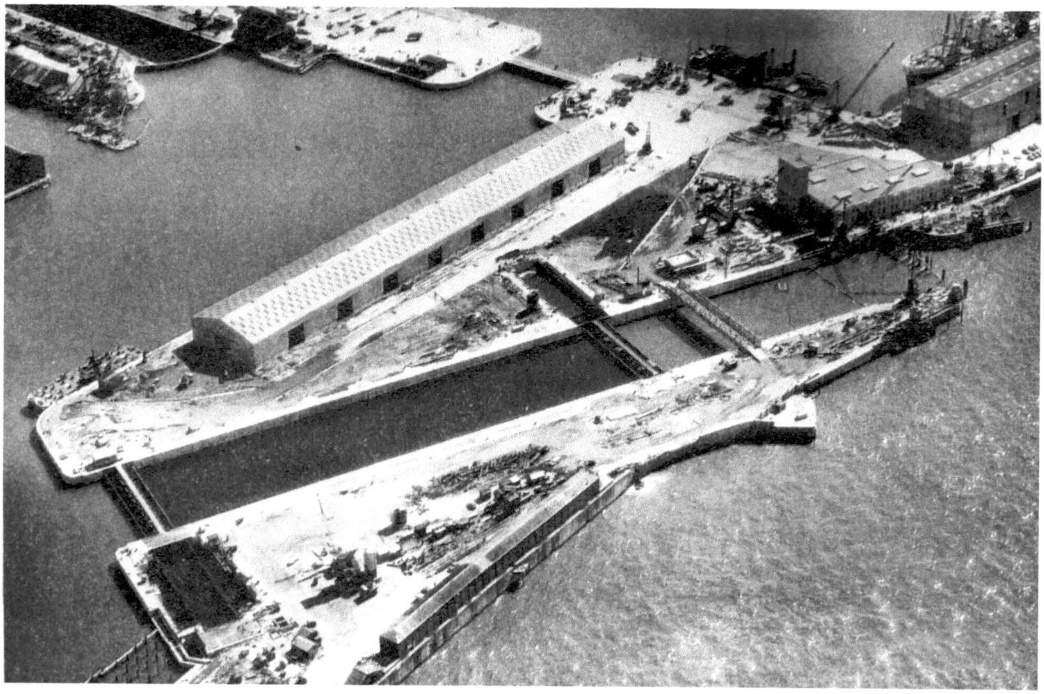

Above: Langton river entrance nears completion in 1963.

Below: Langton Lock entrance.

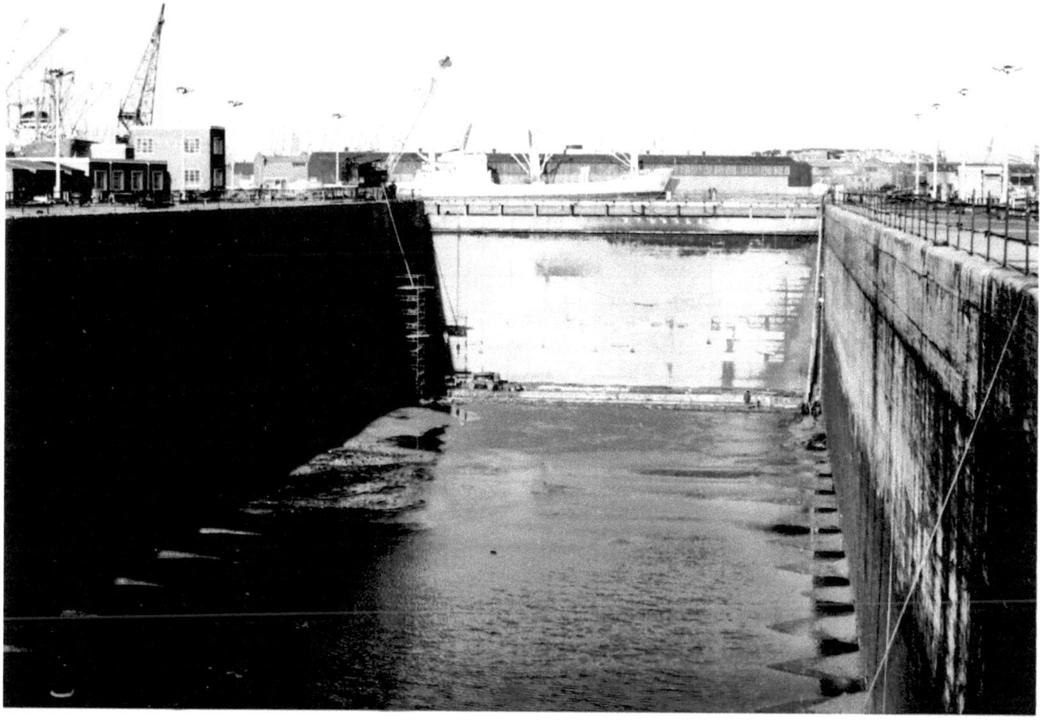

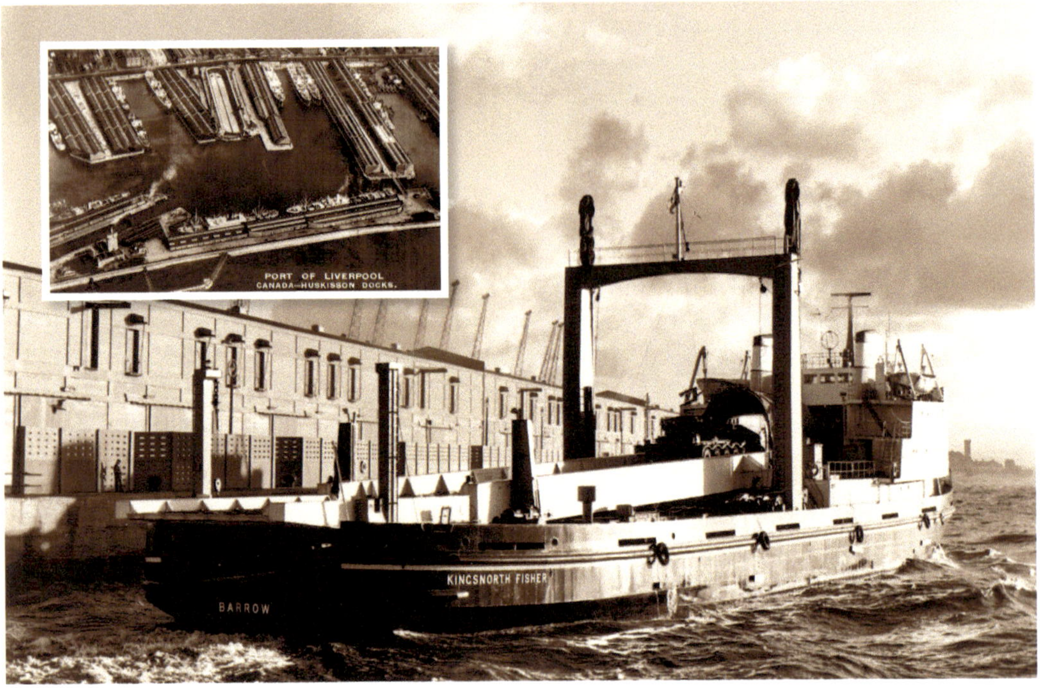

Kingsnorth Fisher sails from Langton Dock (*above*). She was owned by James Fisher & Sons Limited and became *New Generation* in 1990 and *New Gen* in 2001. She arrived at Alang to be broken up on 19 December that year. By 2011 the warehouses have been demolished and the berths in Canada Dock are now used for the export of scrap metal (*below*). The inset shows an aerial view of Canada and Huskisson docks.

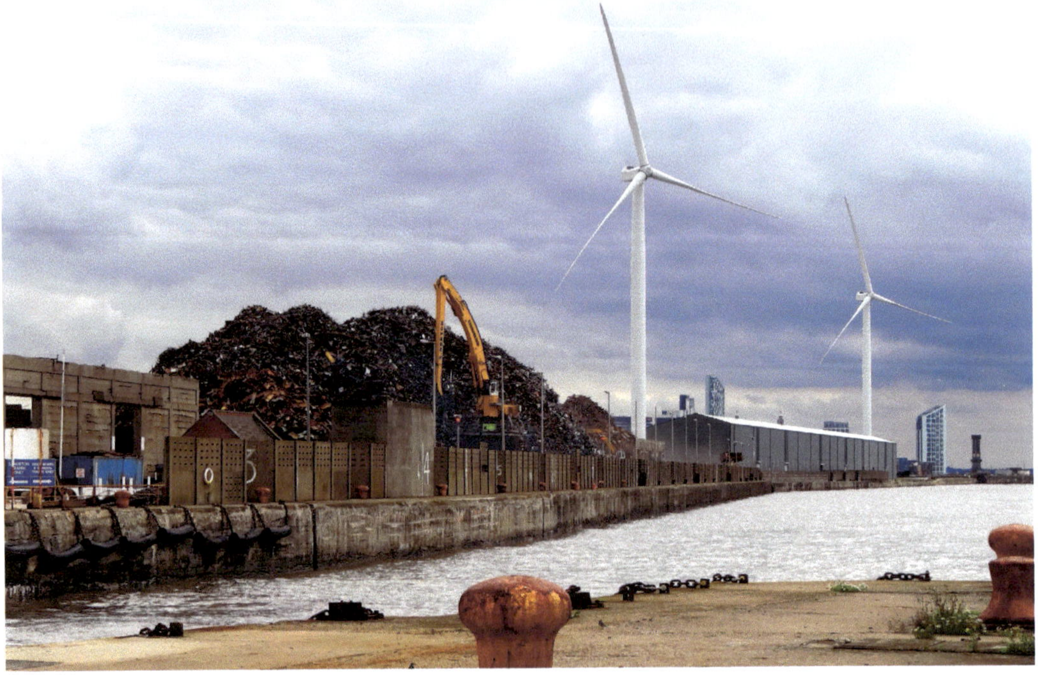

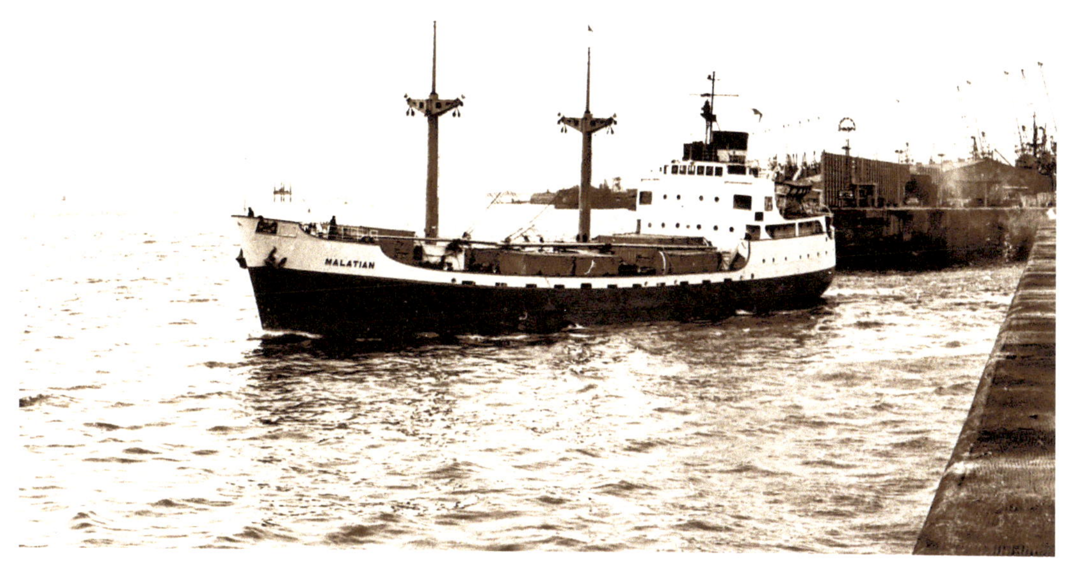

Above: The Ellerman & Papayanni cargo vessel *Malatian* sails to the Mediterranean from Langton Lock. She was built by Henry Robb & Company in Leith in 1958 for the Westcott & Laurence Line and transferred to Ellerman & Papayanni in 1969. She was sold to Maldive Shipping Limited in 1971, becoming *Maldive Victory*. On a voyage from Singapore on 13 February 1981, she struck a reef off Malé harbour and sank. She was later declared a total constructive loss.

Below: Saint Colum 1 prepares to sail to Belfast as she shares Langton lock with *Vigilant* and Alexandra, Lamey and Rea tugs.

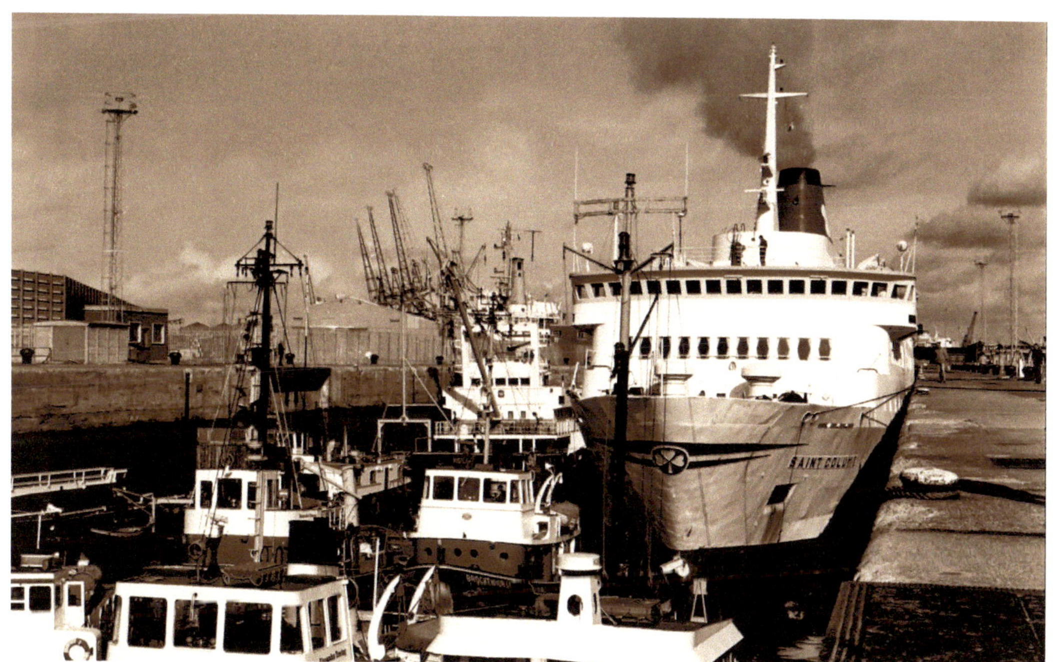

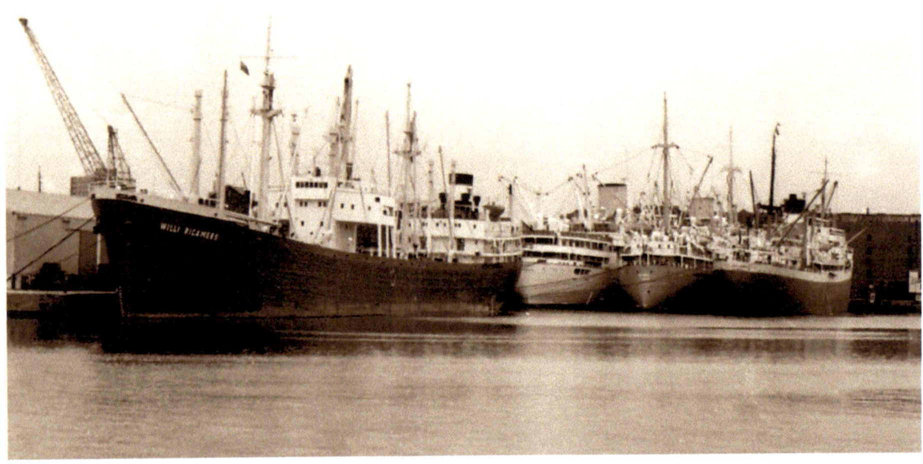

Above: Willi Rickmers, Aureol, Apapa and the *City of Manchester* laid up in Brocklebank Dock during the seamen's strike in 1966.

Below: Seatruck's *Clipper Pennant* loading vehicles for Dublin in 2011. Brocklebank Dock was originally known as Canada Half-Tide Dock when it was opened in 1862, and consists of two branch docks which were originally used for the importation of timber. In 1879 it was named after Ralph Brocklebank, who was chairman of the Mersey Docks & Harbour Board between 1863 and 1869.

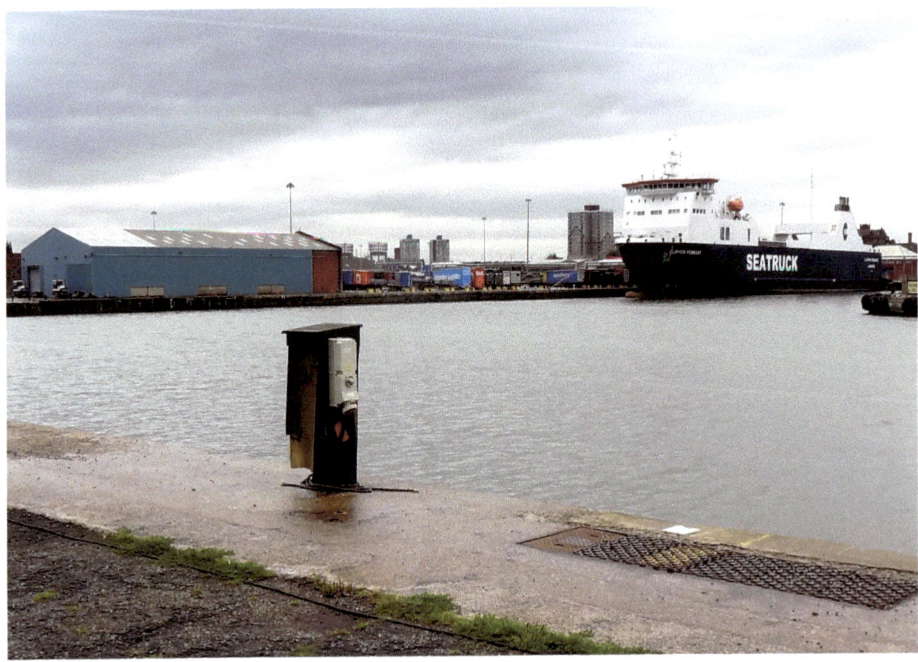

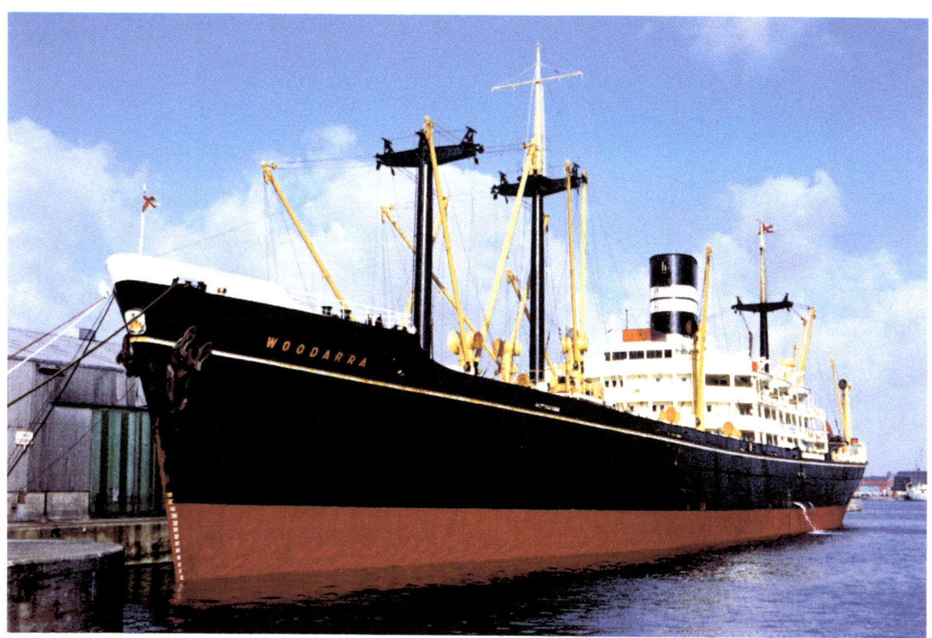

Above: An unusual visitor to Liverpool was the British India cargo vessel *Woodarra,* seen here berthed in Brocklebank Dock. She was built in 1956 and became *Pando Gulf* in 1968 and *Benalbanach* in 1974, when she was sold to the Ben Line. She arrived at Inchon to be broken up on 21 May 1978.

Below: The same berth in 2011 is now used by Peel Ports for maintenance services.

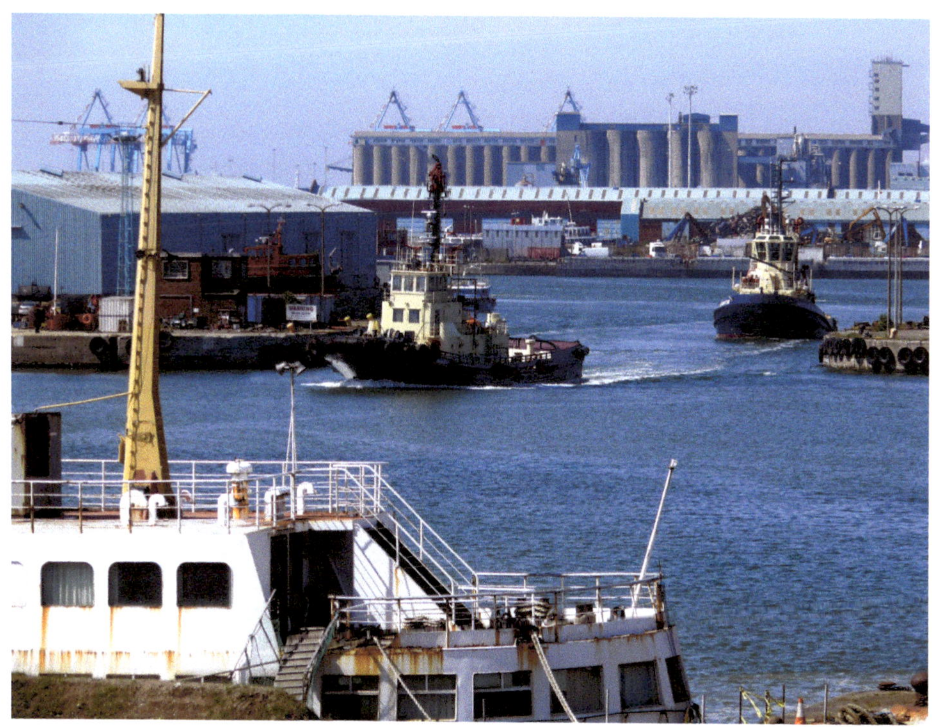

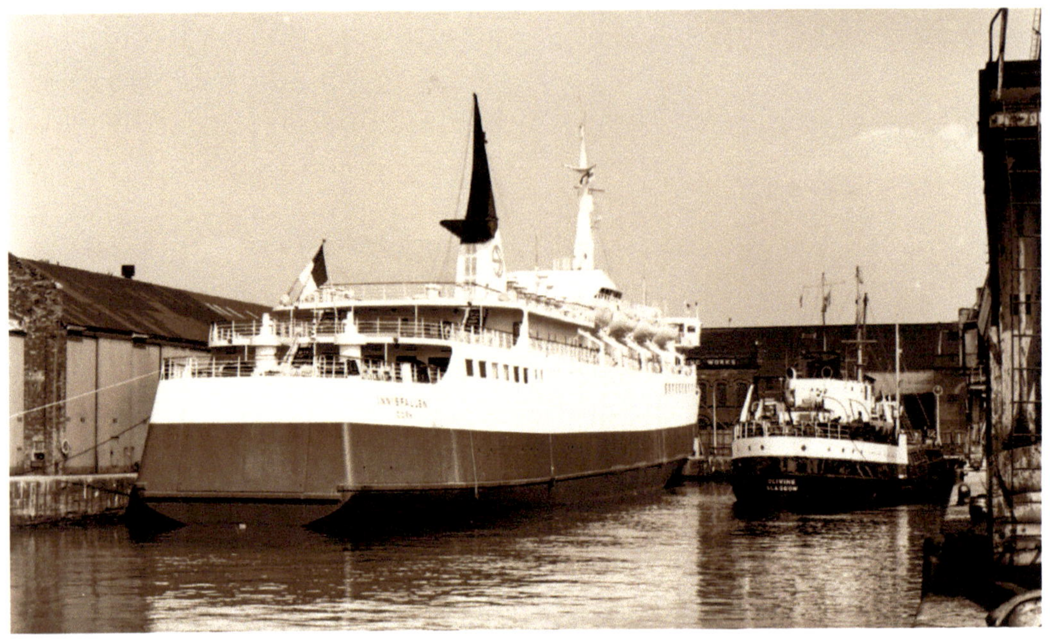

Above: The B+I passenger car ferry *Innisfallen* and *Olivine* in Carriers Dock. The car ferry berth in Carriers Dock was operational from 15 May 1968 until the sailing by *Munster* on 30 September 1972. Sailings were made from the new terminal in Trafalgar Dock the following day.

Below: The Cargill works on the site of Carriers Dock has been operating since 1995. It is a rapeseed crush plant and refinery which produces mid protein meal and crude rape oil and has facilities to outload oil for export.

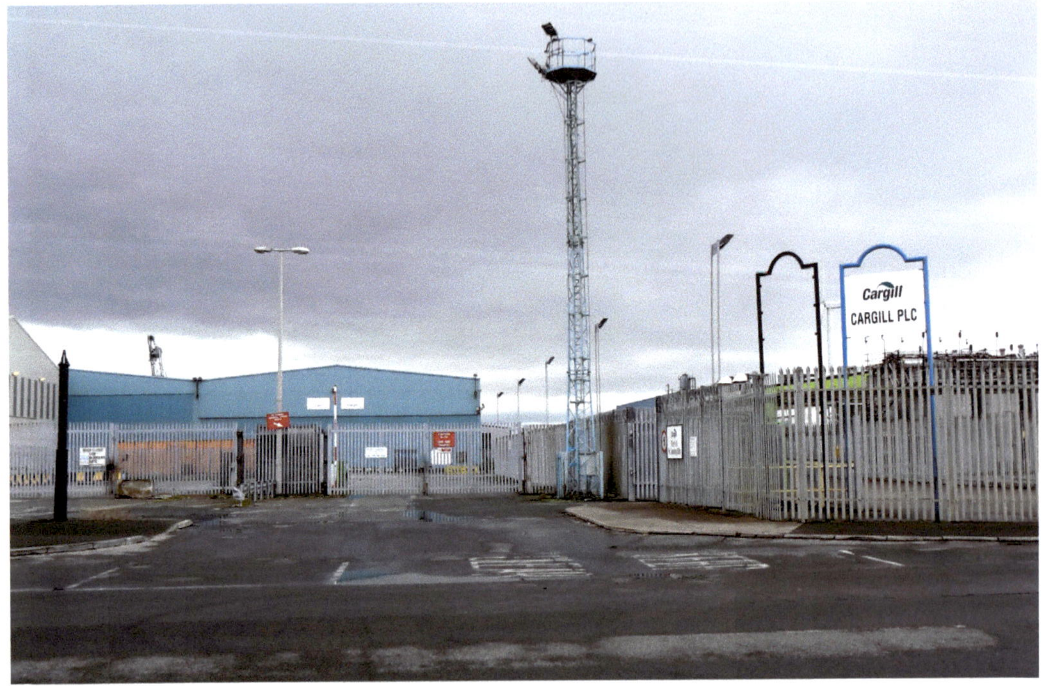

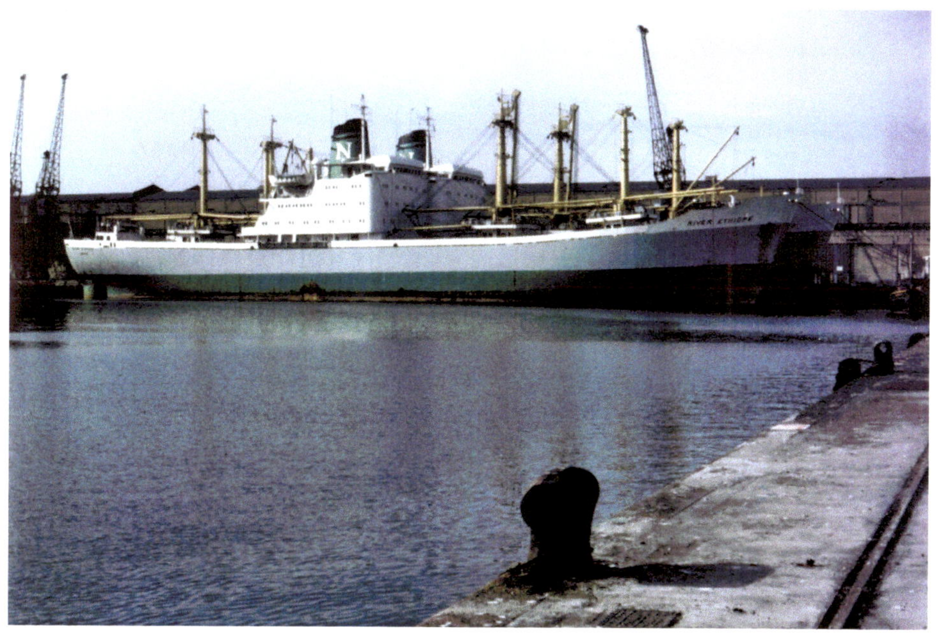

Nigerian National Lines vessels laid up in Canada Dock. The Nigerian National Line was formed in 1957, with 33 per cent of the shares held by the Elder Dempster Line and 16 per cent by the Palm Line, and the Nigerian Government holding 51 per cent. All the shares were acquired by the Nigerian Government in 1961, and by 1964 the line owned sixteen vessels. Following the Nigerian Civil War, the Nigerian Government encouraged the line to develop its fleet and nineteen new vessels were ordered in 1977. However, by the early 1990s the line suffered serious financial problems and many of the company's ships were arrested in various parts of the world. The Nigerian National Line went into liquidation in 1995 and the fleet of cargo vessels were sold.

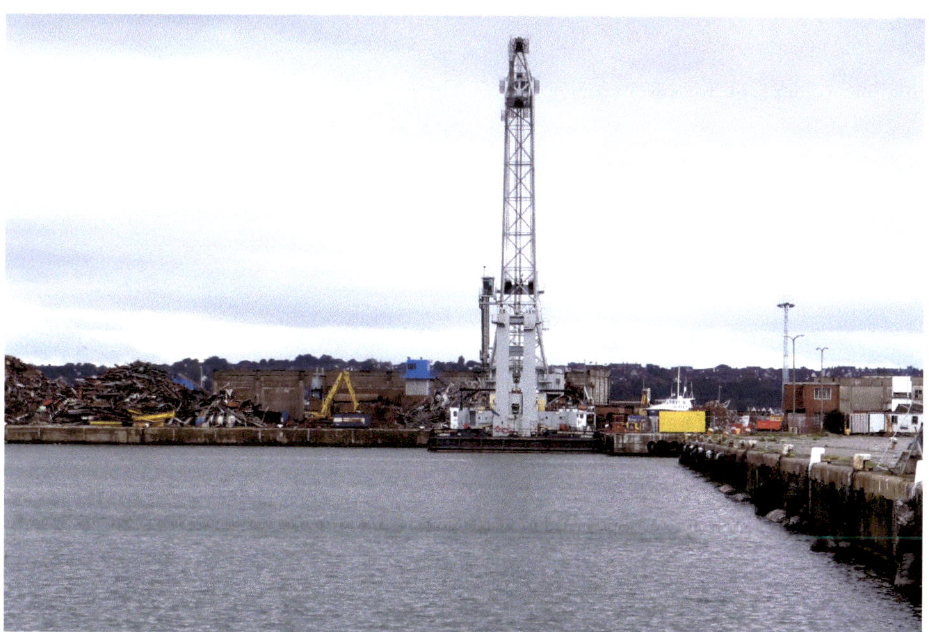

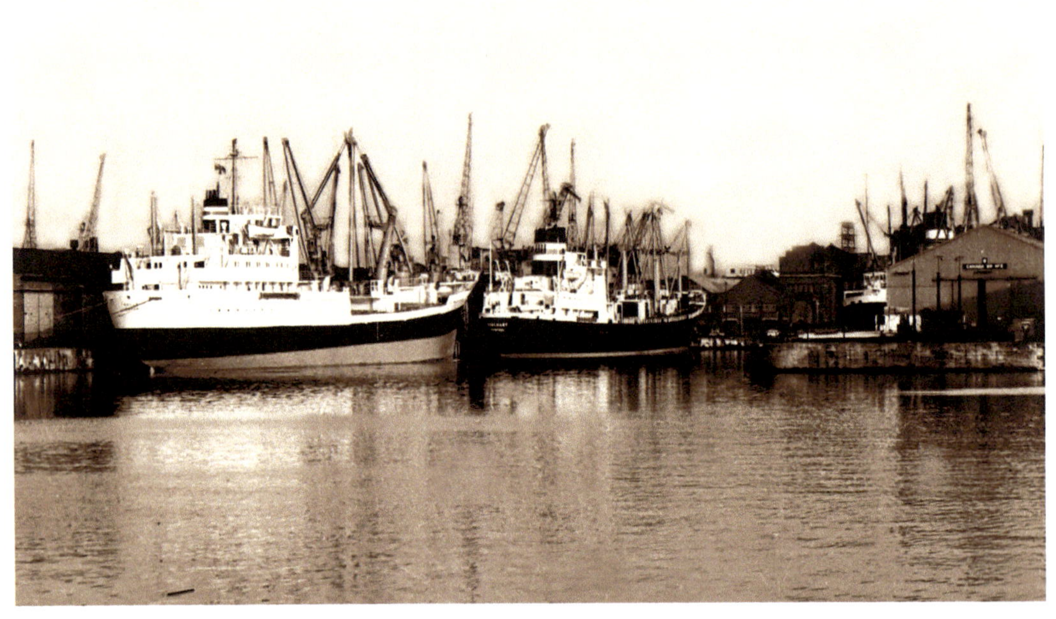

The Harrison Line cargo vessels *Trader* and *Merchant* loading at Canada Branch No. 1 Dock. *Trader* was built by A/B Lindholmes Varv. at Gothenburg in 1966 and was sold by the line in 1980, becoming *Bangpa-In*, and was broken up at Rayong in 1986. *Merchant* was built for Cunard Line service by Cammell Laird & Company at Birkenhead in 1964 as *Scythia*, and was purchased by the Harrison Line in 1969. After ten years' service she was laid up, sold in 1979 and renamed *Sisal Trader*. In April 1984 she was driven ashore on Mayotte Island, off Madagascar, in Cyclone Kamisy and was later refloated and taken to Mombasa, where she was sold for scrap.

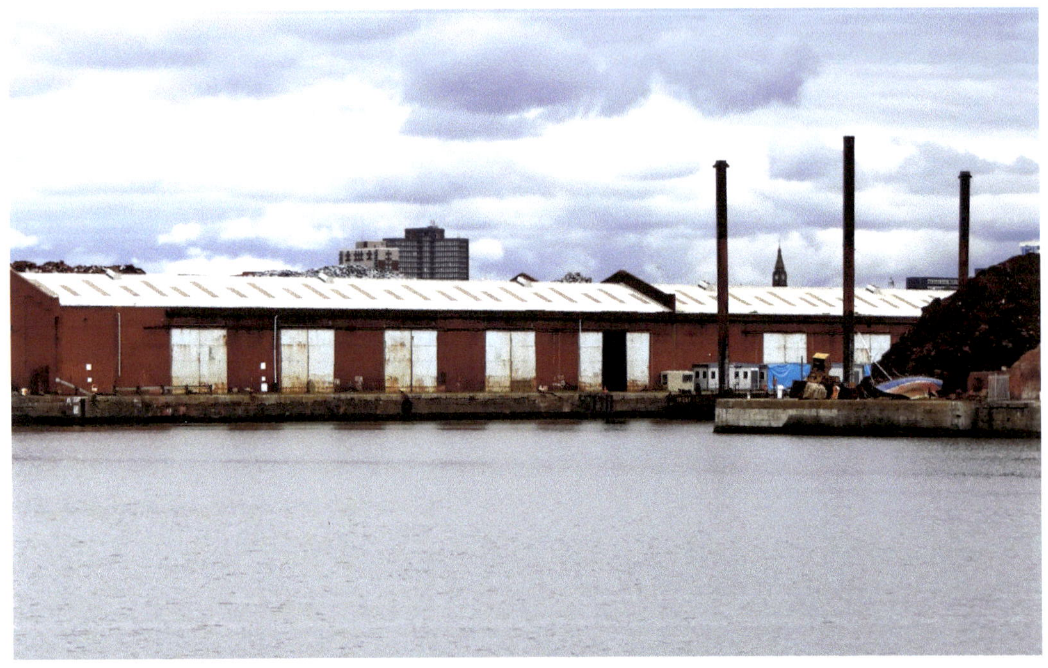

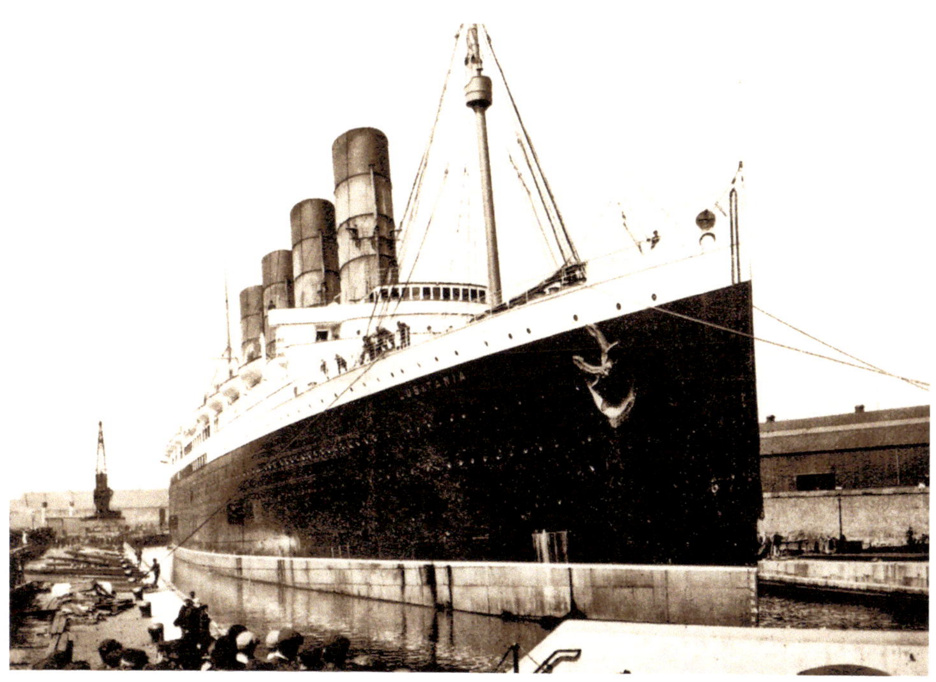

Above: The Cunard liner *Lusitania* in Canada Graving Dock. *Lusitania* was built by John Brown & Company at Clydebank and sailed on her maiden voyage from Liverpool to New York on 7 September 1907. She achieved 23.99 knots on her second voyage, taking the Atlantic speed record. Leaving Liverpool on 4 August 1914, the day war was declared, it was announced that she would remain in service, sailing each month. On 1 May the following year, she sailed from New York with 1,257 passengers aboard, and 702 crew, and was torpedoed by the German U-boat U-20 on 7 May, off the Old Head of Kinsale. She sank within eighteen minutes; 1,198 people were drowned and 761 people survived.

Below: Canada Graving Dock has been used to scrap several Royal Naval vessels in recent years.

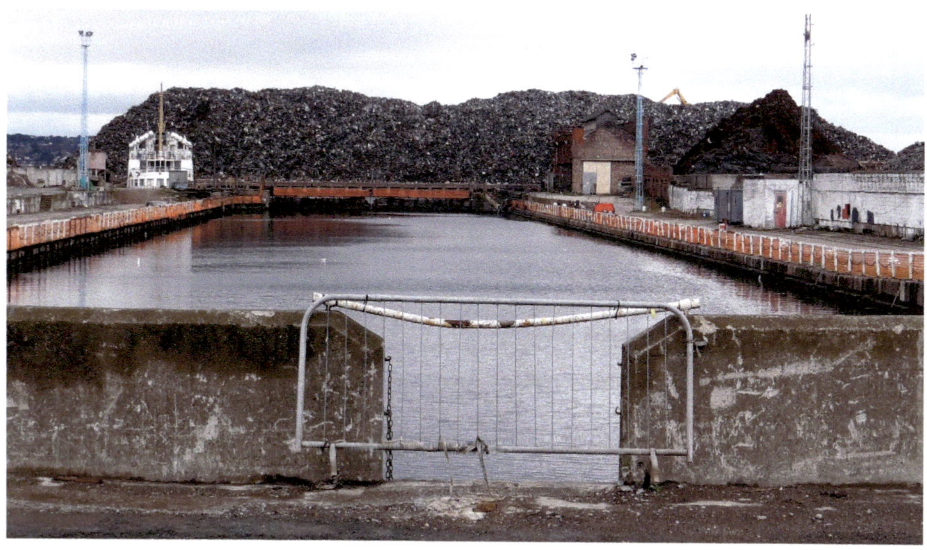

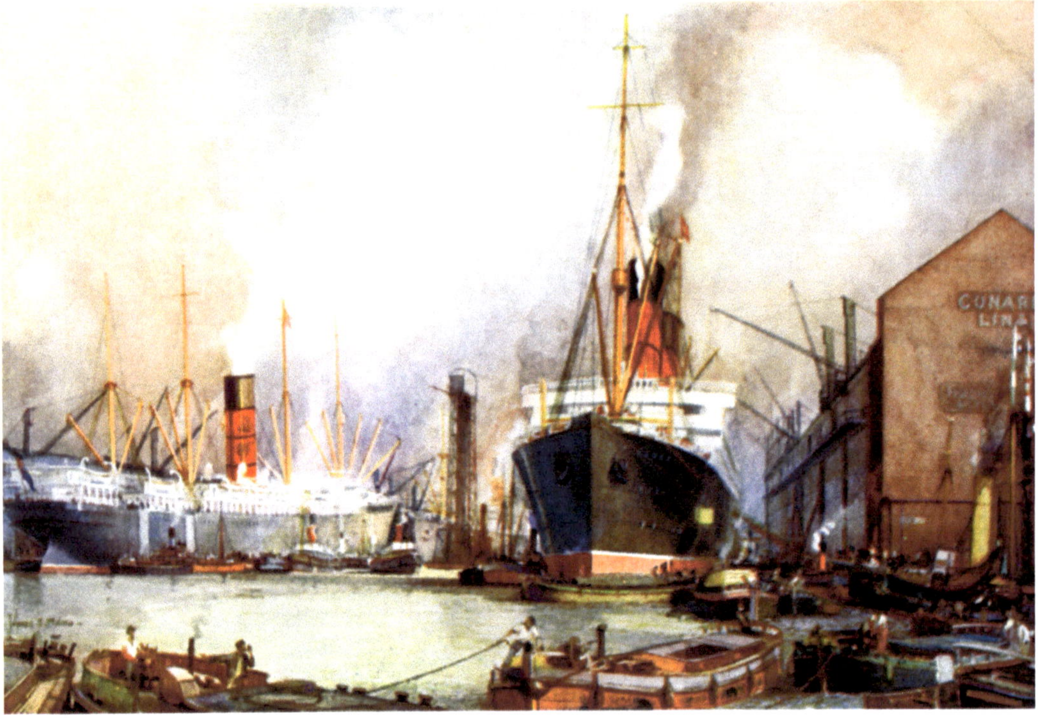

Cunard Line passenger ships in Huskisson Dock Branch No. 1, north and south berths. Huskisson Dock was designed by Jesse Hartley and was named after a former Member of Parliament and Treasurer of the Navy, William Huskisson. It was originally involved in the timber trade and later grain was imported through the dock.

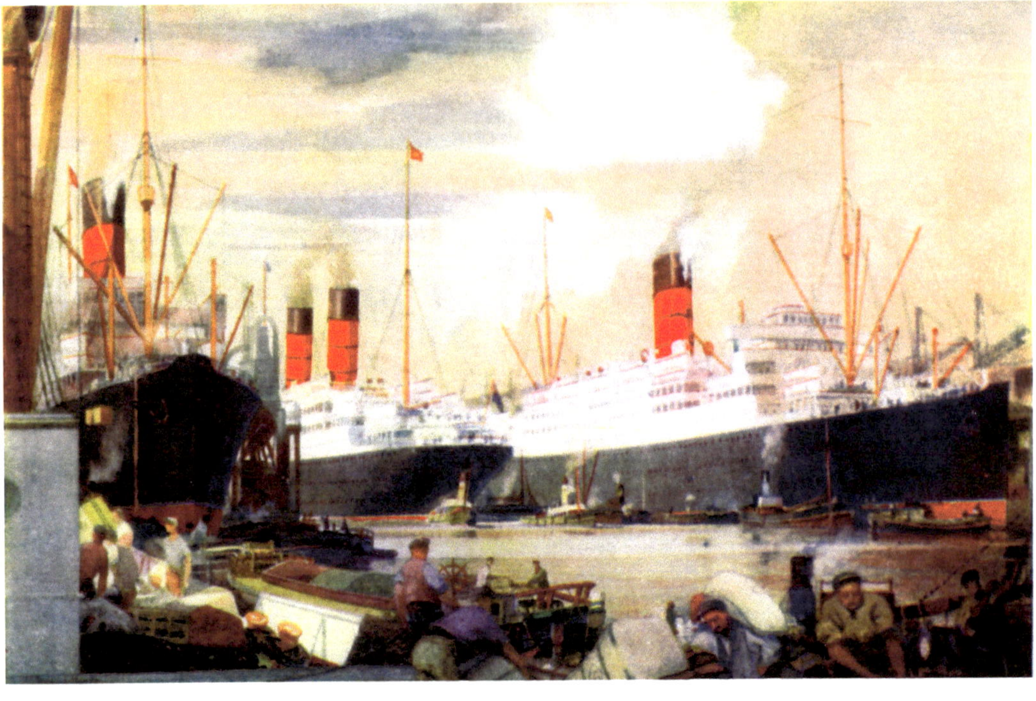

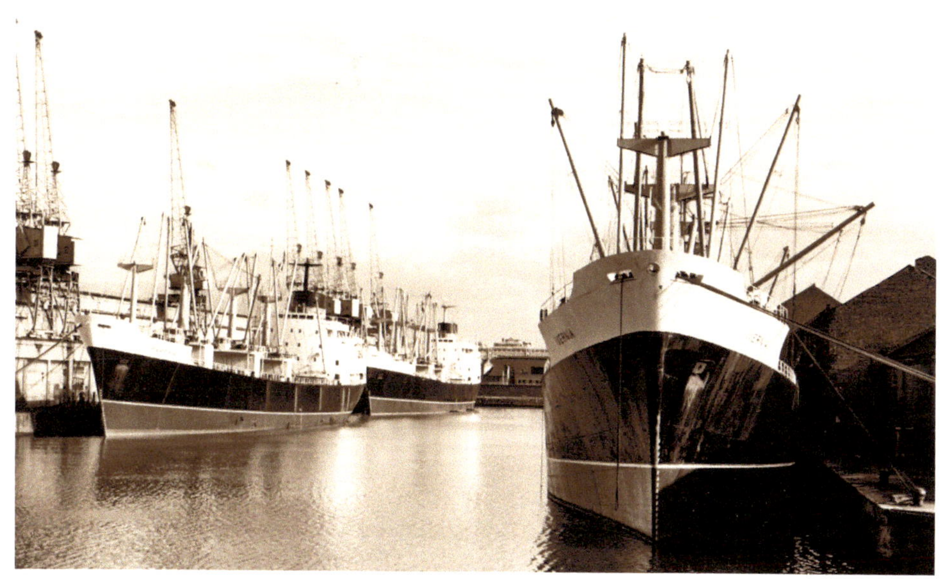

Above: Parthia, Saxonia and *Ivernia* in Huskisson Branch No. 1 Dock. *Saxonia* was built in 1964 and was lengthened in 1970 by Swan Hunter at South Shields and renamed *Maharonda* for Cunard-Brocklebank service. She was renamed *Concordia Foss* briefly in 1972 during a charter, reverting back to *Maharonda*. Sold in March 1978, becoming *New Deer* and broken up in China in 1983. *Ivernia* was built in 1964 for the Liverpool to New York cargo service. She was also lengthened in 1970, renamed *Manipur, Concordia Manipur* and *Manipur* again in 1971. Sold in 1977, becoming *Philippa* and broken up at Chittagong in 1985.

Below: The dredger *Shoalway* berthed at Huskisson Branch No. 1 (south). She is managed by Boskalis Baggermaatschappij, Papendrecht, and was completed in 2010.

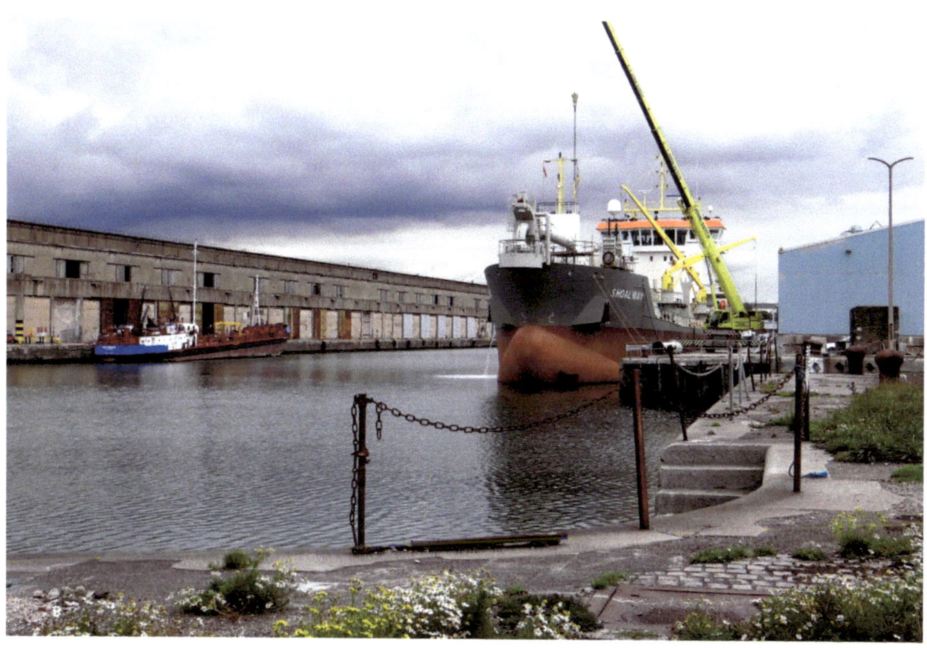

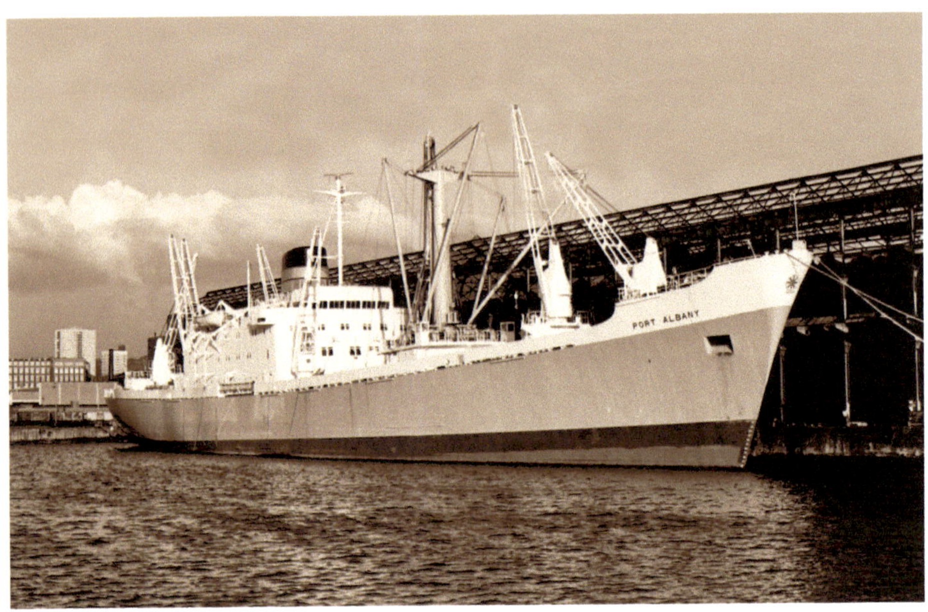

Above: Port Albany at Huskisson Branch No. 1, south berth. She was delivered to the Cunard Line, on charter to Port Line in 1965 and transferred to Port Line ownership three years later. The following year she operated on the Atlas Line Australia to Japan route and was owned by the Trafalgar Group in 1971. In 1972 she was sold, becoming *Marietta, Artemon* in 1990 and was broken up at Alang, where she arrived on 15 May 1992.

Below: Huskisson Branch No. 1, south dock.

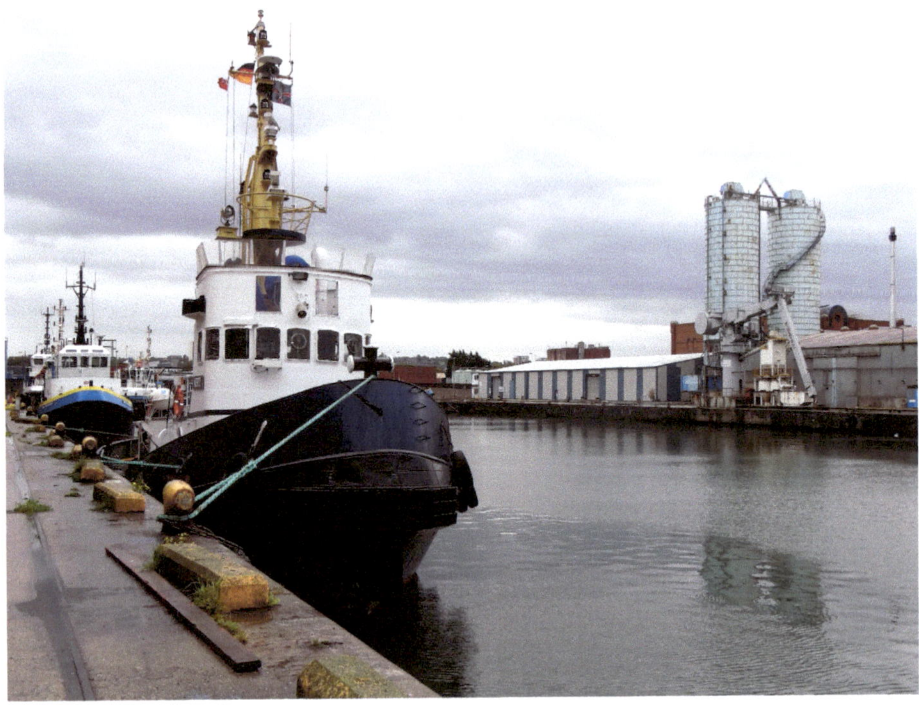

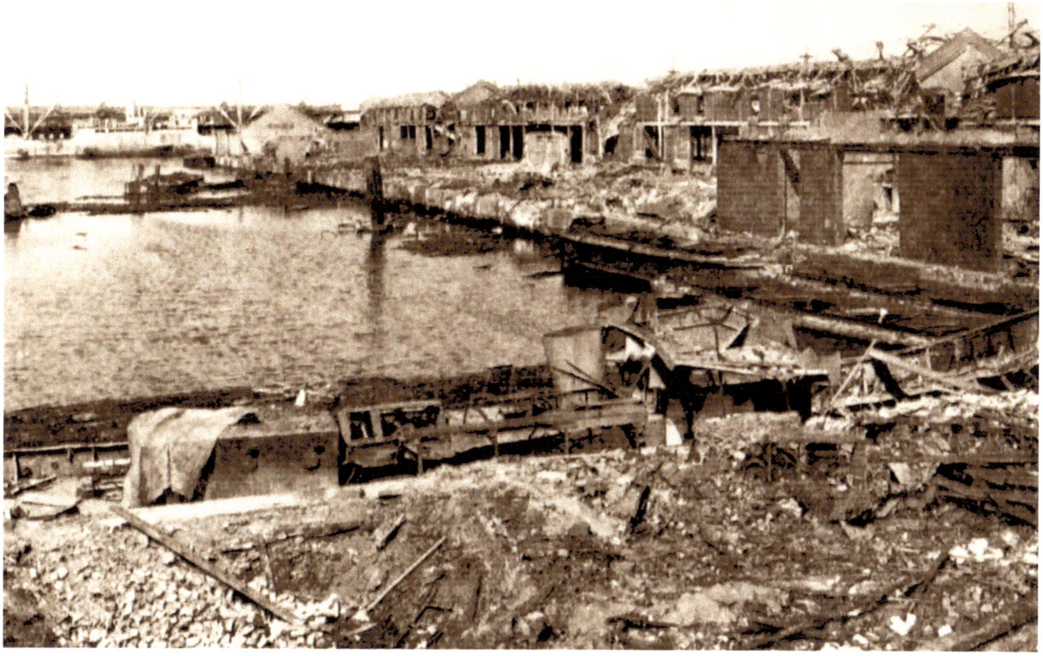

On the night of 3/4 May 1941, Liverpool suffered one of its worst air raids. *Malakand* was berthed in Huskisson Dock with a cargo of ammunition, incendiary and high explosive bombs. It was estimated that there were over 500 German planes bombing Liverpool that night and the people of Wirral said that it looked as if the whole of the city centre was on fire. A deflated barrage balloon slipped from its moorings and then became tangled with *Malakand*'s rigging. It then fell on the deck and burst into flames. A shower of incendiaries had ignited some of the sheds and the flames quickly enveloped *Malakand*. An attempt was made by the crew to scuttle the ship and the captain gave the instruction to abandon ship but the vessel exploded, causing extensive damage to the whole of the Huskisson Dock system.

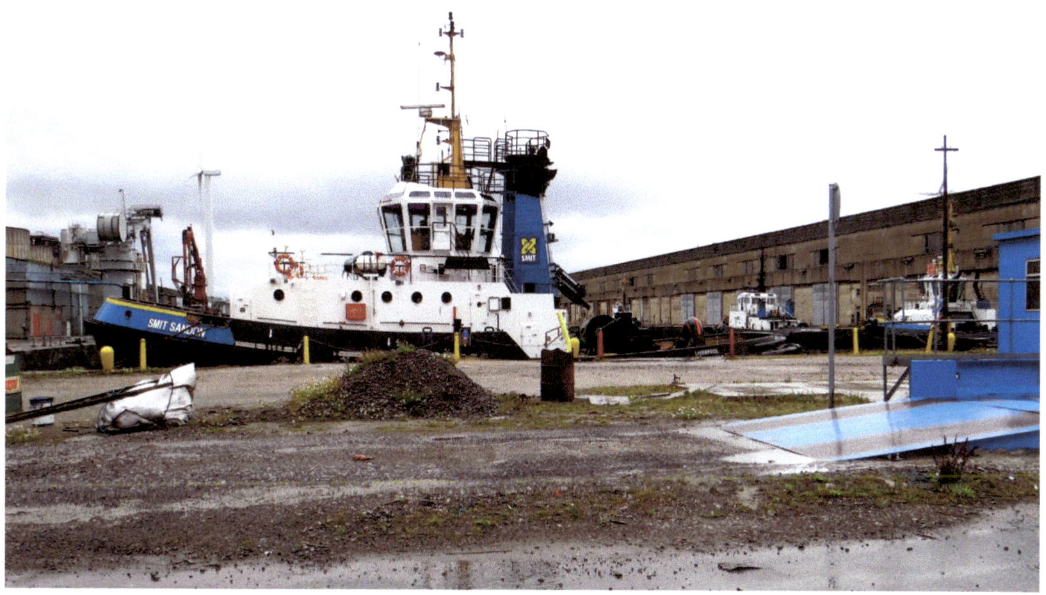

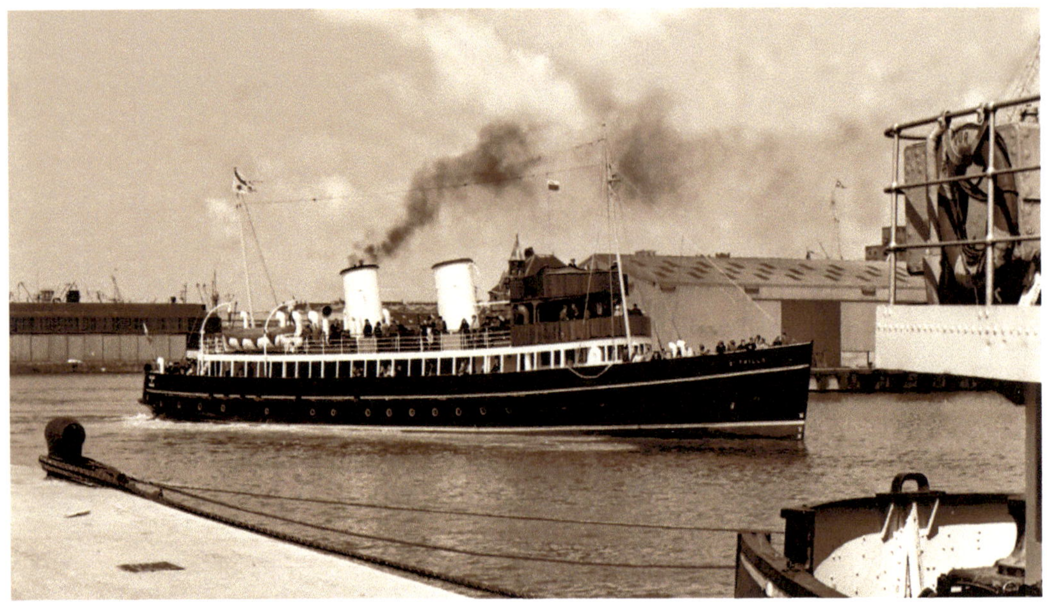

Above: The P&A Campbell passenger vessel *St Trillo*, on charter to the Mersey Docks & Harbour Board to promote the port to its customers in May 1964. *St Trillo* originally operated on short cruises from Llandudno in North Wales to Anglesey for the Liverpool & North Wales Steamship Company. She was purchased by P&A Campbell for service in the Bristol Channel, converted to a floating restaurant in 1972 and broken up at Dublin three years later.

Below: The small coastal cargo vessel *Loach* passes through the dock system, proceeding to her berth in Sandon Dock. She was built in 1968 by the Bay Wharf Construction Company and is employed carrying cargoes, mainly grain, from Liverpool to various destinations on the Manchester Ship Canal.

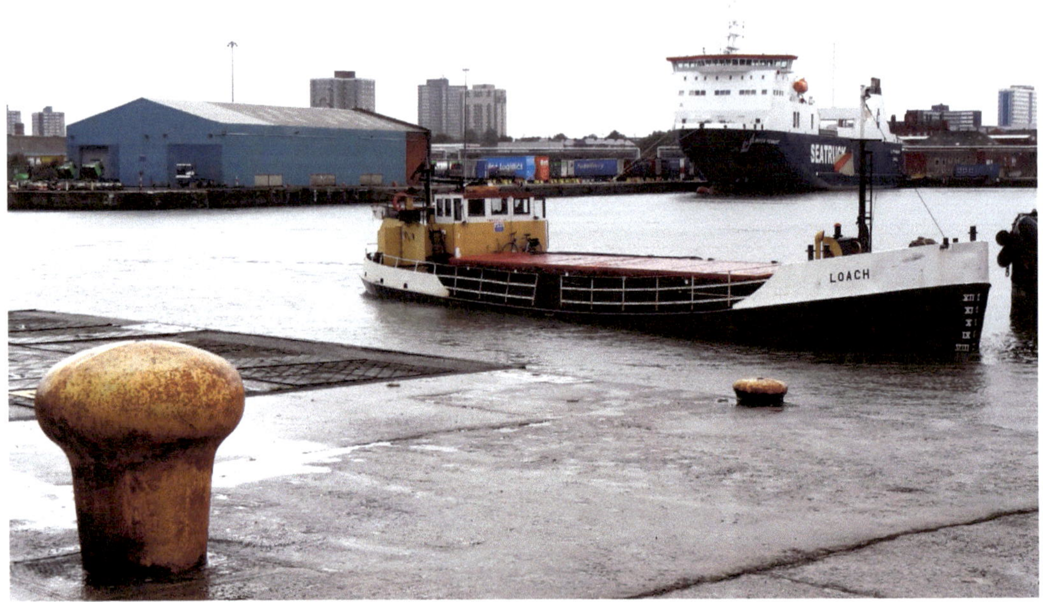

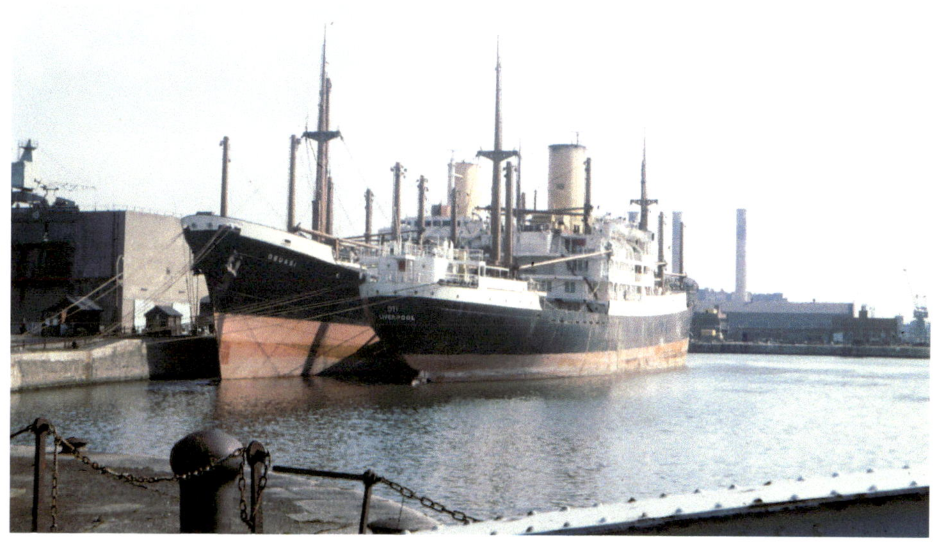

Above: Oti and *Obausi* laid up in Sandon Dock. *Oti* was built in 1957 for the Blue Funnel Line as *Menelaus*. She was transferred to Elder Dempster Lines in 1972 and renamed *Mano*, operating for the Guinea Gulf Line, *Oti* in 1977, and placed on Elder Dempster services to West Africa. She was sold the following year, renamed *Elstar* and broken up in Korea in 1979. *Obuasi* was built as *Machaon* for the Blue Funnel Line, becoming *Obuasi* in 1977 for the West African services. She was sold the following year, becoming *Elsea* and *Med Endeavour*, and was broken up at Kaohsiung in 1979.

Below: Samaria in Sandon Dock. She was owned by the Cunard Line and was built by Cammell Laird at Birkenhead in 1965. *Samaria* was sold to the Harrison Line in 1969, becoming *Scholar* and *Steel Trader* in 1980. In August 1980 she was damaged by shell-fire at Khorramshahr during the Iraq/Iran war and was abandoned. Sandon Dock was also designed by Jesse Hartley and the original dock was enclosed when Sandon Half-Tide was built. Part of Sandon Dock has been filled in and is the site of a sewage treatment plant and pumping station (*inset*).

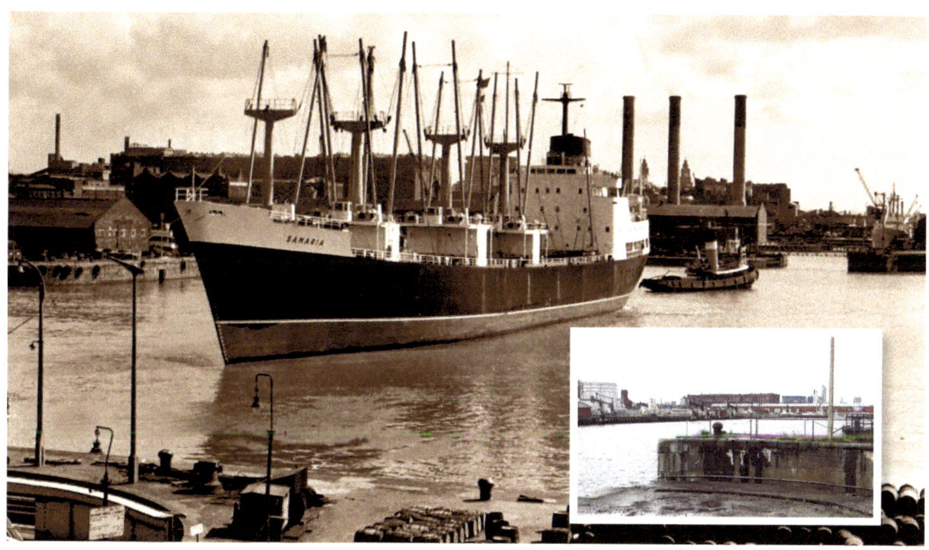

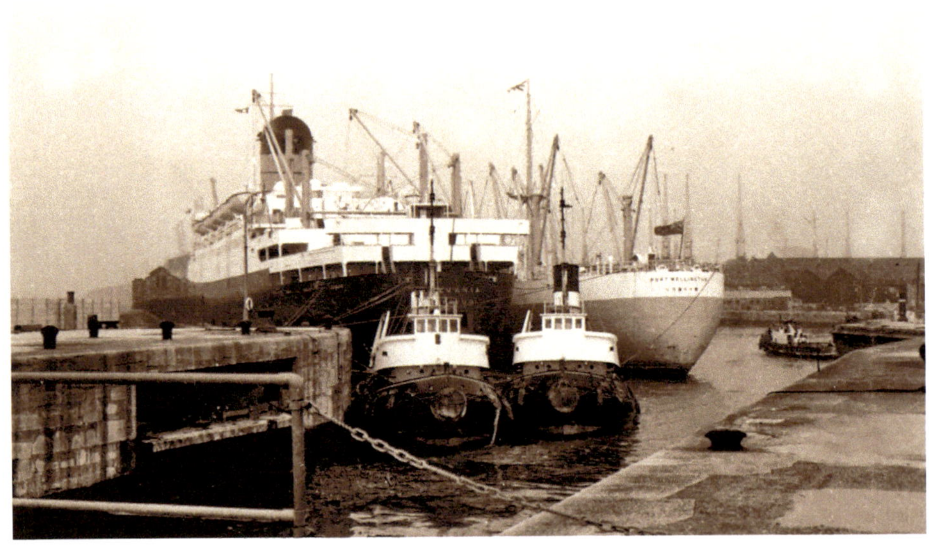

Sylvania and *Port Wellington* await the tide in Sandon Dock. *Sylvania* was the last of four similar passenger liners built for the Cunard Line and was delivered in 1957, for the Liverpool to New York service. She was sold to the Sitmar Line in 1968 and renamed *Fairwind, Dawn Princess* in 1988 and *Albatros* in 1994. She arrived at Alang on 10 January 2004, under the name of *Genoa*, to be broken up. *Port Wellington* was built in 1946 and was Port Line's first post-war ship. She remained in their fleet until 1971, when she was sold and broken up in Spain.

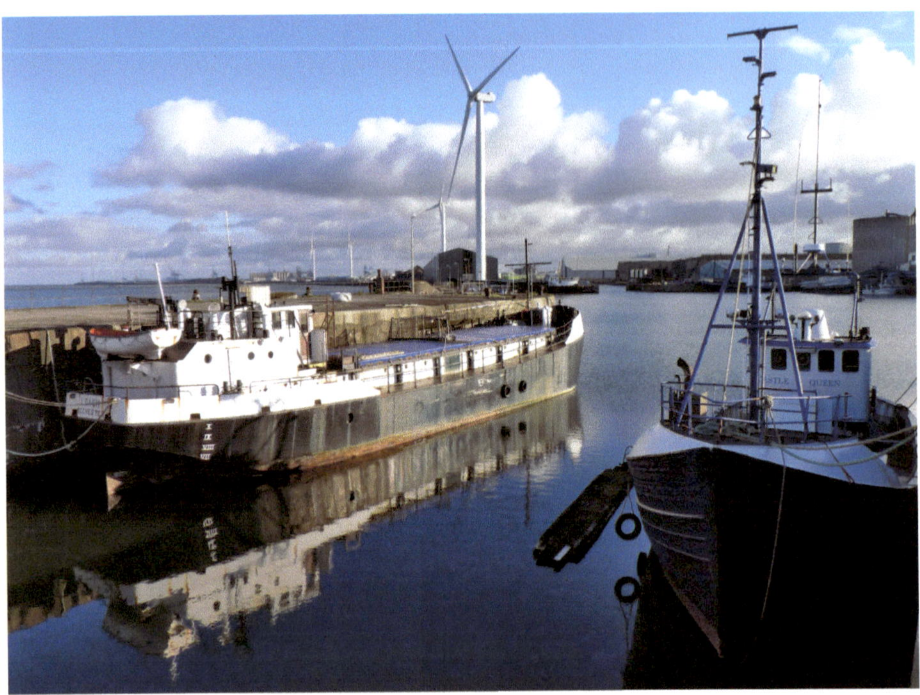

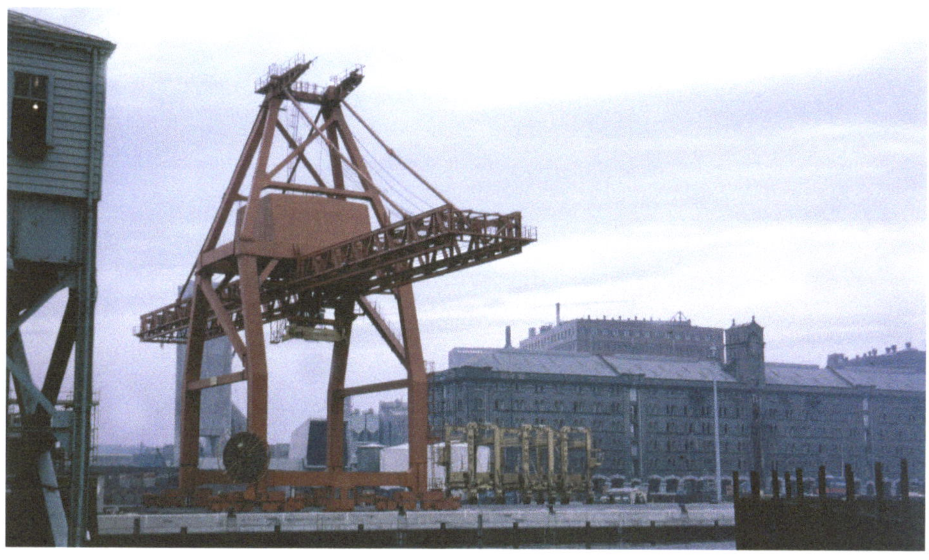

Above: Trafalgar Dock was also used as a container terminal for the B+I Line services to Dublin.

Below: The British & Irish Steam Packet Company operated a car and passenger ferry service from Trafalgar Dock. The reception and waiting rooms were built adjacent to the berth and received a design award when they were built at a cost of £2.1 million. It was constructed on 15 acres of land with the in-filling of the Victoria Dock and Trafalgar Branch Dock. The terminal opened on 1 October 1972. On 1 February 1983 weather conditions were so bad that the ferry *Leinster* was prevented from sailing by hurricane-force winds and she was trapped in Trafalgar Dock for over sixteen hours, with 300 passengers on board. The car ferry *Connacht* made the last sailing from the terminal on 18 October 1983, when Waterloo river entrance was closed to traffic. Demolition of the Terminal building commenced in 2001 but this was not completed until 2005.

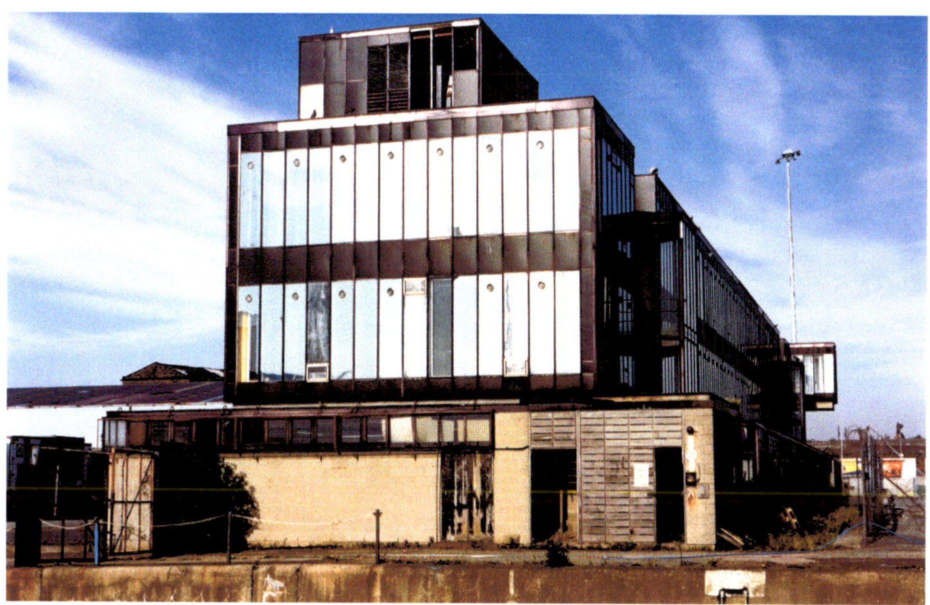

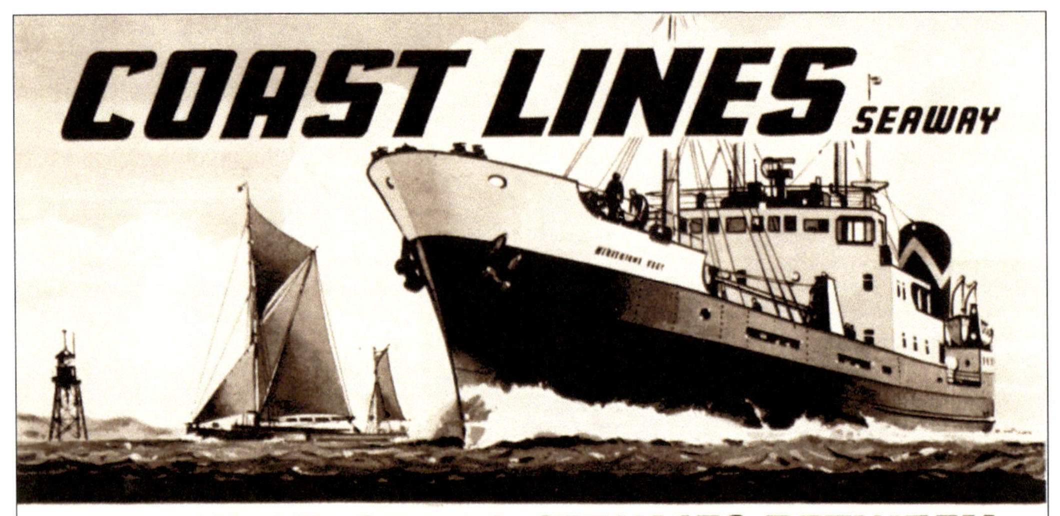

The Coast Line (Link Lines) berths in Trafalgar Dock next to Clarence Dock Power Station. Clarence Dock, designed by Jesse Hartley, was connected to Trafalgar Dock and was named after William, Duke of Clarence, who became William IV. The dock was in-filled in 1929 and a power station with three large chimneys was constructed. This was demolished in the 1990s.

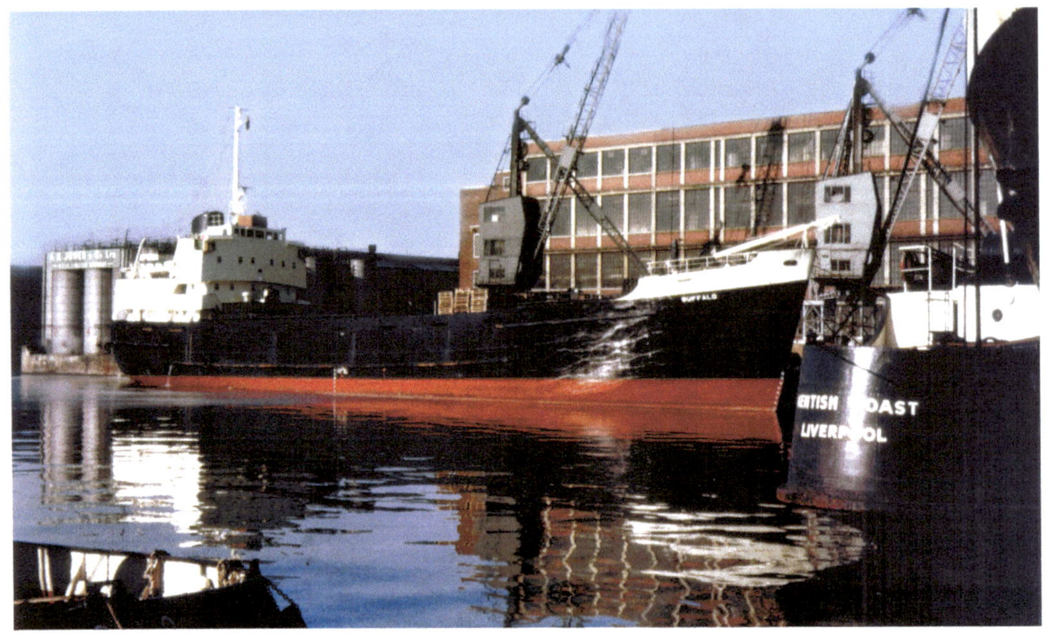

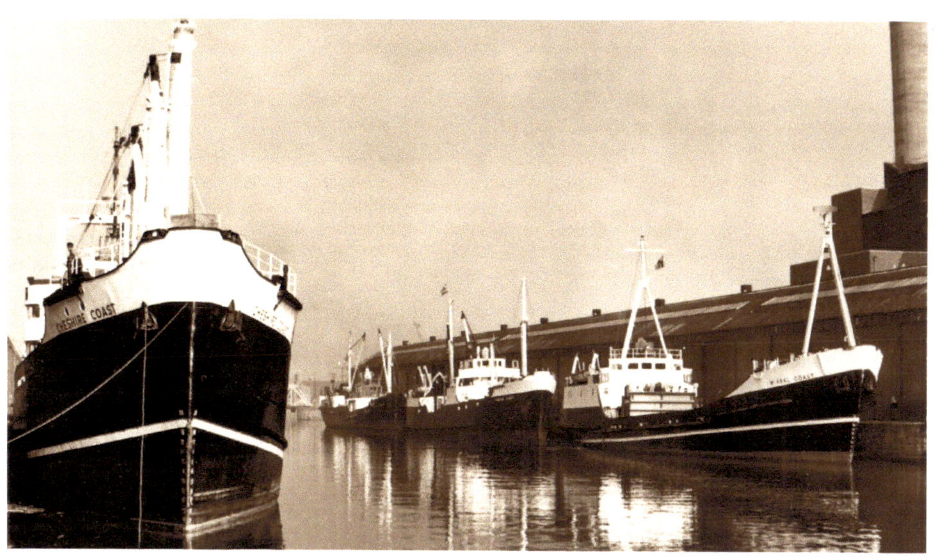

Above: The Coast Lines berths in Trafalgar Dock. *Cheshire Coast, Inniscarra, Kentish Coast* and *Wirral Coast. Cheshire Coast* was built in 1954, becoming *Malabar* on charter to the Brocklebank Line, and *Spartan Prince* on charter to Prince Line in 1967, *Cheshire Coast* and *Venture* in 1971 and *Azelia* three years later. She was broken up in 1980. *Inniscarra* was owned by the B+I Line and was built in 1948 as *Brittany Coast*, renamed *Inniscarra* in 1950, *Elni* in 1970, *Ria* in 1972, before being broken up in Italy in 1981. *Kentish Coast* was built in 1946 as *Ulster Duchess* and *Jersey Coast* the following year, *Ulster Weaver* in 1954, *Kentish Coast* in 1964 and *Salmiah Coast* in 1968. She was sold to the Kuwait Coast Line in 1970, Iranian interests in 1975 and was deleted from Lloyd's Register in 1999. *Wirral Coast* was built by Cammell Laird at Birkenhead in 1962, becoming *Shevrell* in 1972, *Portmarnock* in 1974 and *Nadia 1* in 1979. On 27 November 1985 she sank at Khalde and was declared a total loss.

Below: The small Shell-Mex and BP oiler *City* in Waterloo Dock in 1966. She was used to supply oil to vessels using the port. Waterloo Dock was opened in 1834 and was named after the Battle of Waterloo. The dock was divided into two separate basins, East Waterloo Dock and West Waterloo Dock, in 1868. It was closed to traffic in 1988 and the warehouses have been converted to residential apartments.

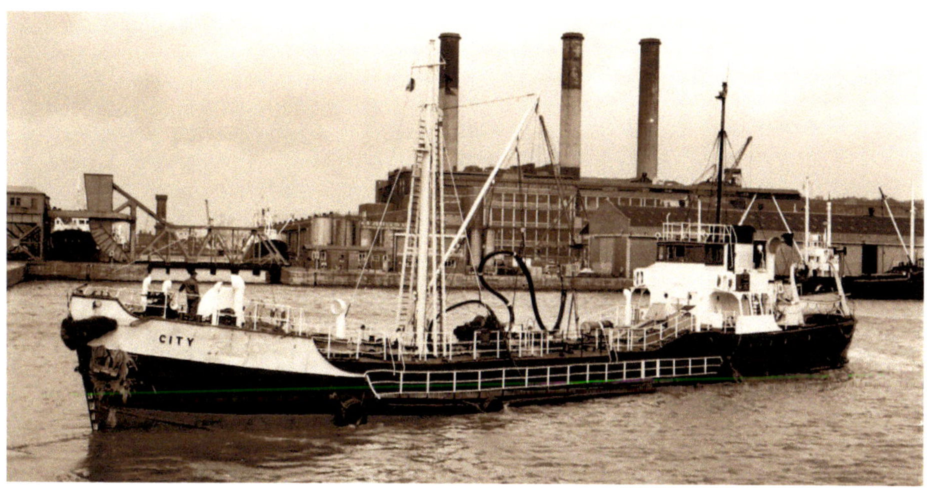

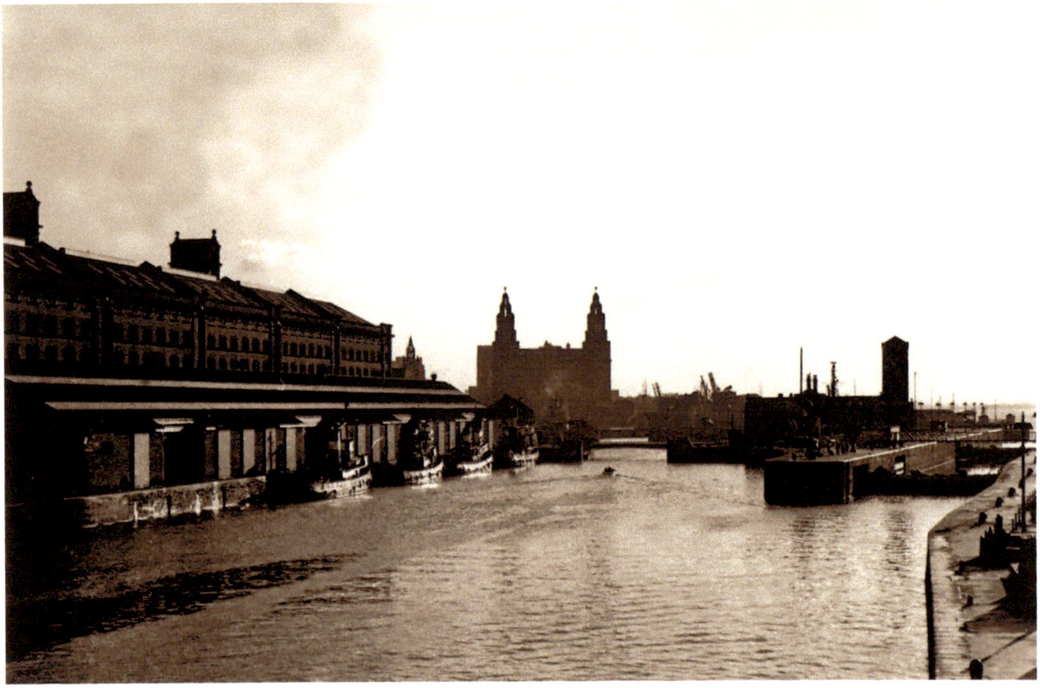

Waterloo Dock entrance, which was closed to traffic in 1983. The lock was opened in 1949 and was closed and in-filled in 1988.

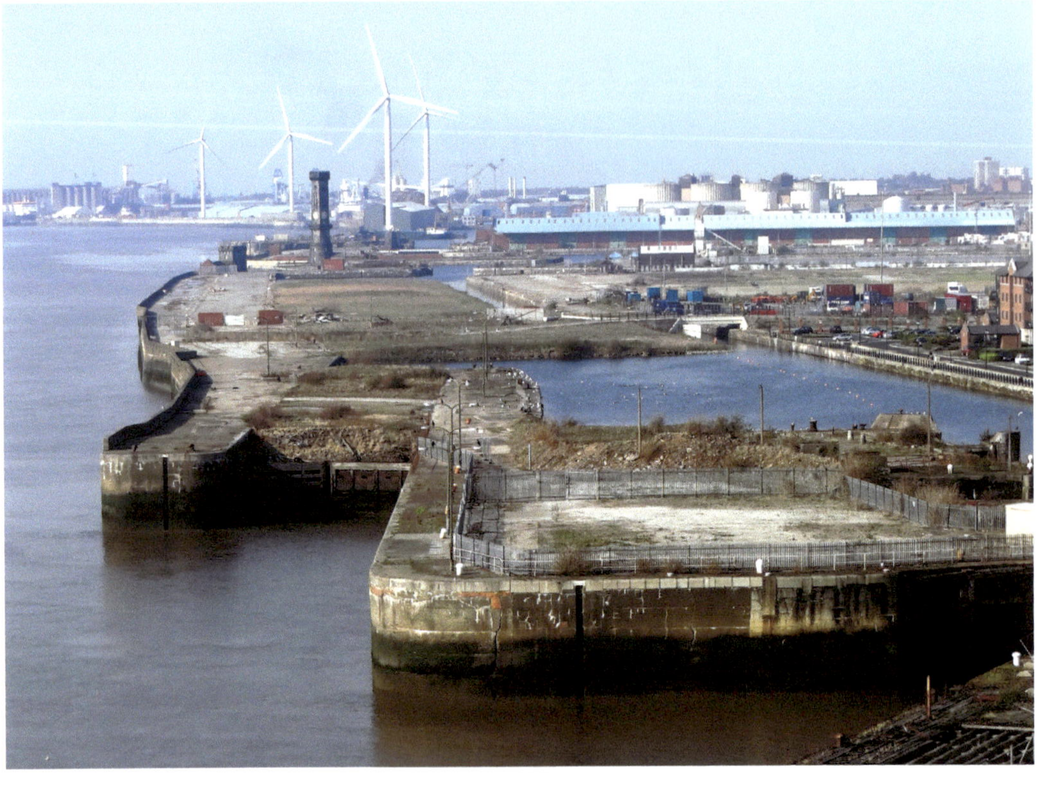

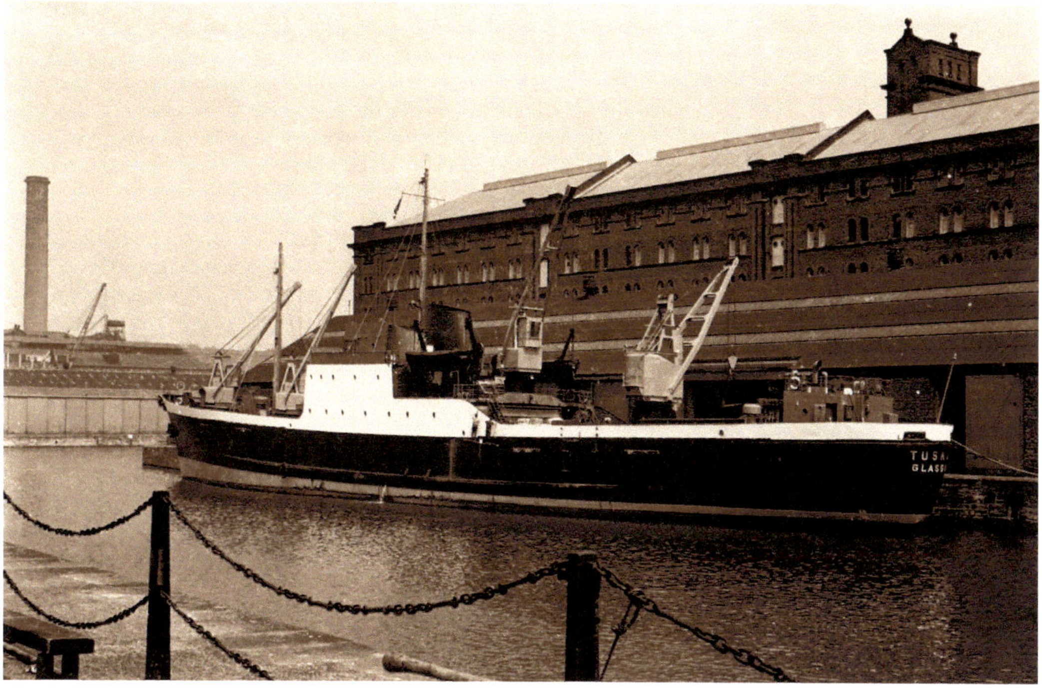

Tuskar in West Waterloo Dock. *Tuskar* was owned by the Clyde Shipping Company and was built in 1962 for the Liverpool to Waterford service. After a very short period on the route, she was sold in 1968 to Losinjska Plovidba OOUR Brodarstvo and renamed *Brioni*. In 1988 she was sold to be broken up.

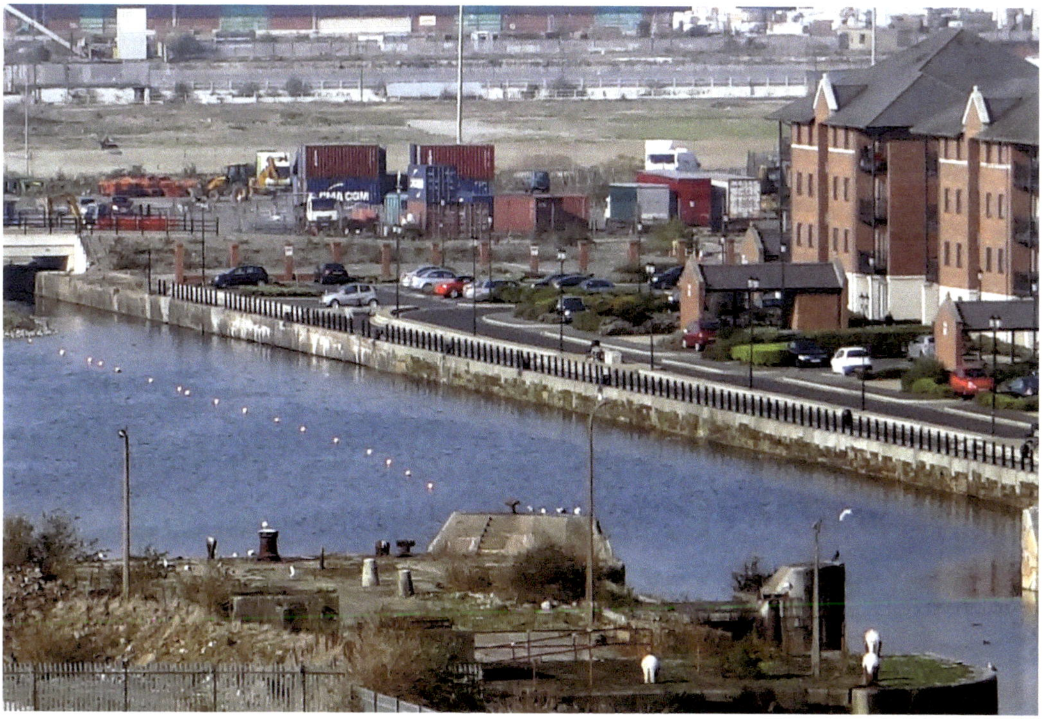

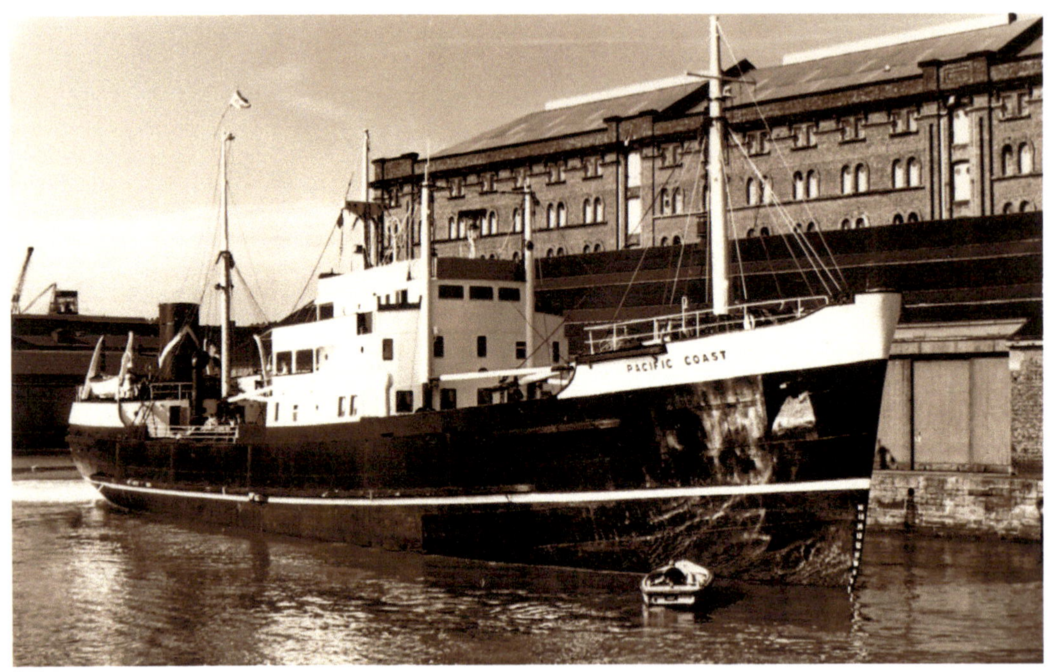

The Coast Line's *Pacific Coast* passing through West Waterloo Dock. She was built in 1947 and was renamed *Kuwait Coast* in 1968, *Mohamed Nassar* in 1974 and *Nassar* the following year. On 29 November 1976 she was abandoned during a gale at Port Rashid. She was refloated the following year and was sunk off a breakwater in shallow water.

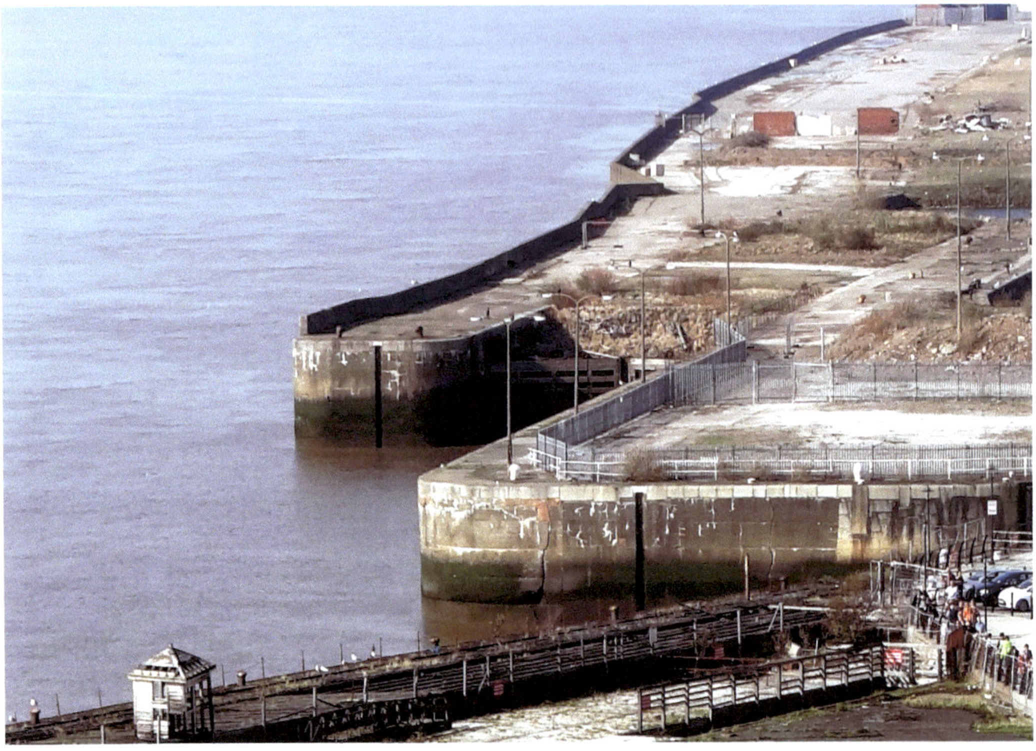

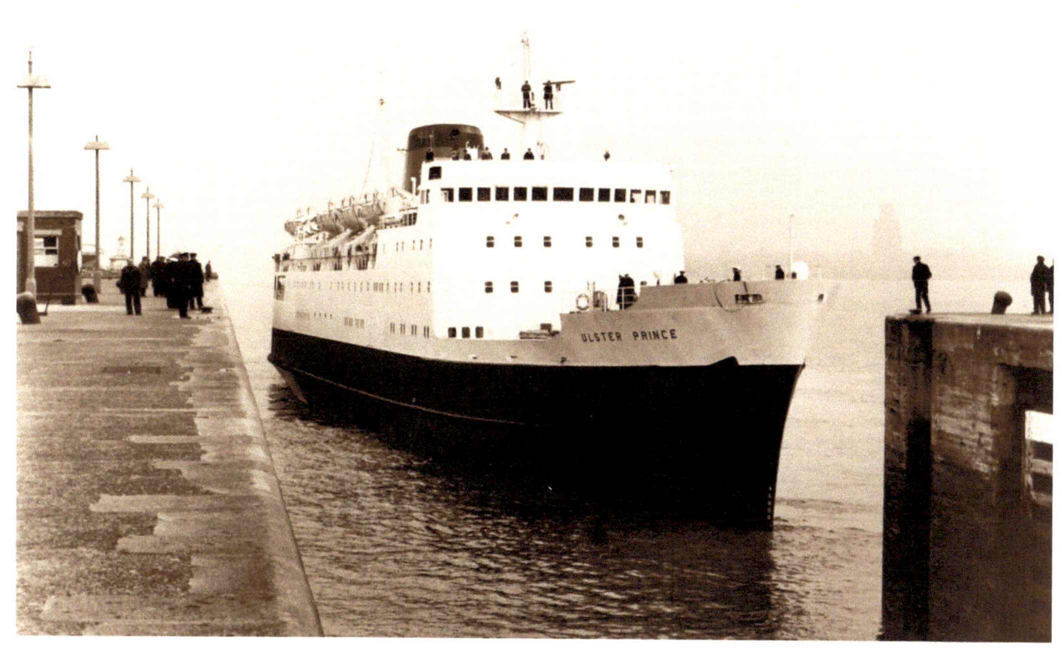

The Belfast Steamship Company car and passenger ferry *Ulster Prince* arriving at Waterloo River Entrance in 1968. She was built in 1967, becoming *Lady M* in 1982, *Tangpakorn* in 1984, *Long Hu* and *Macmosa* in 1988, *Neptunia II, Neptunia* and *Panther* in 1995 and *Vatan* and *Manar* in 2000. She was broken up at Alang in 2004.

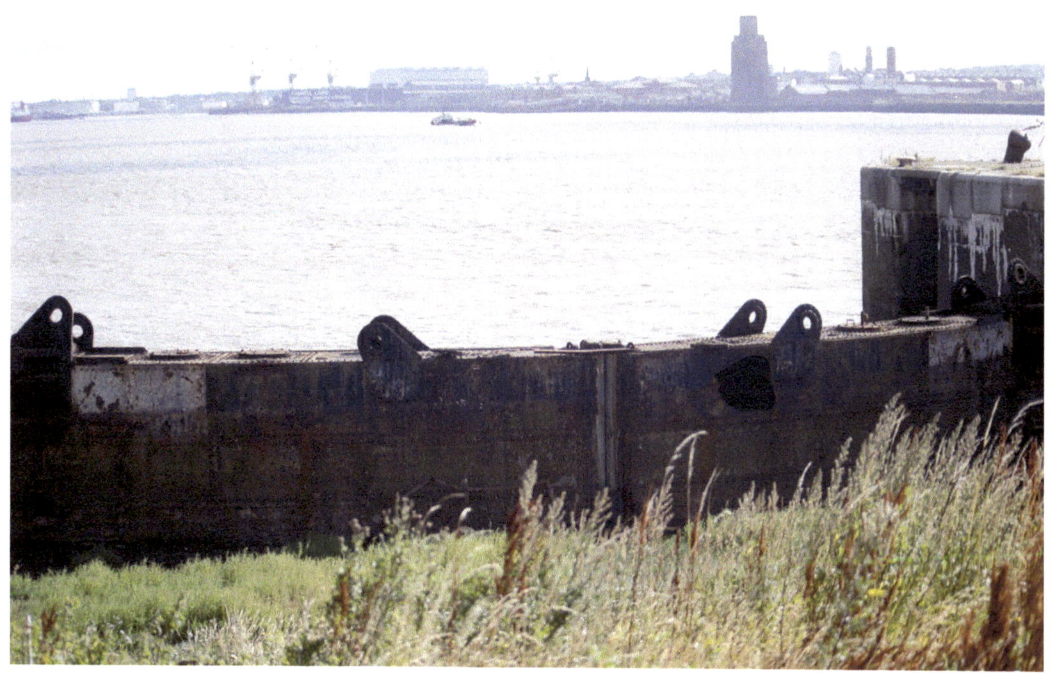

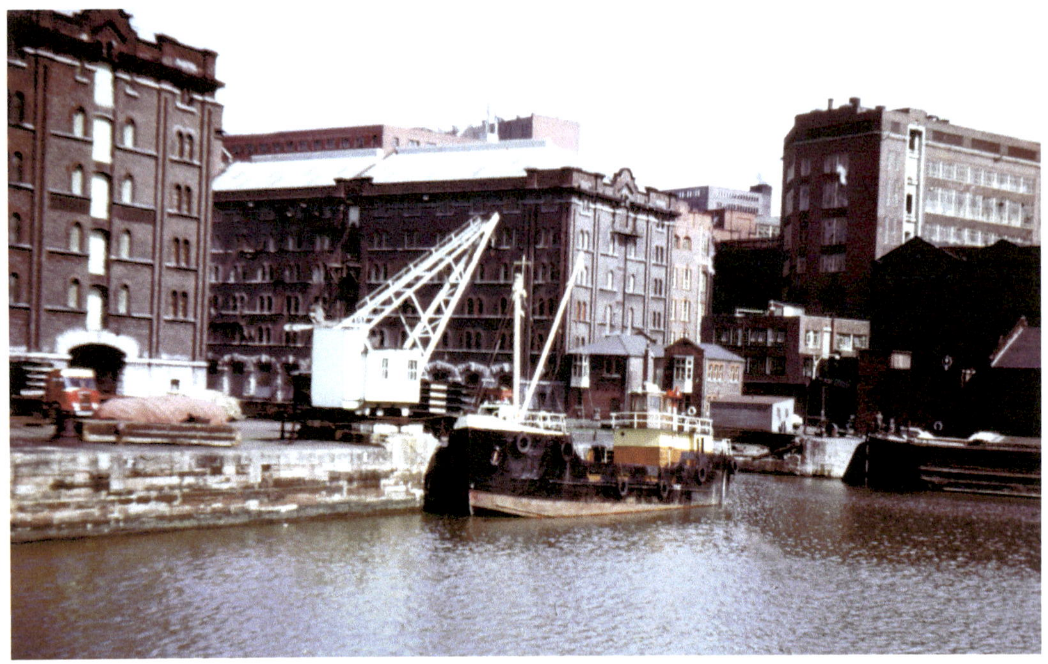

The warehouses at Waterloo Dock are almost identical to those at Albert Dock. Waterloo Dock warehouse now incorporates approximately 114 apartments. Located close to the Pier Head, this warehouse conversion has much of its original features with its exposed brick, original cast iron supporting columns, full length windows and vaulted, barrelled ceilings. The dock was designed by Jesse Hartley and was opened in 1834. An observatory was opened at the dock in 1844, but by 1867 the pollution was so bad in Liverpool city centre that it was decided to move the chronometer to Bidston Hill at Birkenhead. In 1868 the dock was divided into East and West Docks and the grain warehouses were built, which were the first in the country to use mechanical handling equipment.

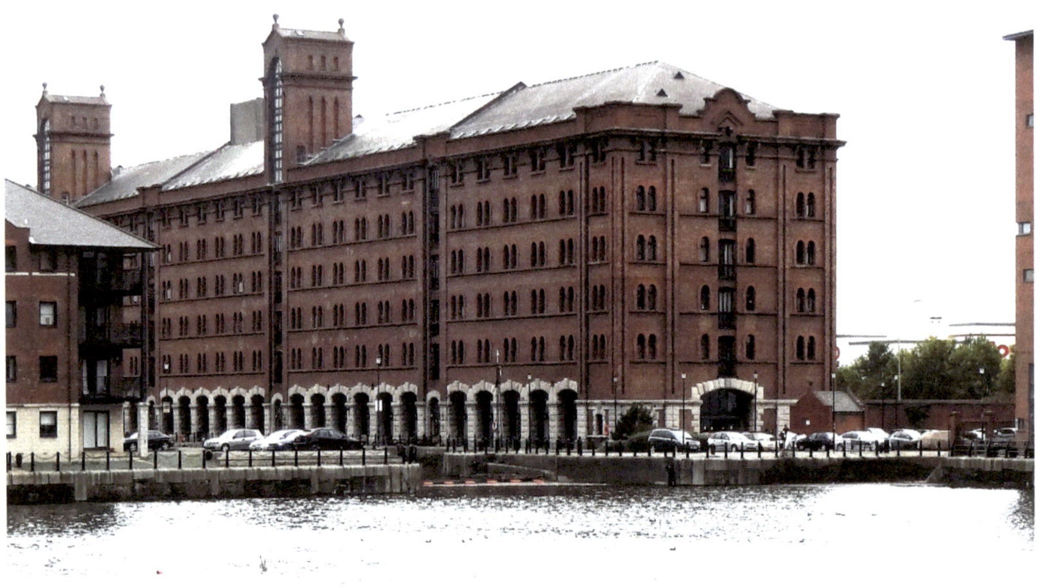

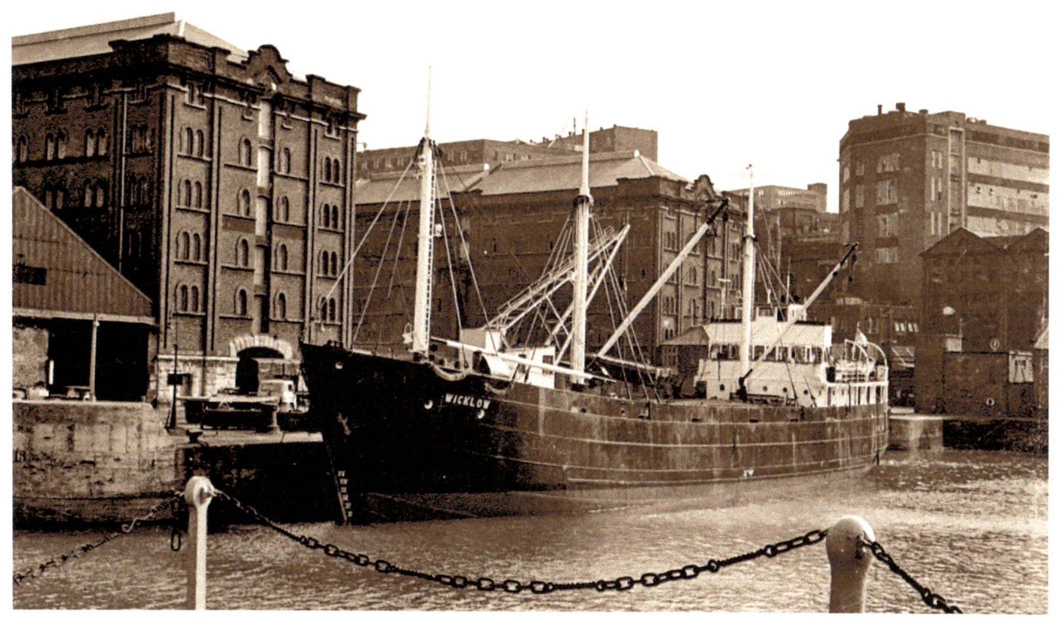

Wicklow in Prince's Half Tide Dock. *Wicklow* was owned by the B+I Line and was built in 1938 as *Sandhill, Valerian Coast* in 1946, *Hebridean Coast* in 1948, *Ulster Chieftain* in 1953, *Durham Coast* in 1956, *Wicklow* in 1960, *Sinergasia* in 1970, *Sonia* in 1973 and *Margarita P* the following year. She was broken up in Italy in 1980.

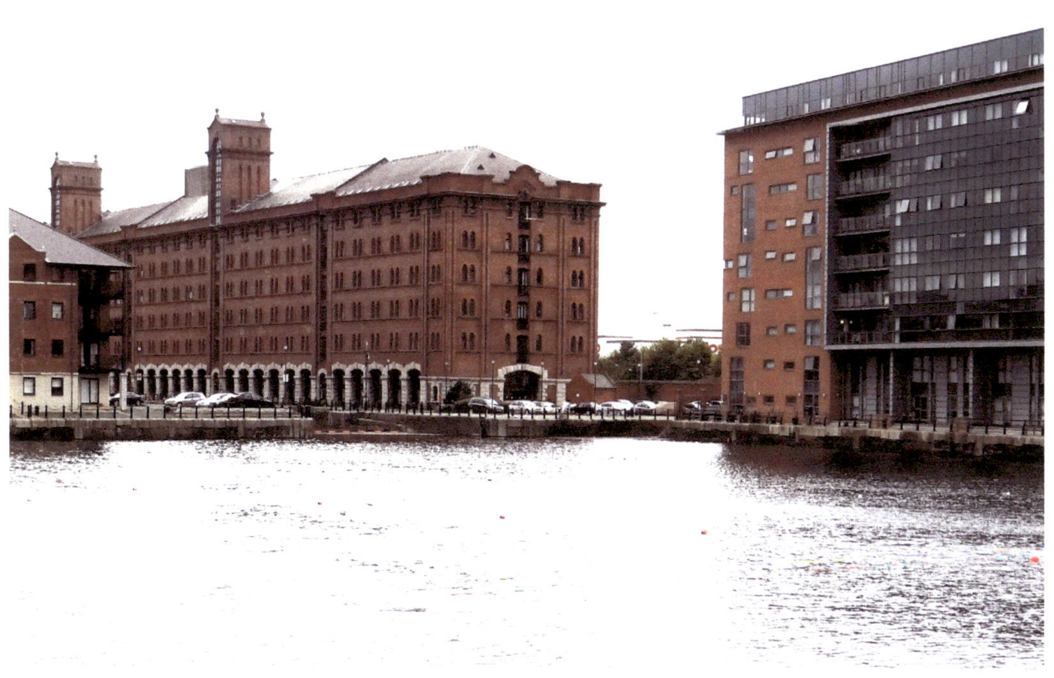

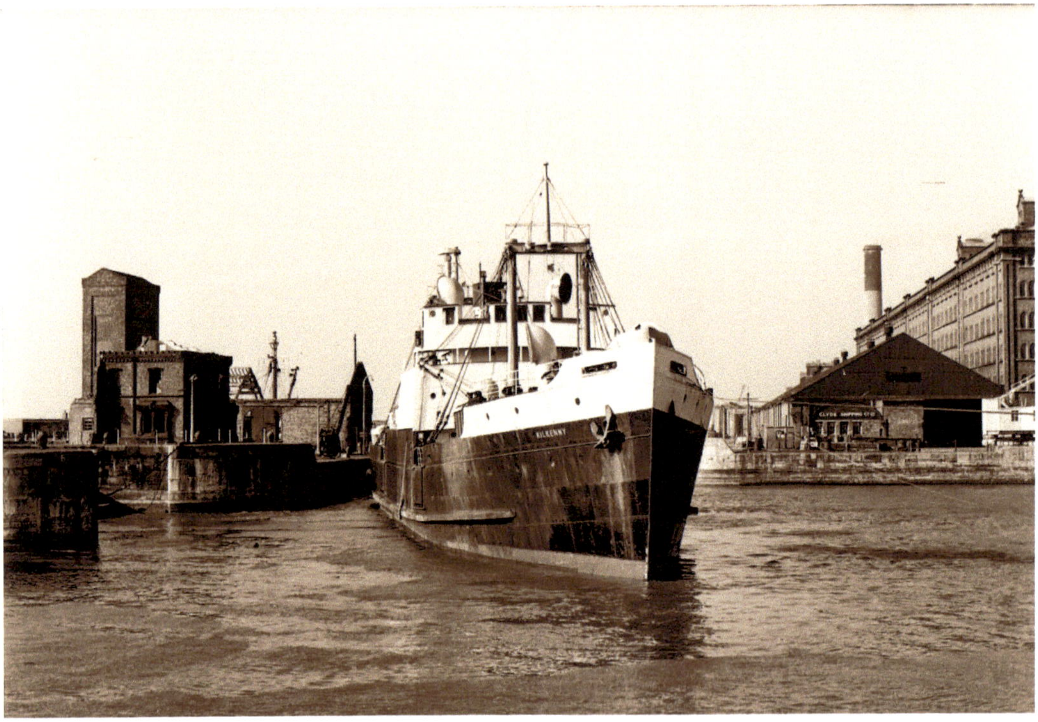

Kilkenny navigates through Prince's Half Tide Dock in 1967.

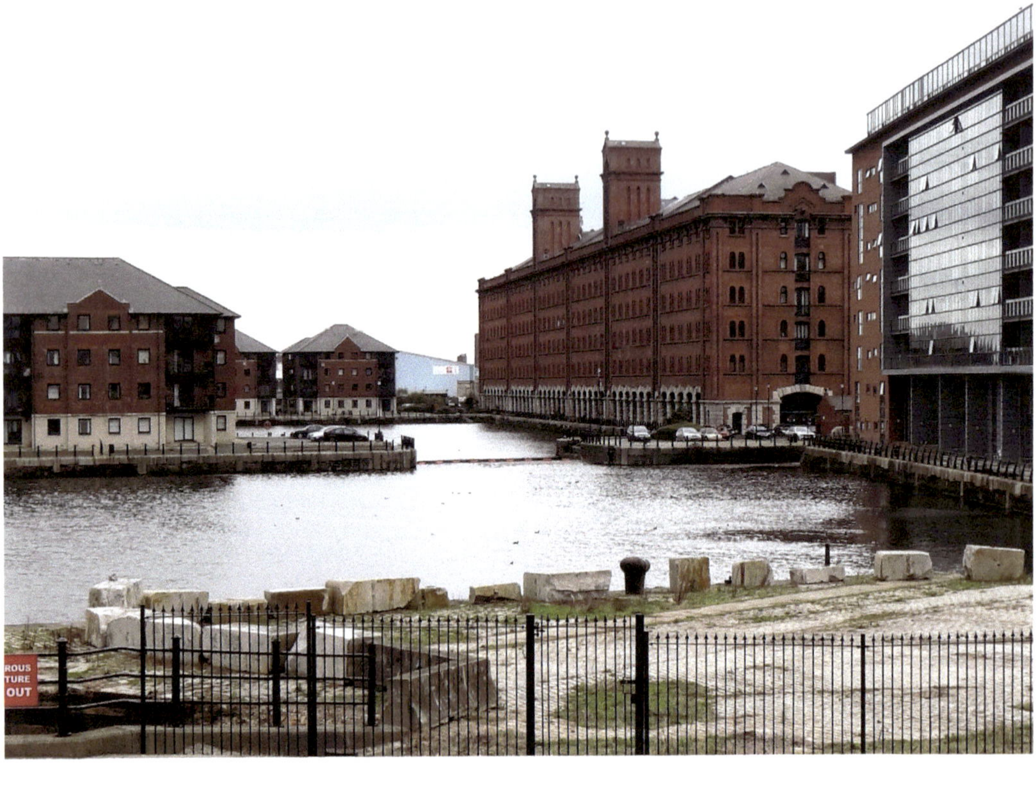

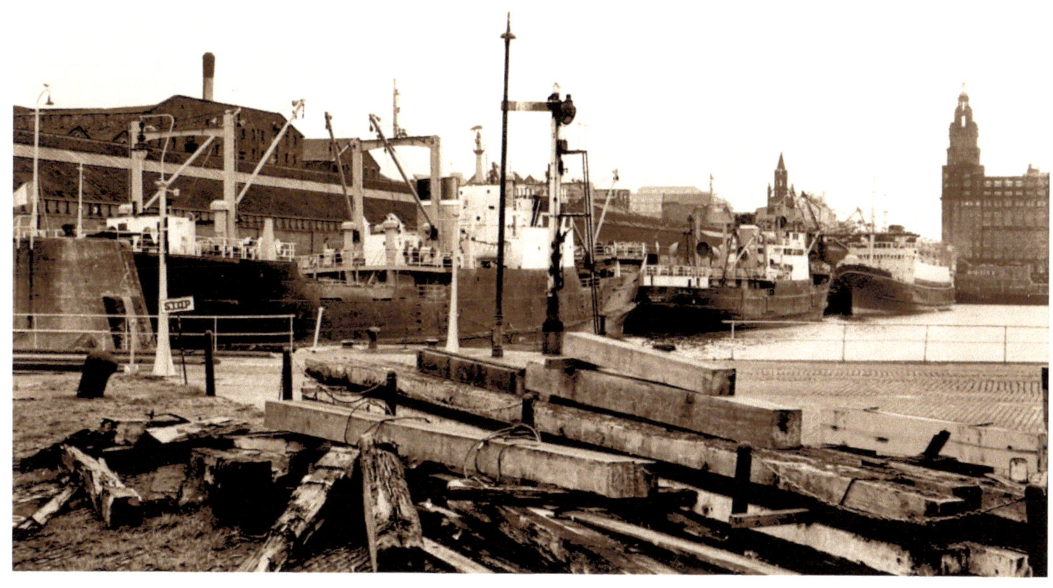

B+I Line vessels *Meath, Kilkenny* and *Munster* at Prince's Dock, east side. *Meath* was built in 1960 for the Dublin to Liverpool route and was sold to the Vickers Shipbuilding Company Limited after thirteen years in service, becoming *Vickers Viscount* in 1975. She was renamed *British Viscount* in 1980 and *British* in 1990, when was sold to be broken up at Alang. *Munster* and her sister *Leinster* were introduced in 1948 and were transferred to Irish Government ownership in 1965. On arrival of a new car ferry she was renamed *Munster I* in 1969 and was sold to Greek interests, becoming *Theseus* and then *Orpheus*. After thirty years' service as a cruise ship in the Mediterranean, she was sold to be broken up at Alang in 2000.

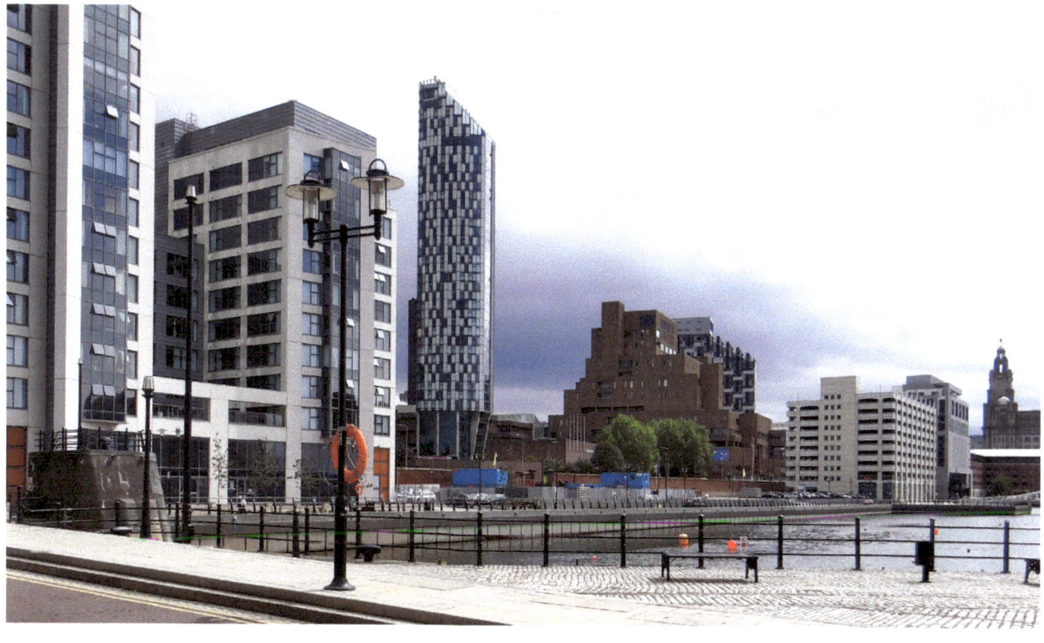

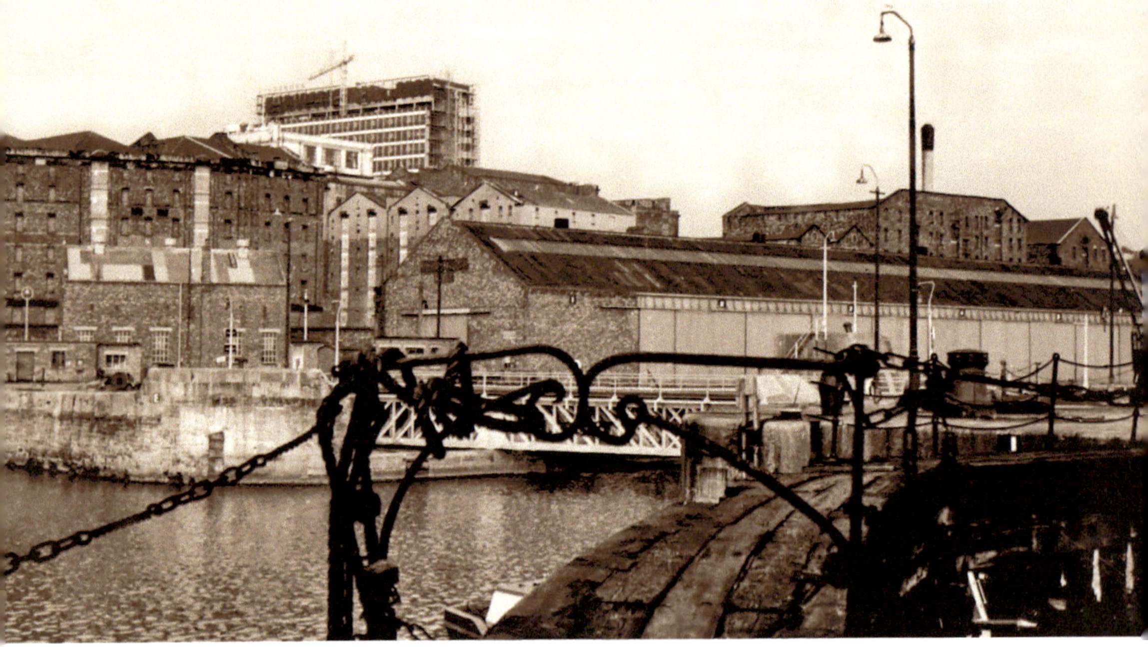

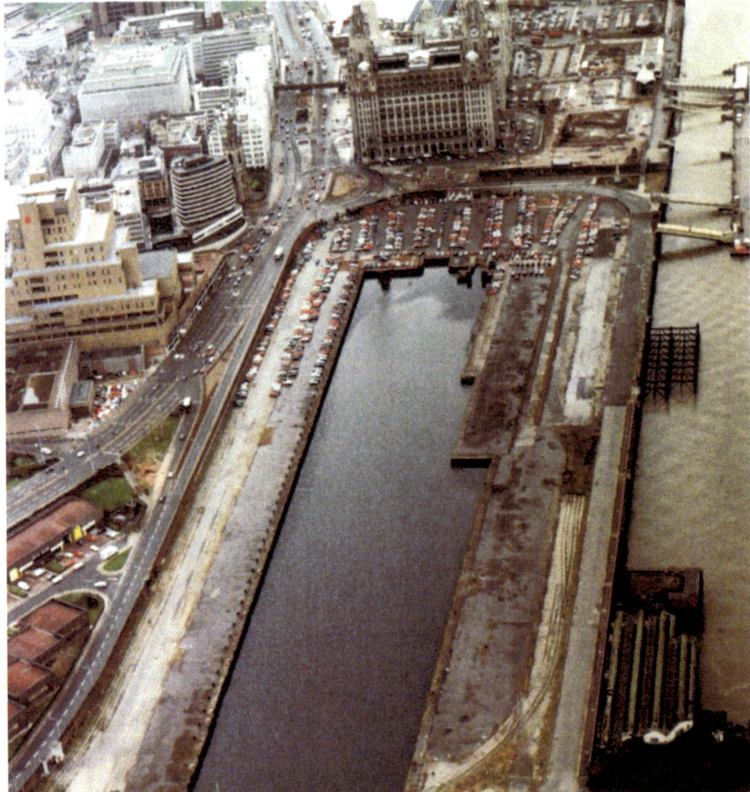

Above: Prince's Dock, east side in 1967. Prince's Dock was named after the Prince Regent and opened the day of his coronation as George IV on 19 July 1821.

Left: The warehouses and Riverside Station have been demolished at Prince's Dock and Prince's Parade.

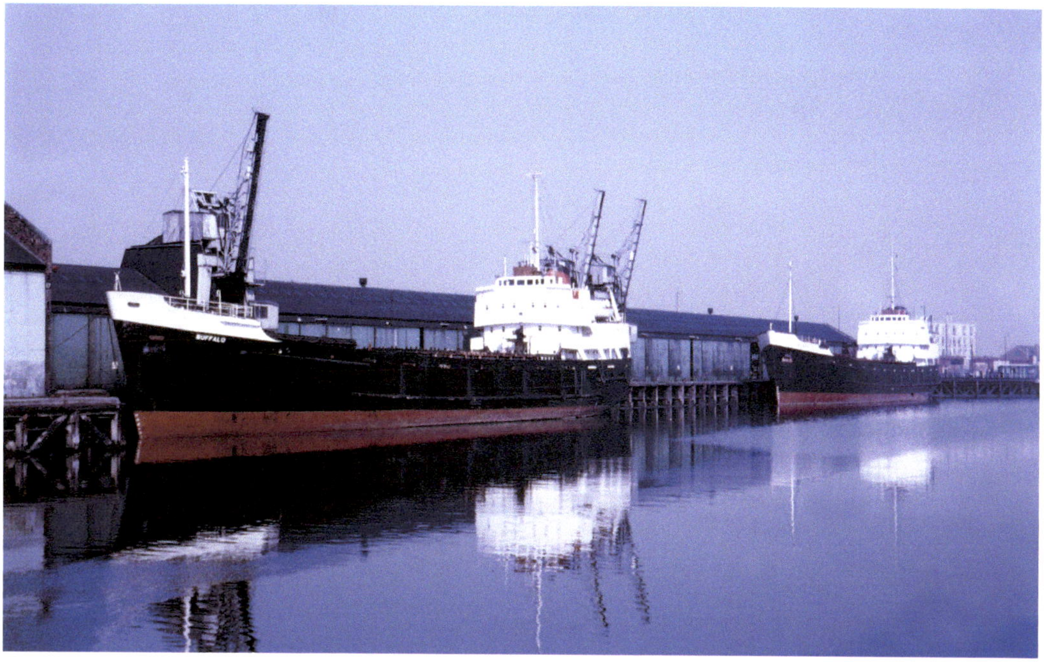

Above: The Link Line vessels *Buffalo* and *Bison* laid up at Prince's Dock, west side. *Buffalo* was built in 1961 and became *Norbrae* in 1972, *Roe Deer* in 1974, *Newfoundland Container* in 1977, *Caribbean Victory* in 1985, *Lefkimmi* in 1986, *St George* in 1988 and *Container Express* in 1992. She was abandoned in 1993.

Below: Narrow boats are now able to navigate through Prince's Dock from the Leeds–Liverpool Canal, and through to Albert Dock past the Pier Head.

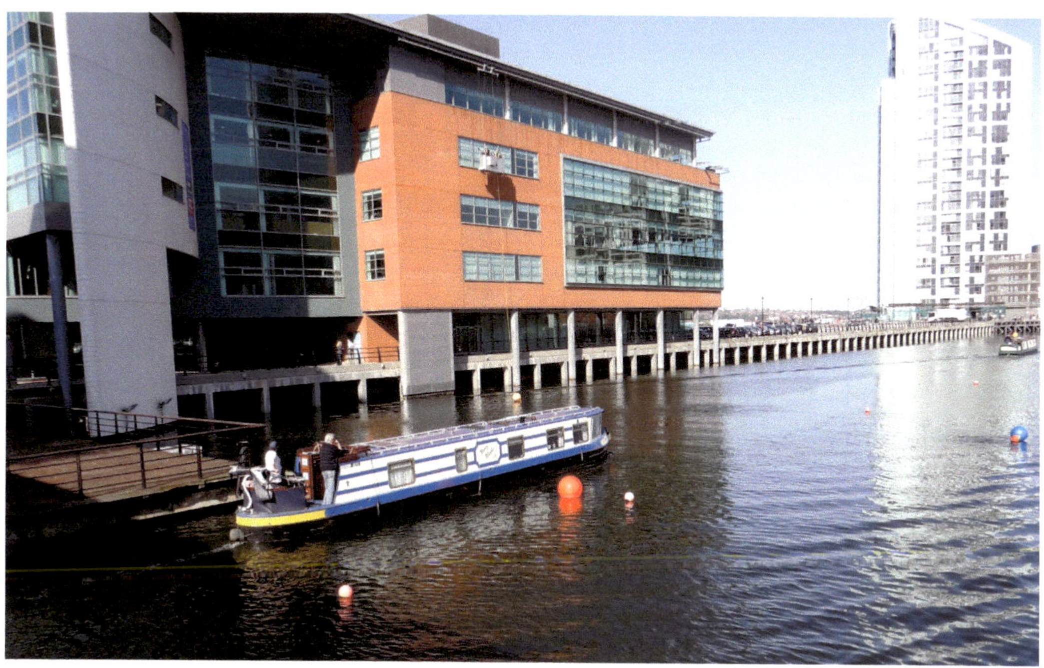

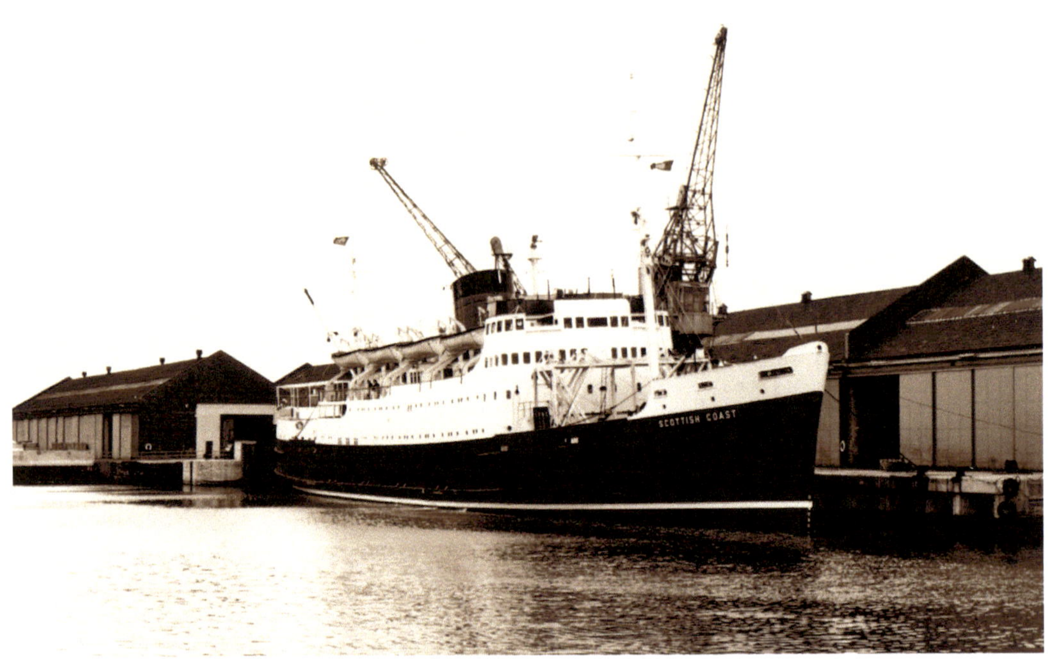

The *Scottish Coast* at Prince's Dock, west side berth, relieving the normal vessel on the Belfast service. *Scottish Coast* was sold in 1969 and renamed *Galaxias*. She was used as a floating hotel at Vancouver in 1986 and became *Princesa Amorosa* in 1989. She was broken up in 2002.

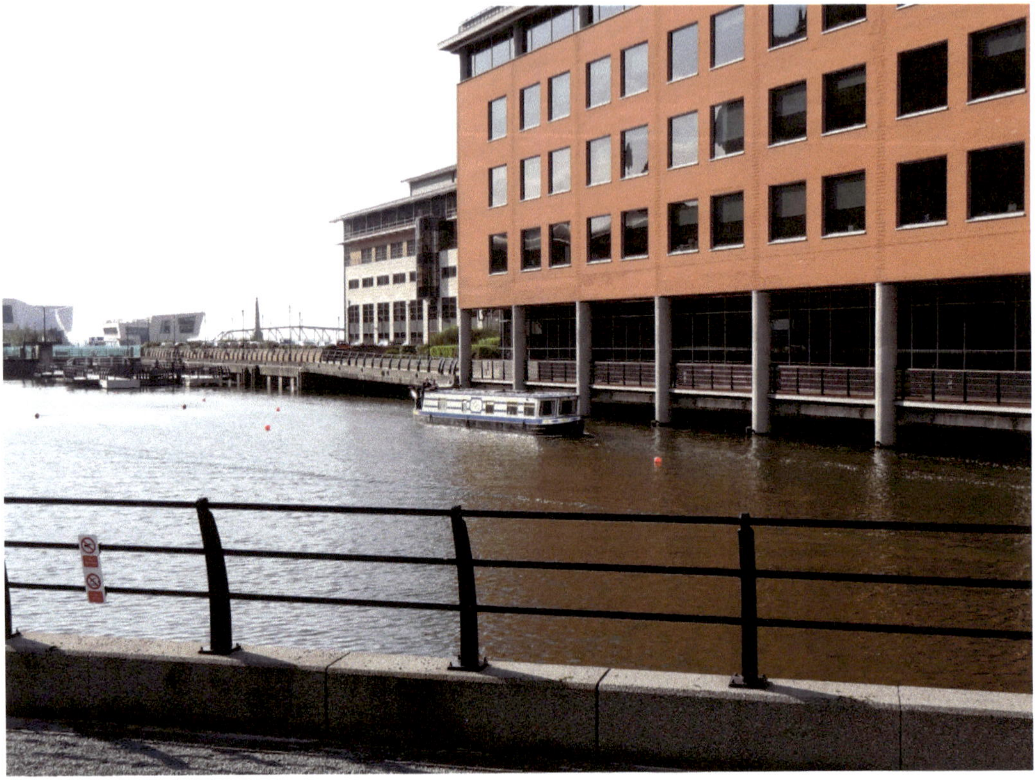

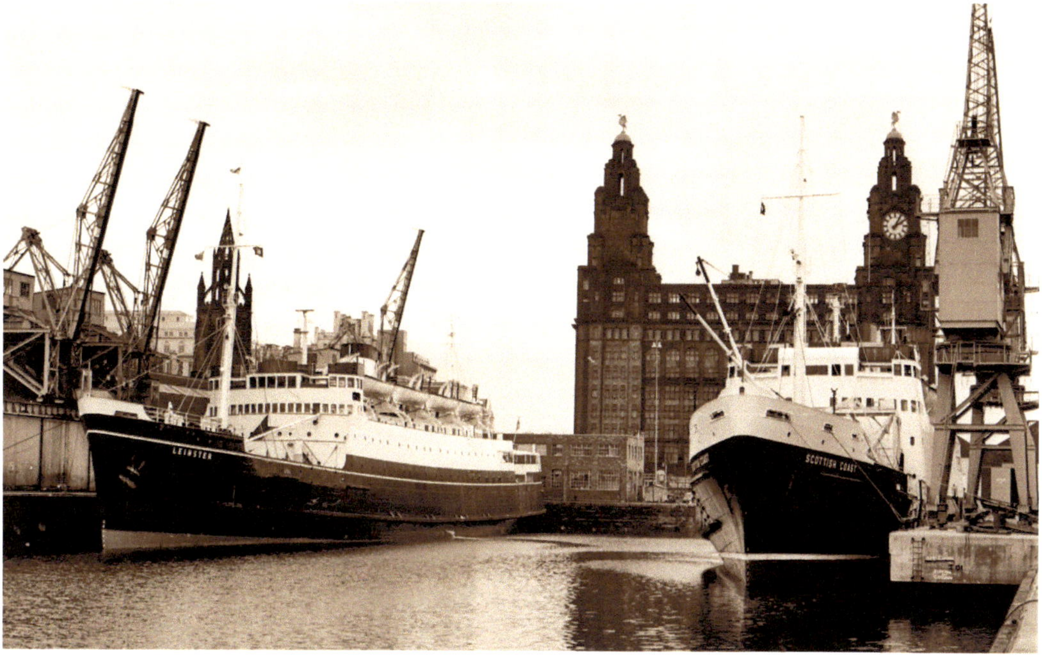

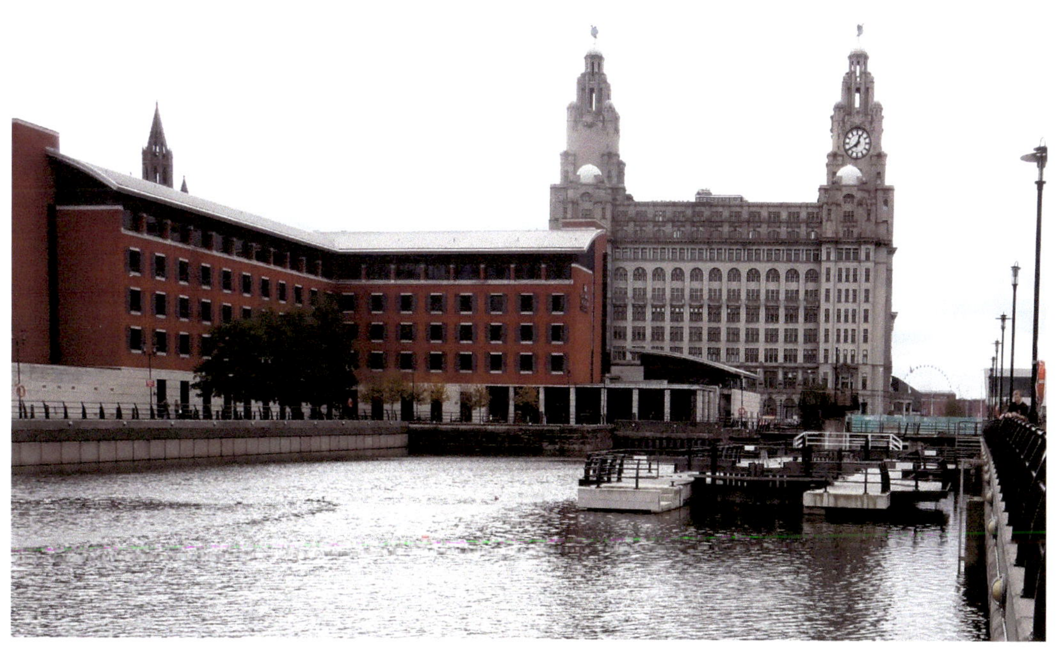

Leinster and *Scottish Coast* loading in Prince's Dock for Dublin and Belfast. *Leinster* operated on the service from 1948 to 1969, when she was renamed *Leinster I* and laid up at Birkenhead on the arrival of a new car ferry for the service. She was sold, renamed *Aphrodite* and was used for cruising in the Mediterranean. She arrived at Aliaga on 11 October 1987 to be broken up. There is now a lock at the site of the Belfast car ferry berth (*below*), where narrow boats lock down to enter a tunnel, which takes them under the road to the Pier Head. The Canal Link was officially opened to boaters on 20 April 2009.

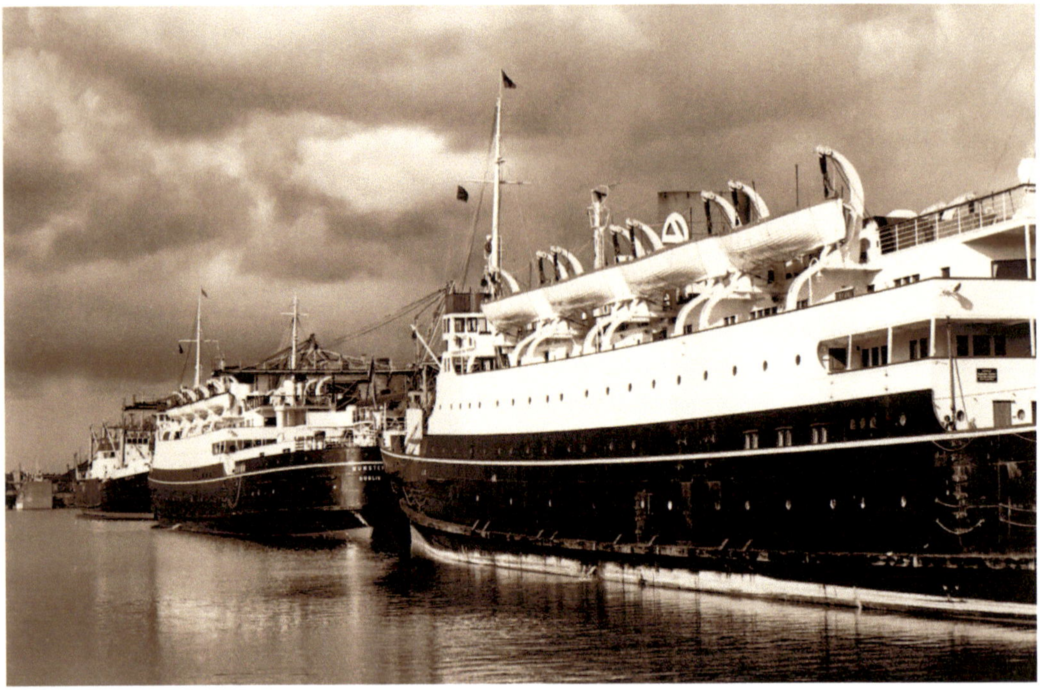

The Dublin passenger vessels at Prince's Dock, east side in the 1960s. The site is now occupied by hotels and a multi-storey car park.

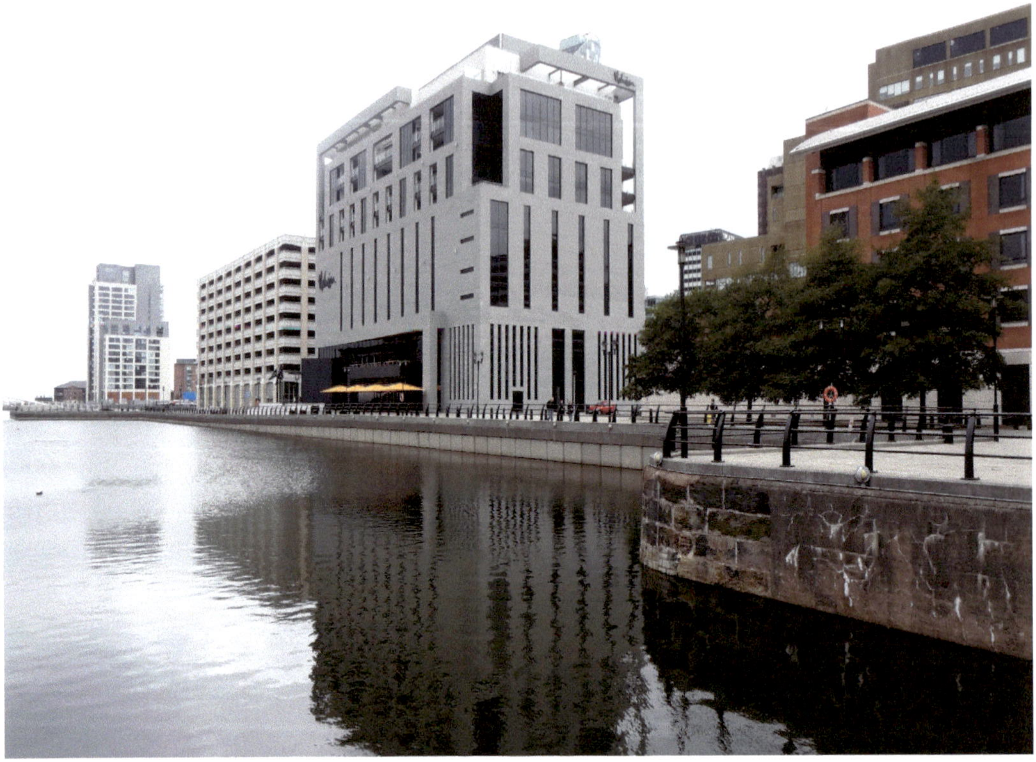

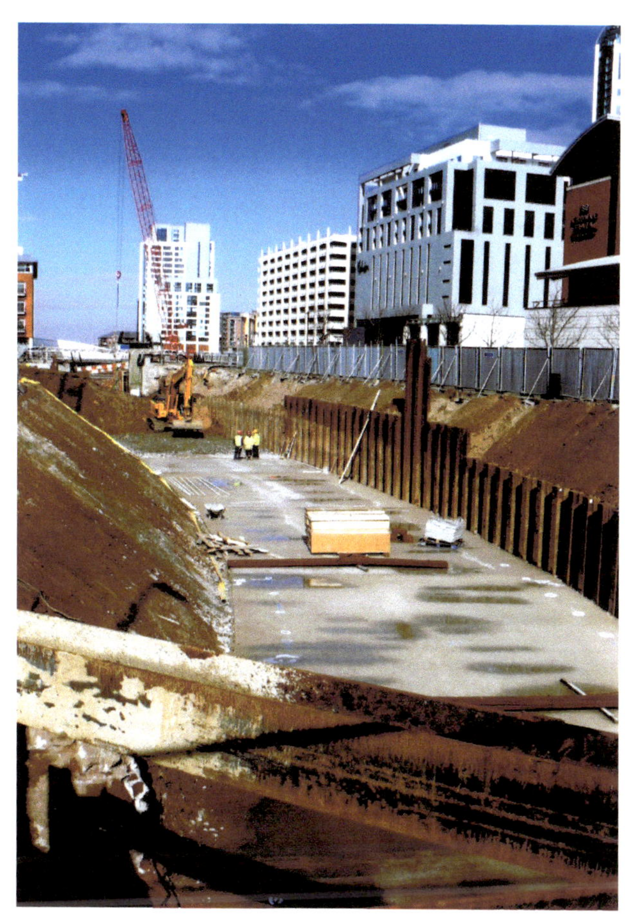

Prince's Dock and the
construction of the new Canal
link to Albert Dock.

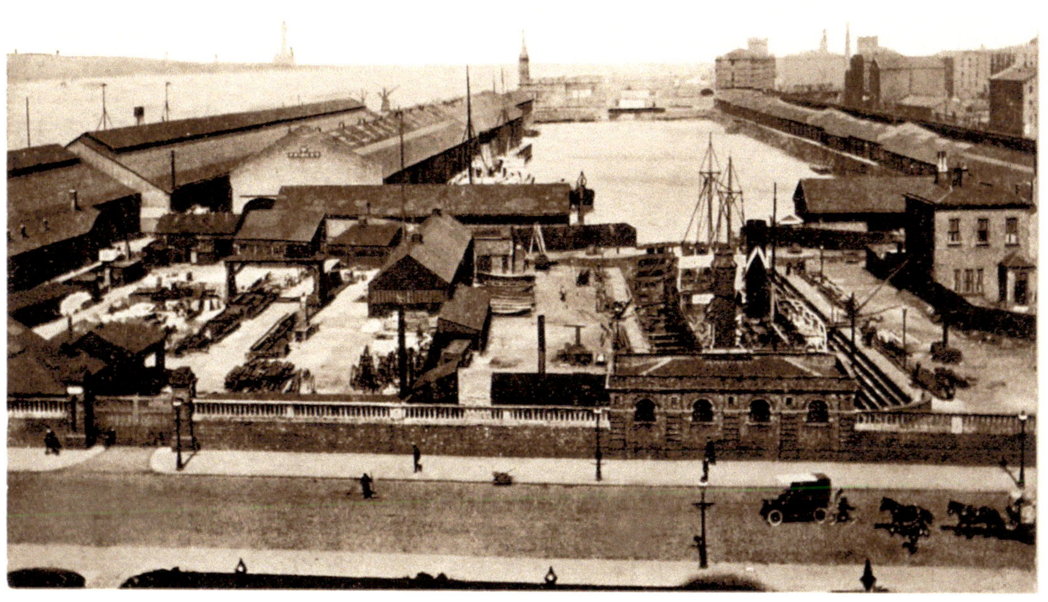

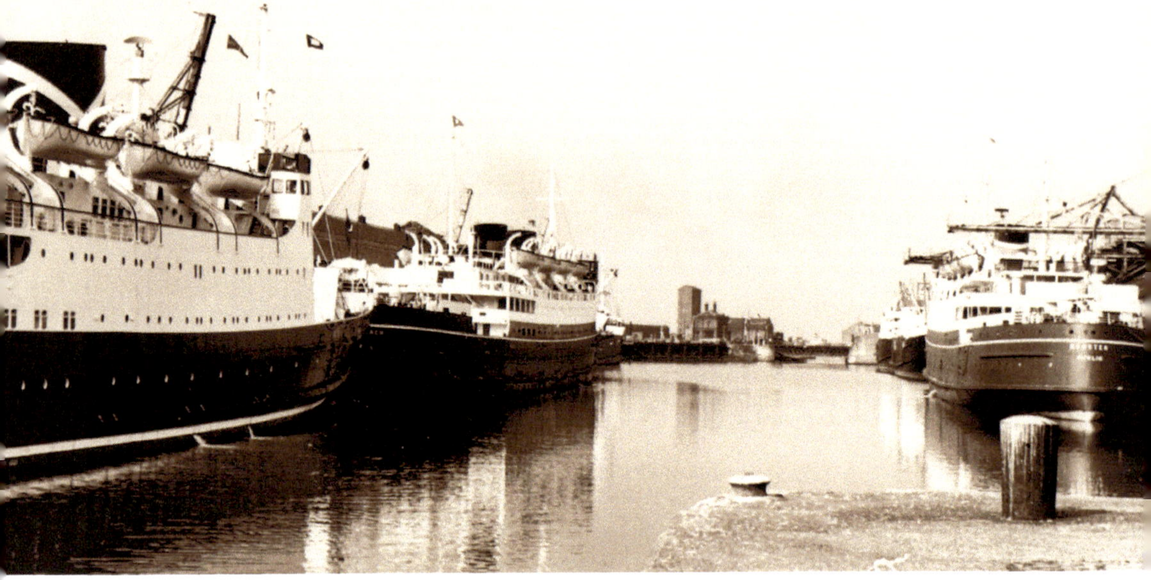

Prince's Dock looking north.

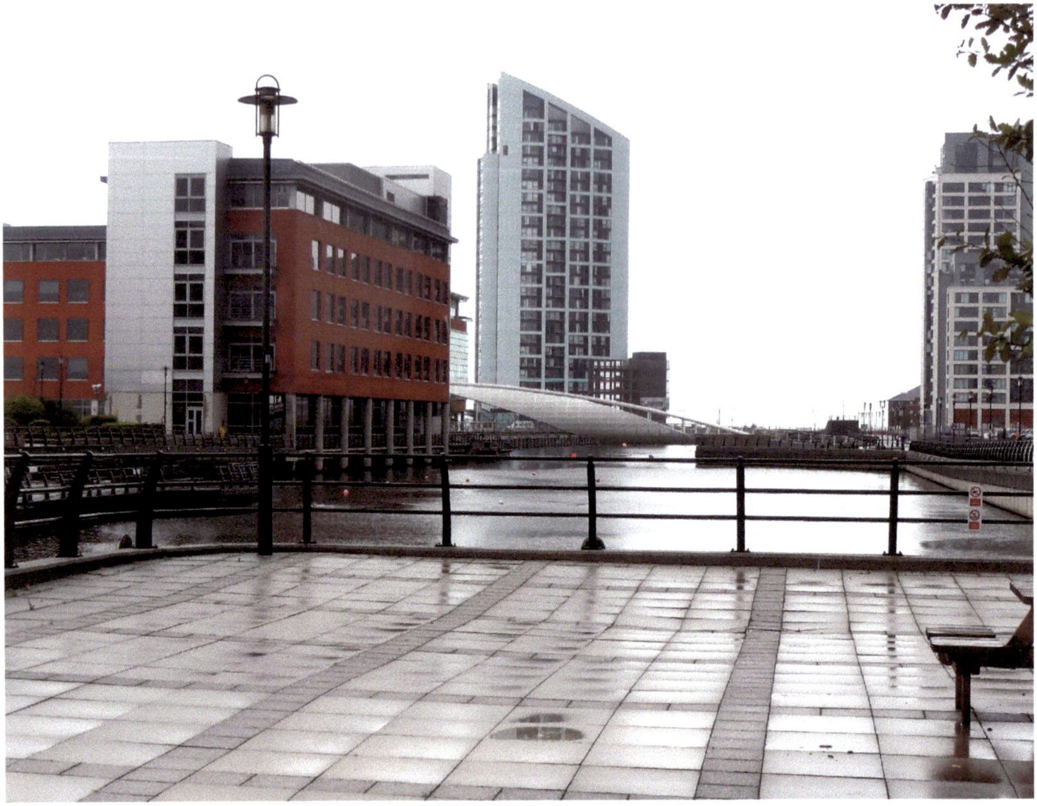

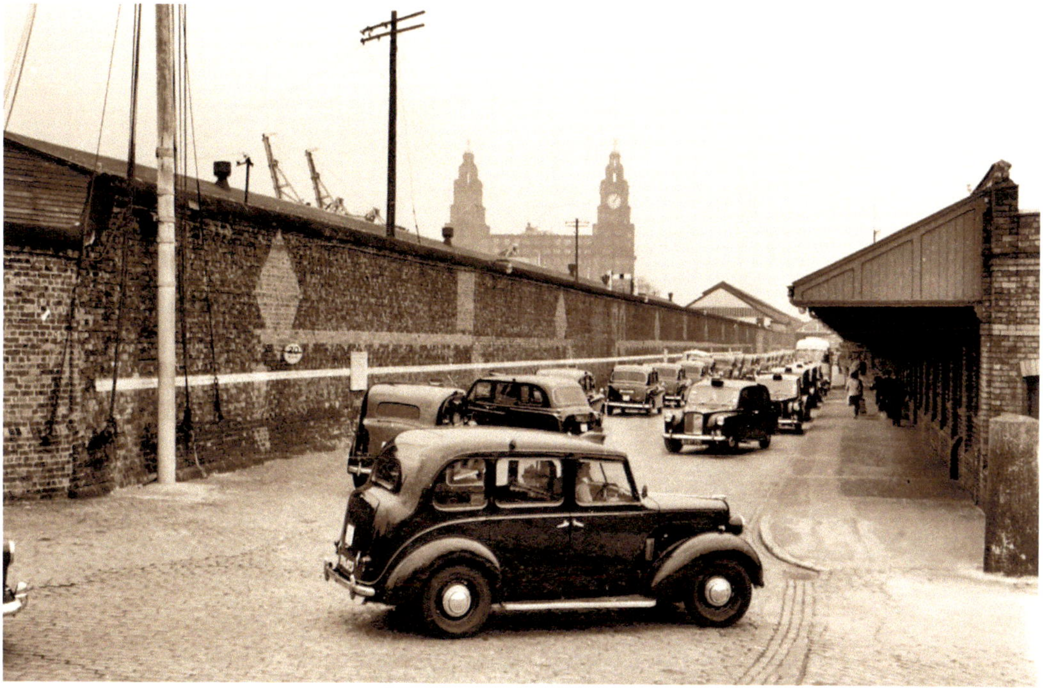

Taxis queue at the end of Prince's Parade to pick up passengers from a Canadian Pacific liner which had arrived from Montreal.

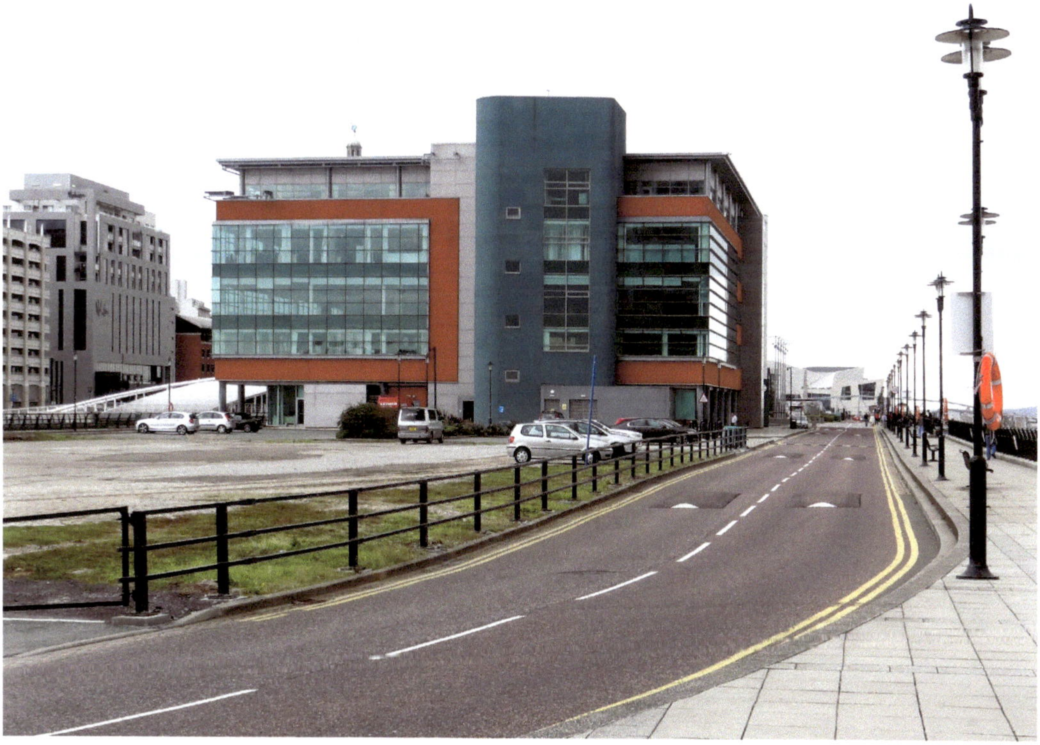

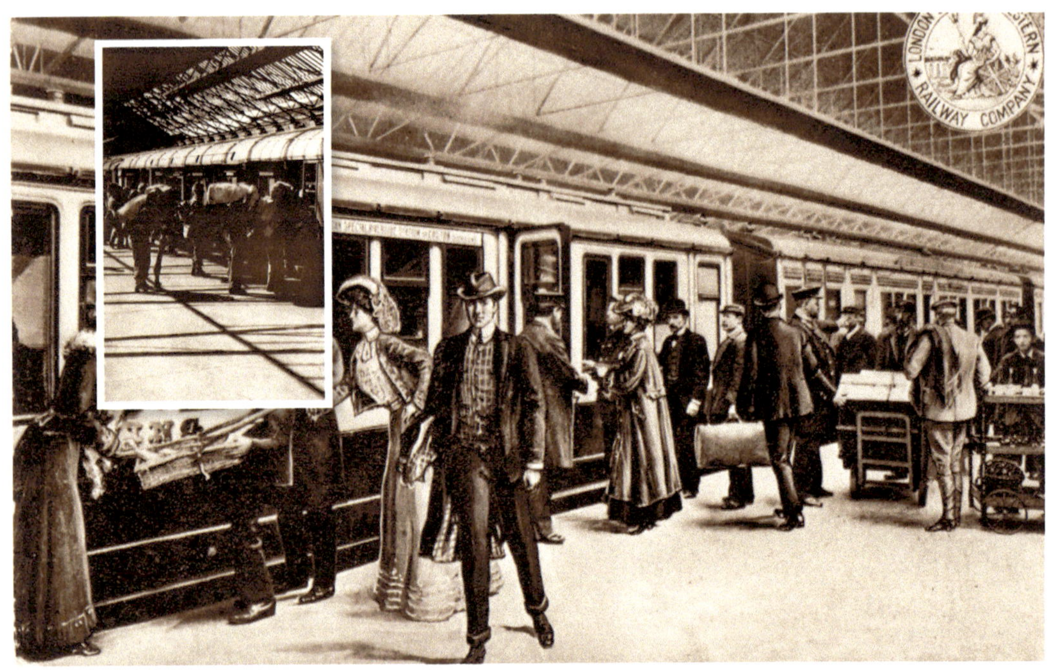

Riverside Station on Prince's Parade at the Pier Head. The station was opened on 12 June 1895 and was used to allow passengers to travel to the ocean liners by rail. It was accessed via the Victoria and Waterloo tunnels and was used during the Second World War, transporting troops from across the country (*inset*). The last train left the station on 25 February 1971 and it was demolished in the 1990s.

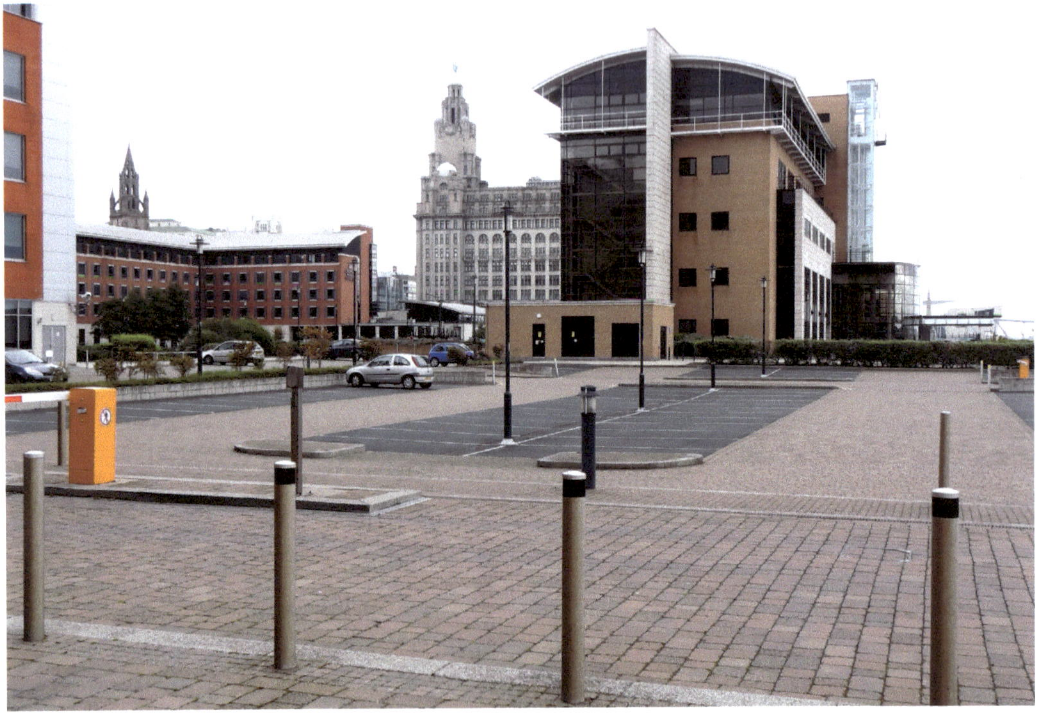

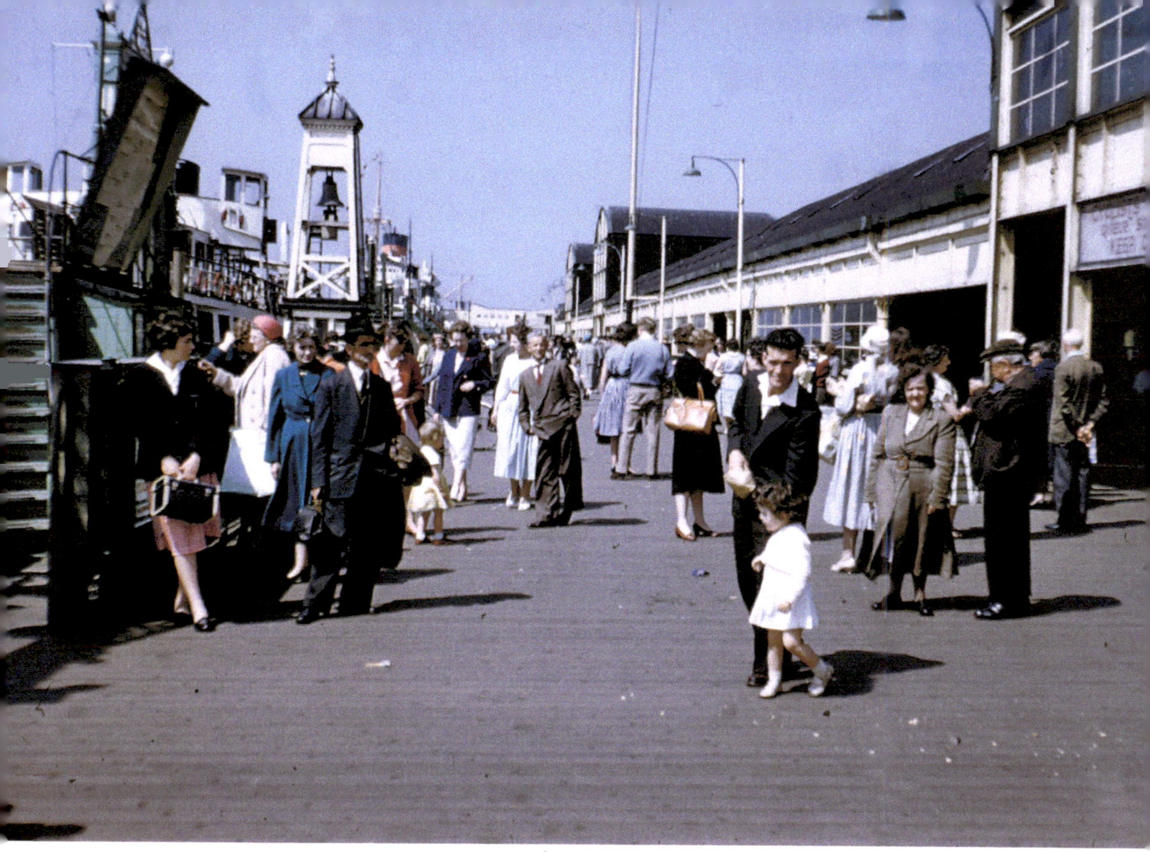

Above and below: The Mersey ferry landing stage in the 1950s and 1960s.

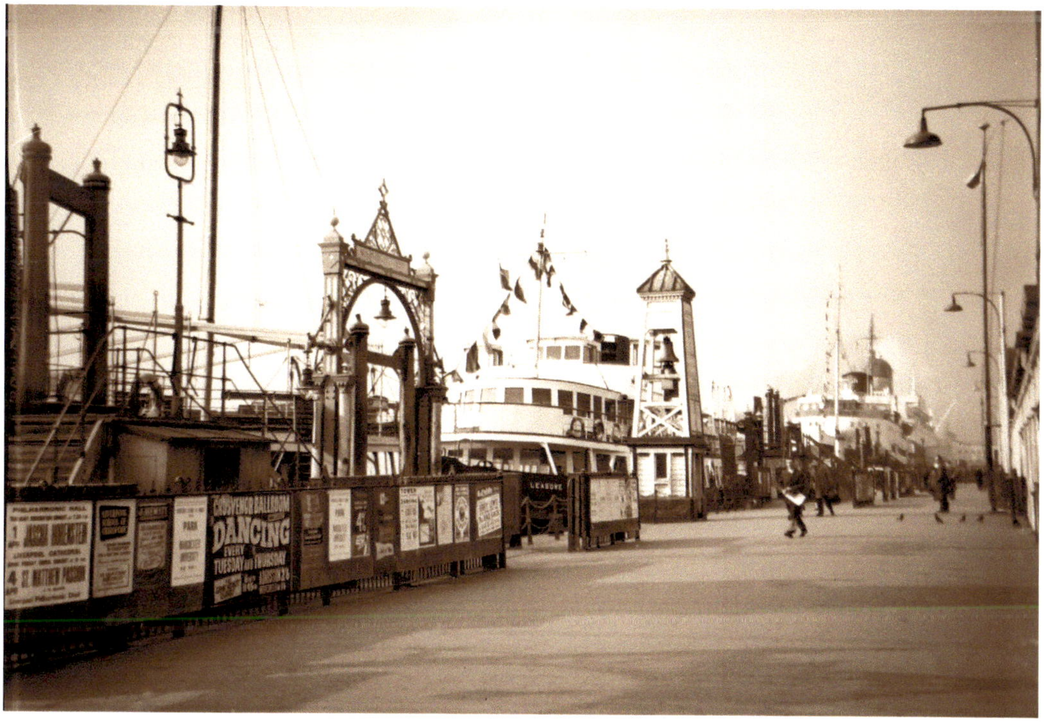

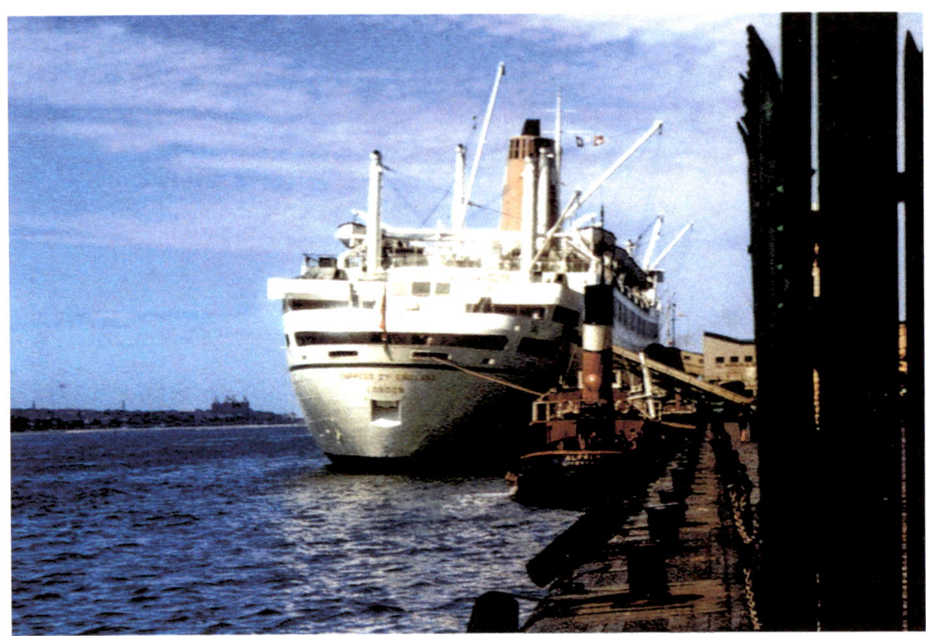

Above: The Canadian Pacific passenger liner *Empress of England* at Prince's Landing Stage, preparing to sail to Quebec and Montreal. She sailed from Liverpool to Canada from 1957 to 1970, when she was sold to the Shaw Savill Line and renamed *Ocean Monarch*. She was broken up at Taiwan in 1975.

Below: The new Cruise Facility was opened in 2008 and is seen with passengers embarking for a Mersey cruise on the ferry *Snowdrop*.

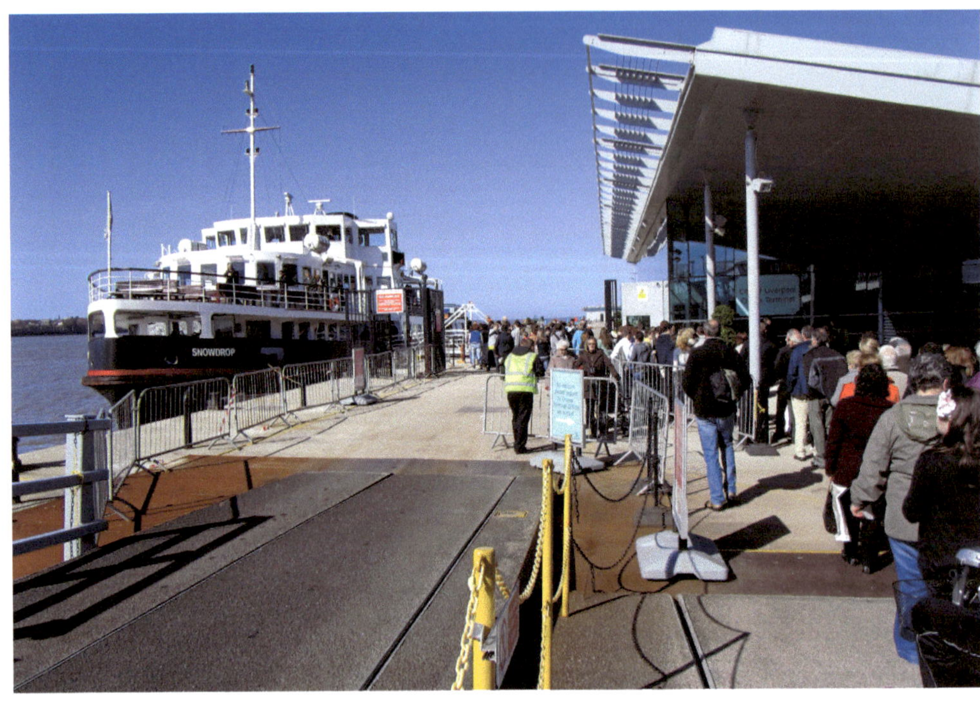

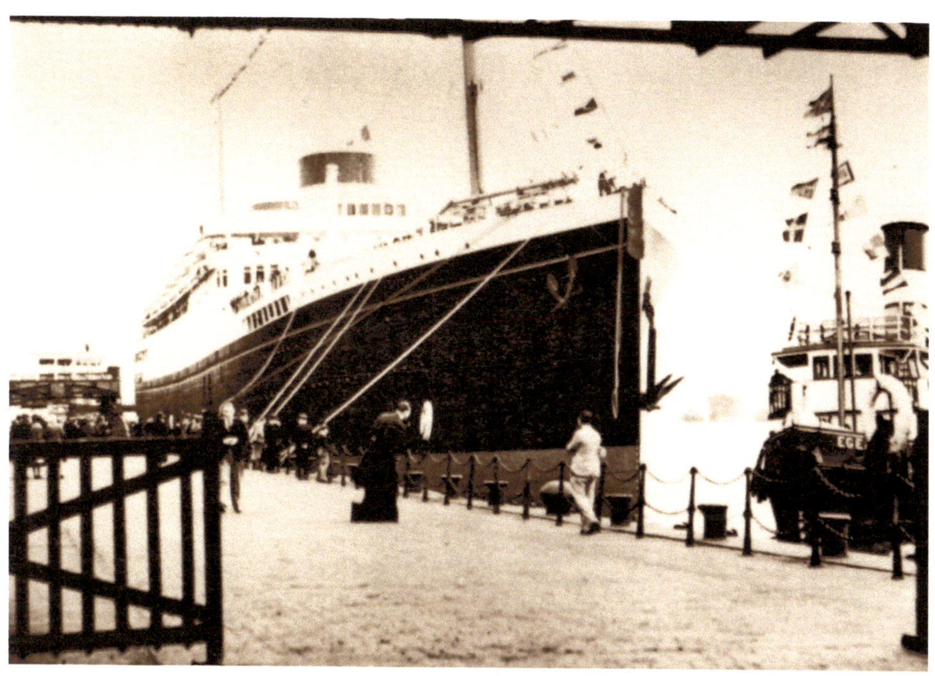

Above: The White Star liner *Georgic* prepares to sail on her maiden voyage from Liverpool to New York on 25 June 1932.

Below: The cruise ship *Discovery* at the new Liverpool Cruise Facility. She was built as *Island Venture* in 1971 and was renamed *Island Princess* the following year, becoming *Hyundai Pungak* in 1999. Renamed *Platinum* in 2001, and *Discovery* in 2002.

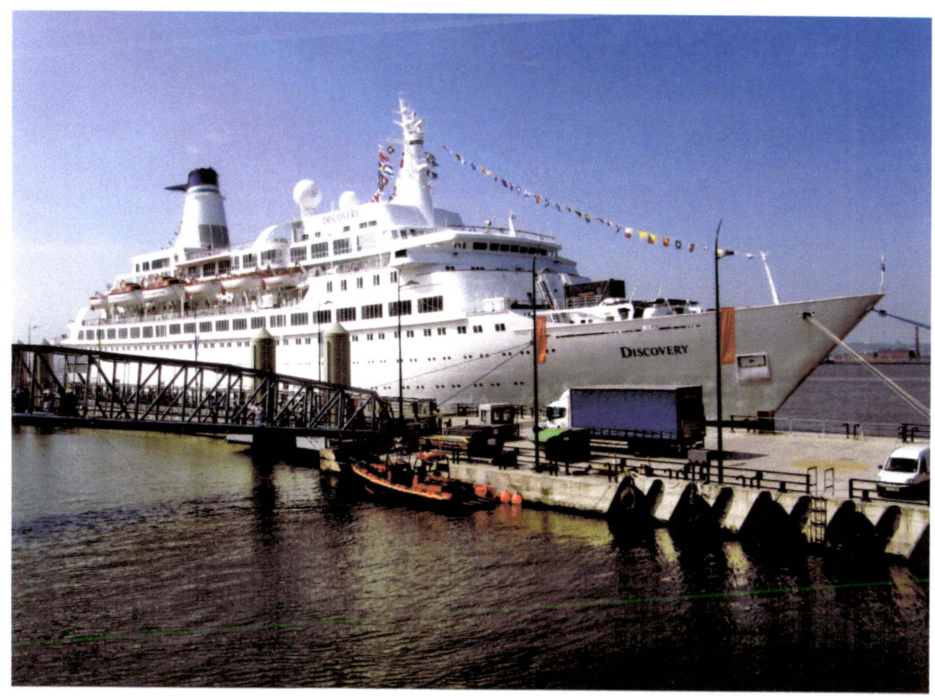

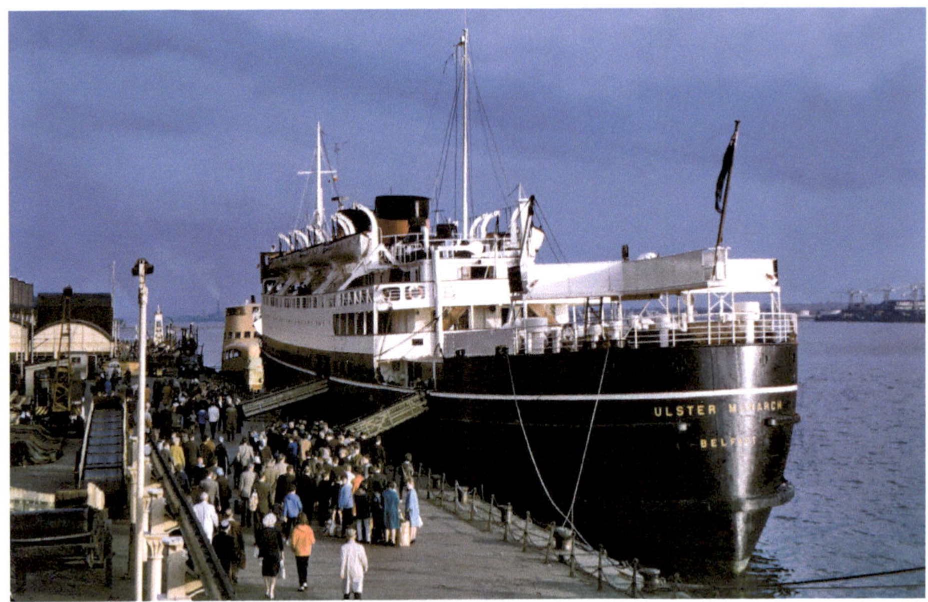

Above: The Belfast Steamship Company's *Ulster Monarch* loading passengers at Prince's Landing Stage in 1964. *Ulster Monarch* was built in 1929 and normally sailed to Belfast from the company's berth at Prince's Dock. However, additional Sunday night sailings were offered in the summer months and she embarked passengers for these sailings at Prince's Landing Stage. *Ulster Monarch* was broken up at Ghent in 1966.

Below: Residensea's *The World*, at the Cruise Facility. She was built in 2002 and incorporates 106 two- and three-bedroom apartments, nineteen one- and two-bedroom studio apartments and forty studios. The apartments are owned by the residents, who live on board and travel the world, staying in ports between two and five days. The facilities on the ship include a store and delicatessen, a boutique, gym, putting green and tennis court. There are five restaurants, a cinema, library and a programme of entertainment takes place in the theatre.

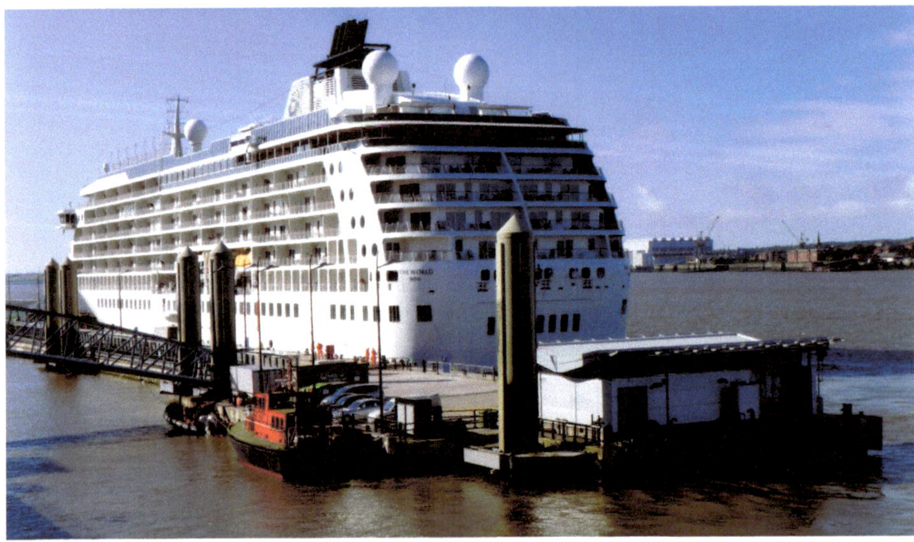

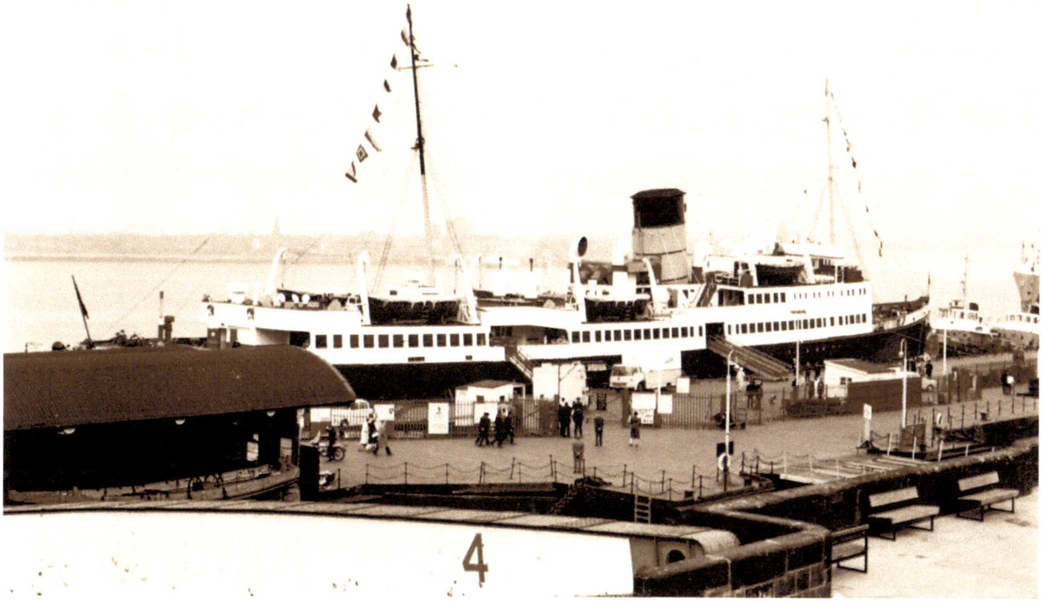

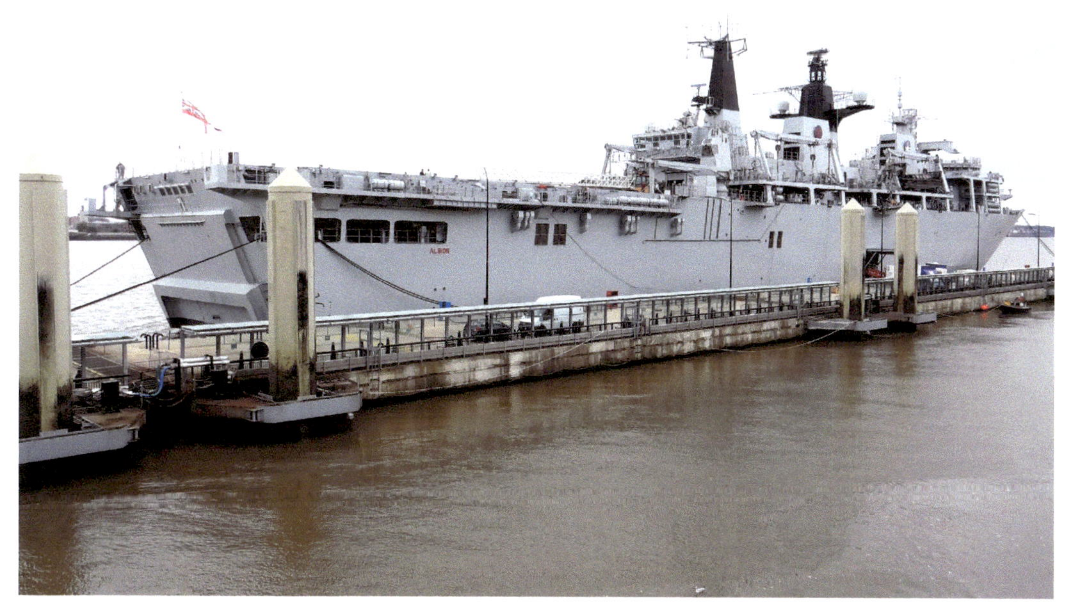

Above: The Isle of Man steamer *Mona's Isle* prepare to sail from the landing stage.

Below: HMS *Albion* on a visit to Liverpool in September 2011.

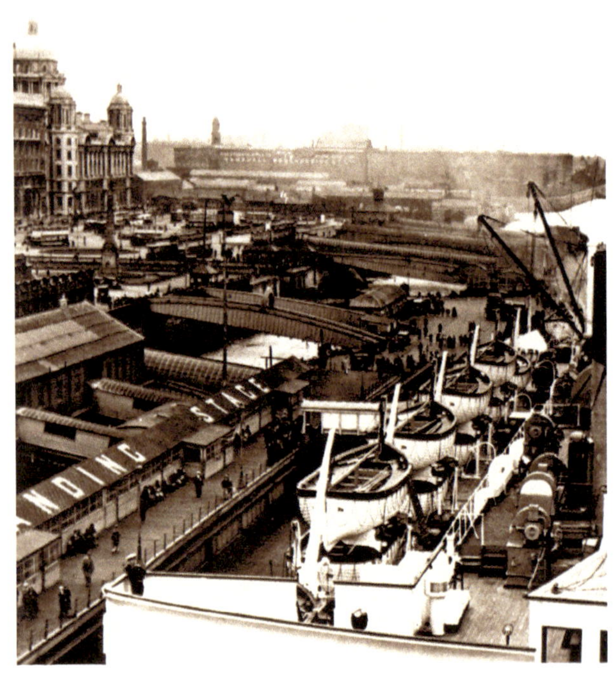

The Pier Head viewed from a
liner (*left*) and the Cunard liner
Queen Mary 2 in 2011.

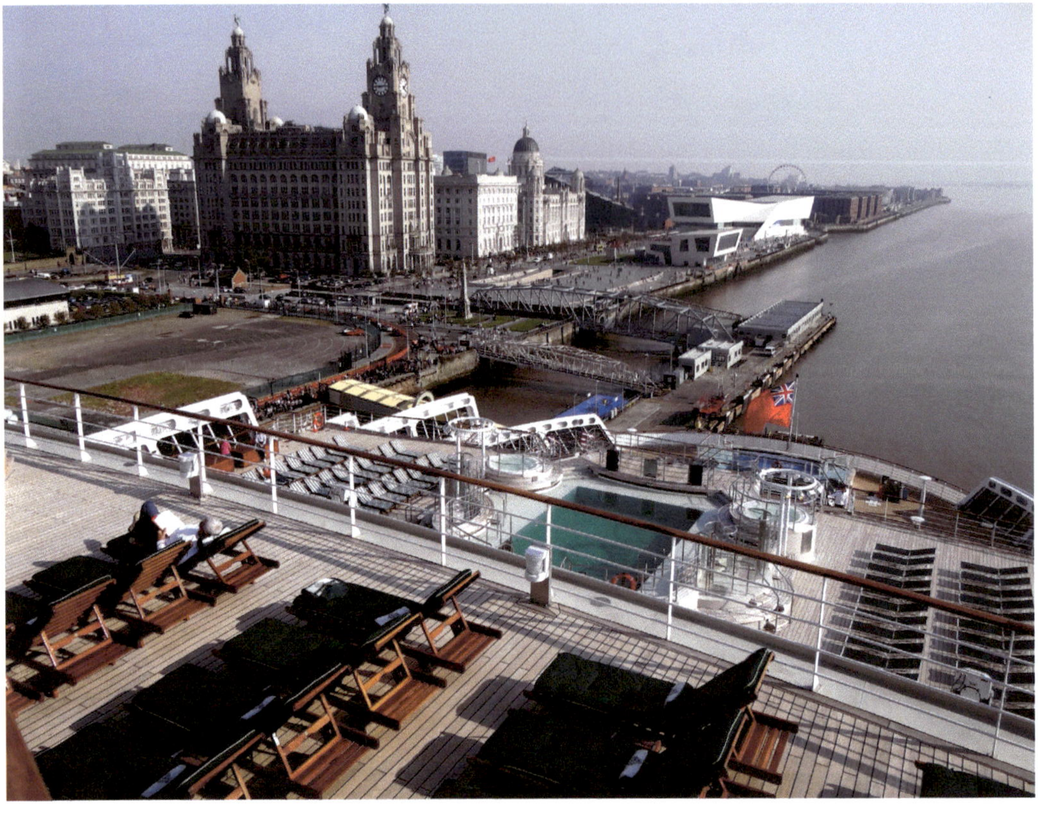

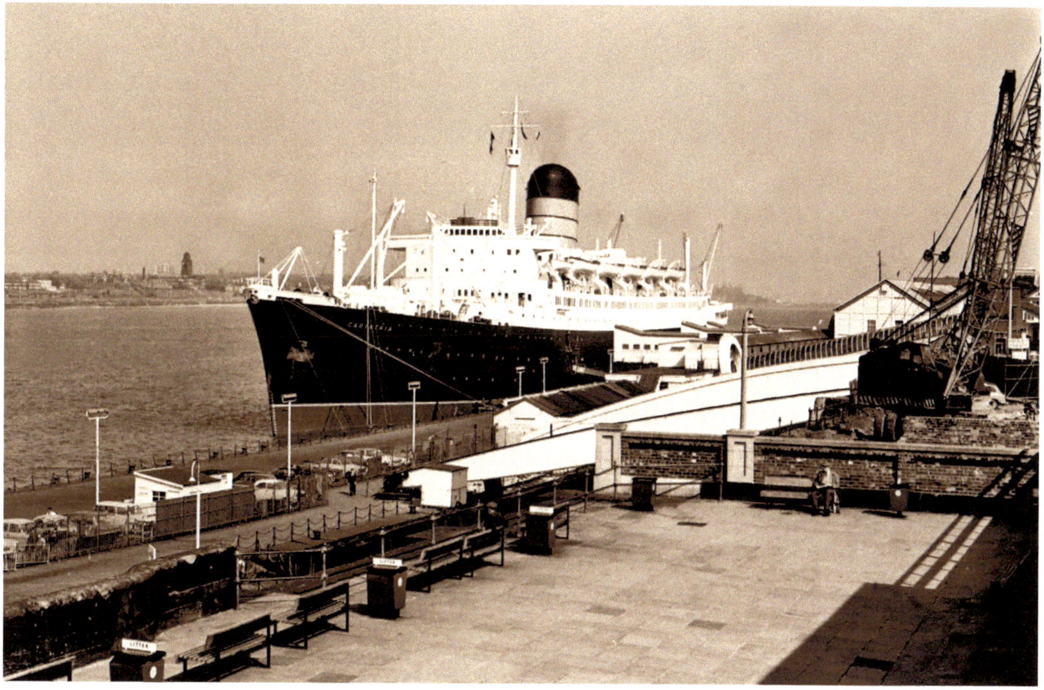

Above: The Cunard liner *Carinthia* at Liverpool Landing Stage in 1964.

Below: The new Cunard liner *Queen Elizabeth* pays her first visit to the Cruise Facility at Liverpool in 2011.

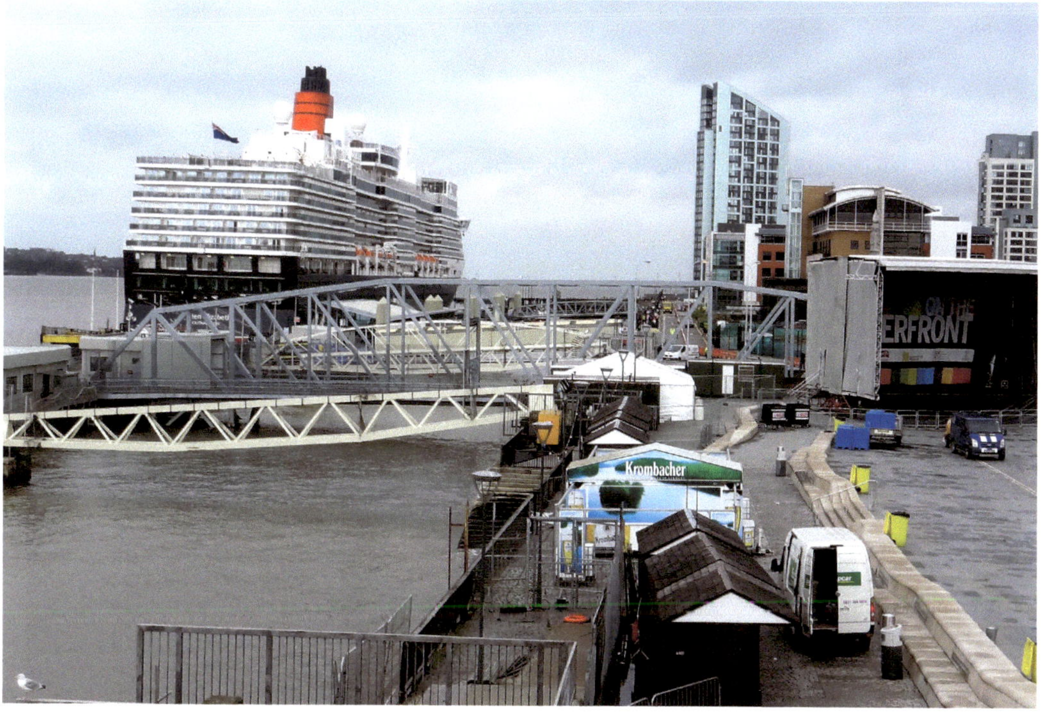

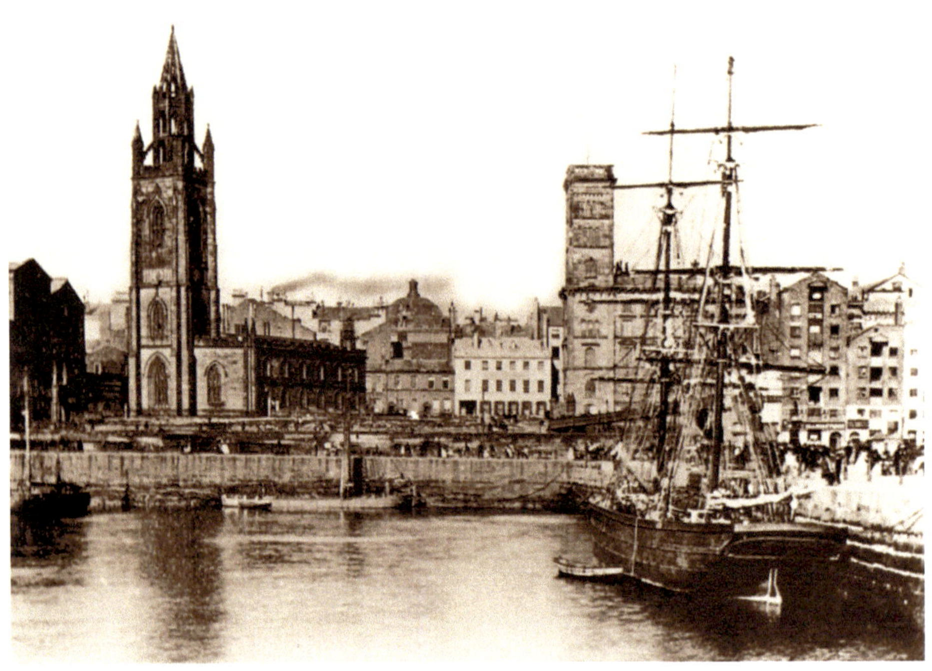

George's Dock was opened in 1771 and the dock, together with the adjoining George's Basin, was filled in to create the Pier Head. The Church of Our Lady and St Nicholas was frequently referred to as 'the sailors' church'. At the beginning of the eighteenth century, when Liverpool became an independent parish, St Nicholas and St Peter's became the parish churches. The church was extended in 1775 and on 11 February 1810, twenty-five people were killed when the spire of the church collapsed. A new tower was built between 1811 and 1815 and the last burials in the graveyard took place in 1849. The church was badly damaged in the Blitz of December 1940 and it was re-consecrated on 18 October 1952.

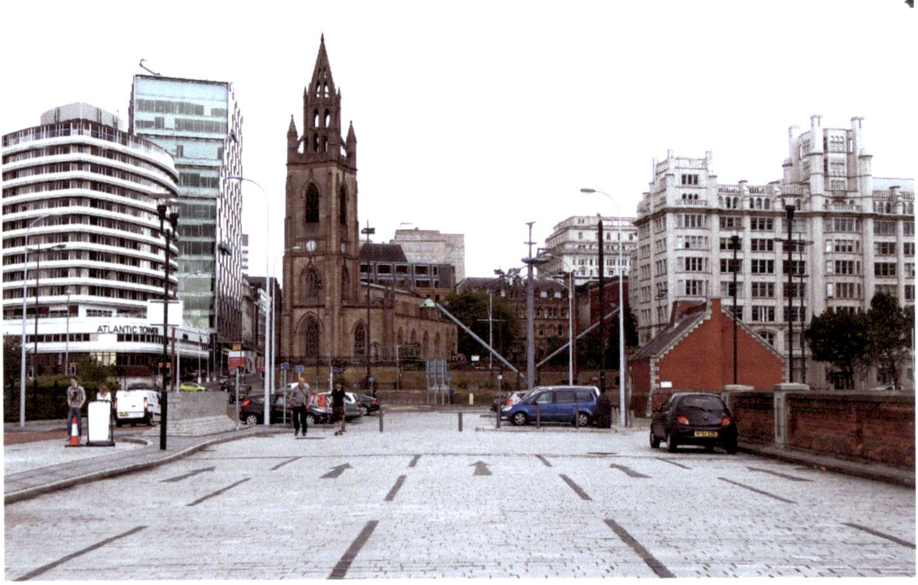

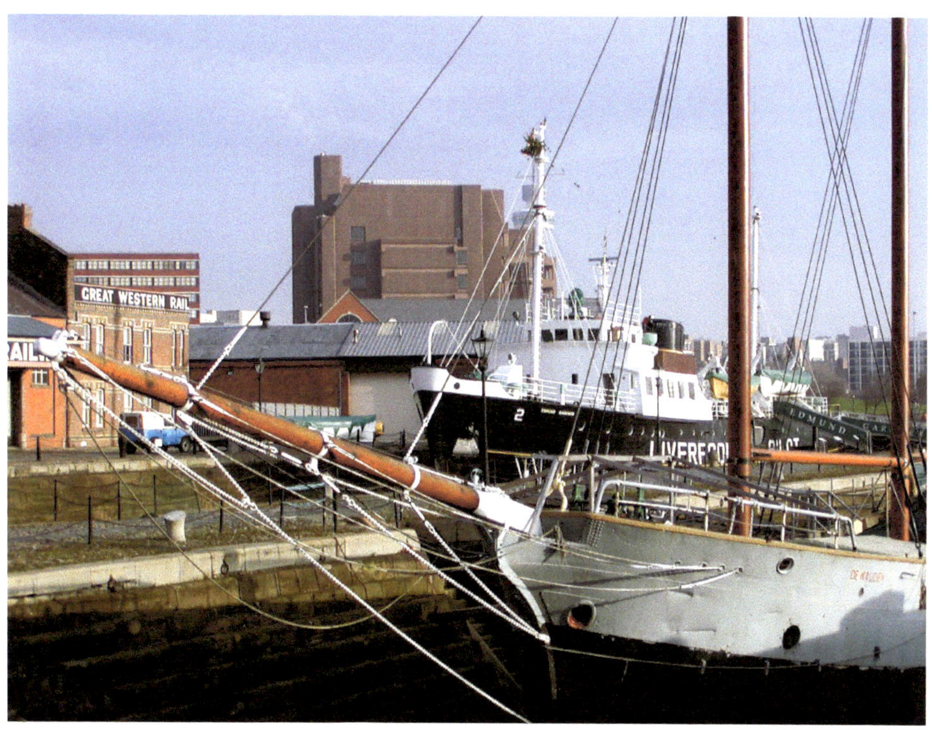

Above and below: The preserved pilot vessel No. 2, *Edmund Gardner,* in dry dock at Albert Dock. She was built by Philip & Son at Dartmouth in 1953 and was sold to Merseyside County Council on 1 August 1971 as a static exhibit at Merseyside Maritime Museum.

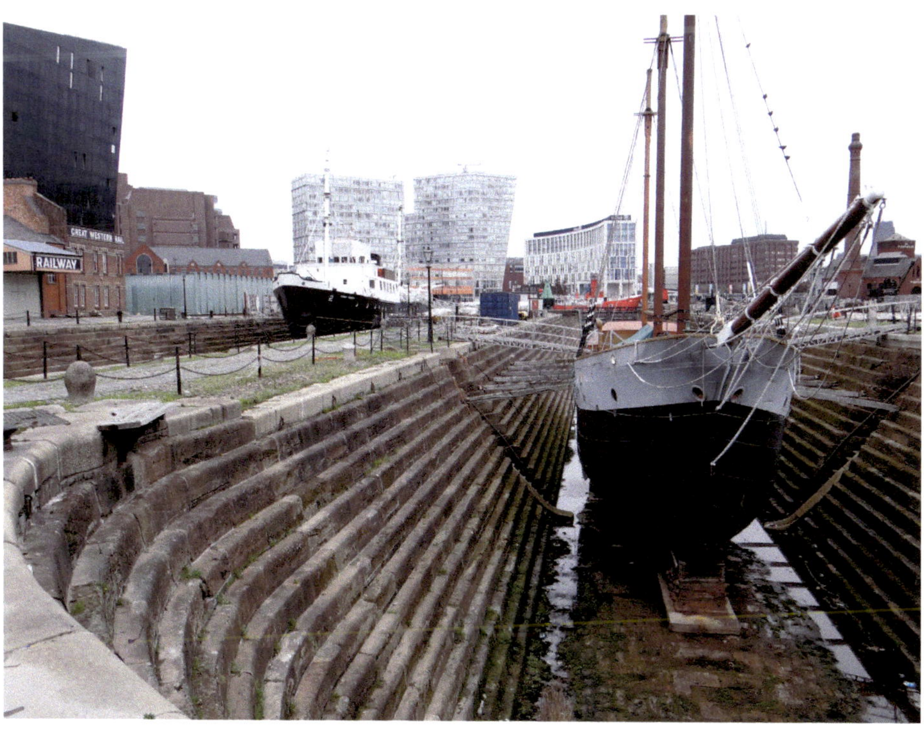

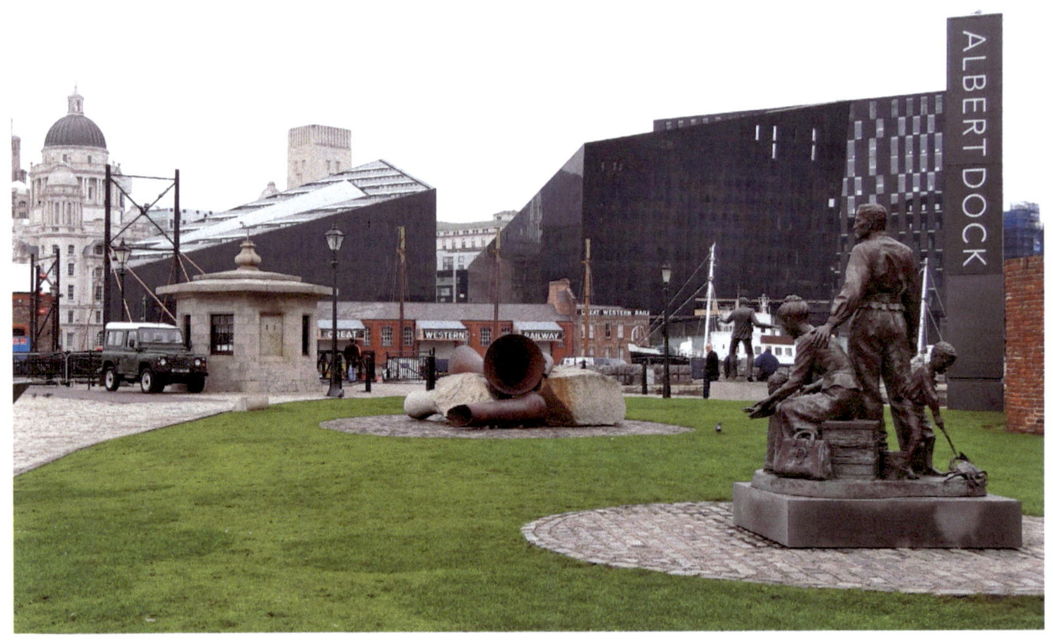

Above: The new Latitude and Longitude buildings and Equator House at Mann Island which were completed in 2011, containing 376 luxury apartments.

Below: The Pier Head, looking north from Albert Dock.

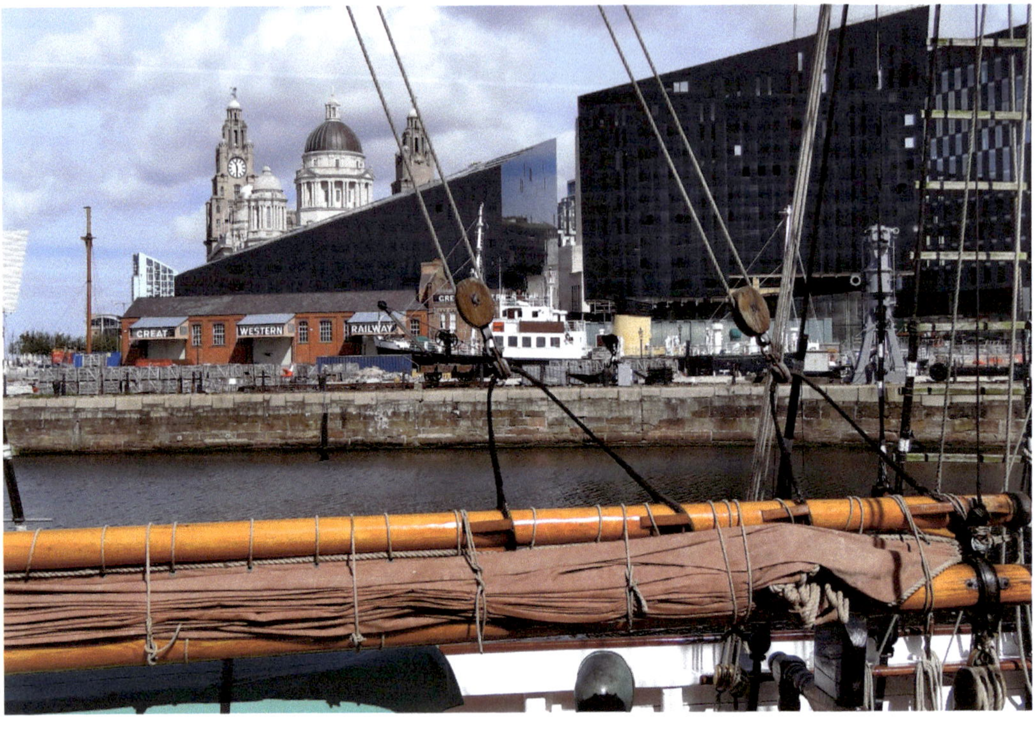

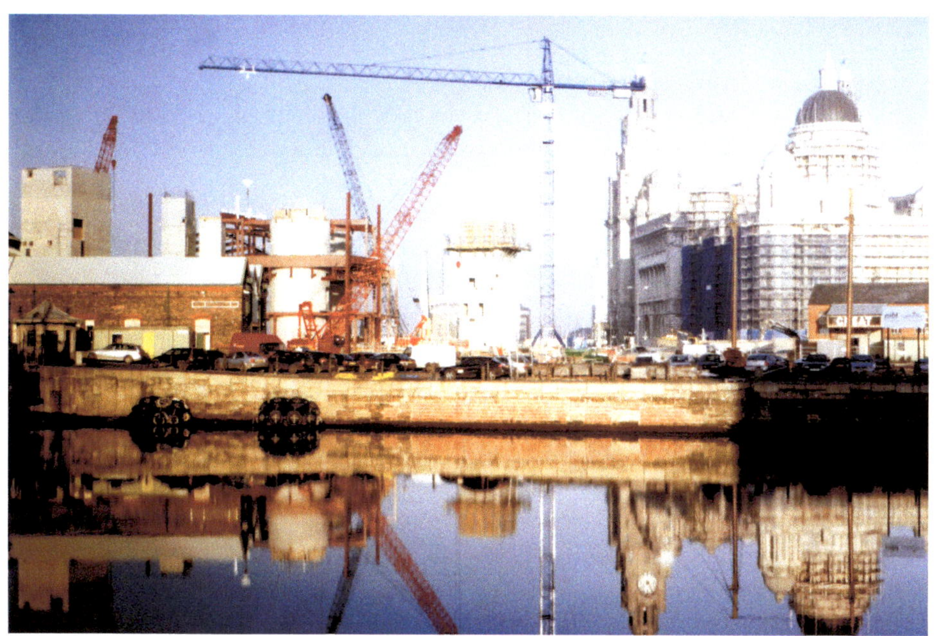

Above: Construction of the new Museum of Liverpool at the Pier Head. The building was opened on 19 July 2011 and was built to reflect the city's global significance through its unique geography, history and culture. Visitors are able to explore how the port, its people, their creativity and sporting history have shaped the development of the city. The galleries include 'Global City', 'Little Liverpool', 'Liverpool Overhead Railway', 'History Detectives', 'City Soldiers', 'The People's Republic', 'Wondrous Place' and the Skylight Gallery.

Below: Another view of Albert Dock. Albert Dock was designed by Jesse Hartley and Philip Hardwick and was opened in 1846 by Prince Albert. This was the first time that a member of the Royal Family had made a state visit to the city. The warehouse complex was the first structure in Britain to be built of cast iron, stone and brick with no wood included in the building. At the beginning of the Second World War in 1939, Albert Dock was used as a base for vessels in the Atlantic campaign and it was extensively damaged in German bombing raids. After the war, the importance of the structure was recognised, in 1952, when it was granted Grade 1 listed building status. In 1983 Arrowcroft Plc and the Merseyside Development Corporation signed a contract creating the Albert Dock Company. The main pavilions were renovated in time for the 1984 Cutty Sark tall ships race, which attracted over one million visitors to the city and to the Albert Dock complex. The Merseyside Maritime Museum opened at the dock in 1986 and Albert Dock was officially opened by Prince Charles two years later. It is now the most popular tourist attraction in Liverpool and the most visited attraction in the British Isles outside London, attracting over four million visitors a year.

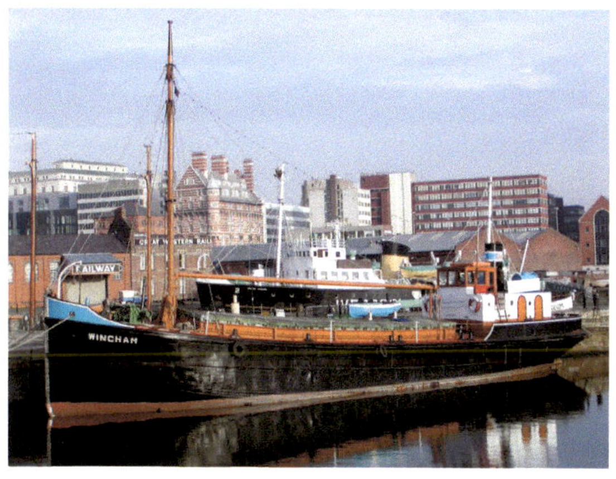

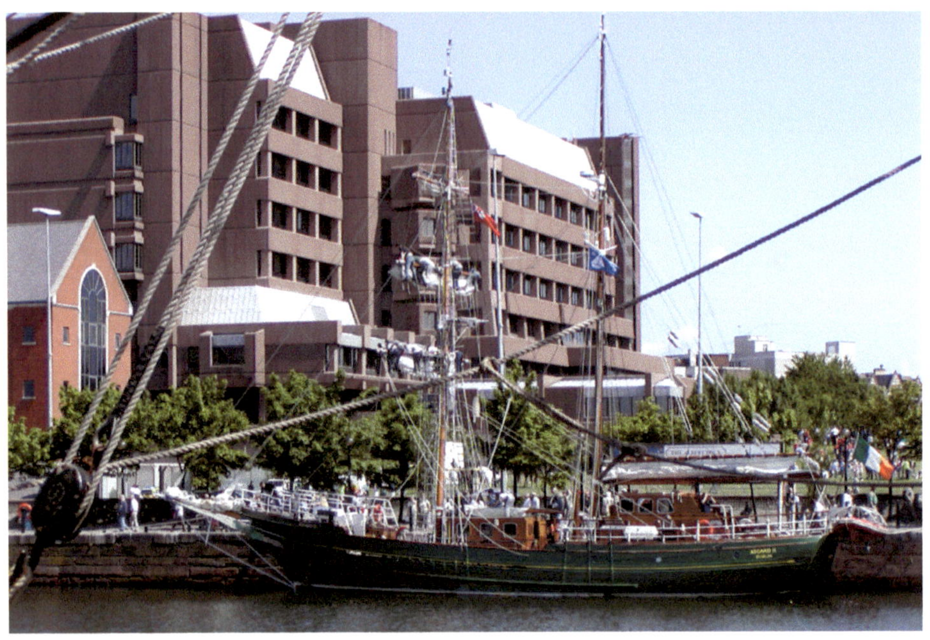

Above: The Irish-registered sailing ship *Asgard II*. The construction and opening of the Liverpool One Shopping Centre has changed the skyline behind the Dock Road, opposite Albert Dock, dramatically. *Asgard II* was the Irish national sail training vessel until she sank in the Bay of Biscay on 11 September 2008, twenty miles south-west of Belle-lle-en-Mer. She was on a voyage from Falmouth to La Rochelle and on board were five crew and twenty trainees, who were forced to abandon the vessel when she started to take on water. As *Asgard II* was lying on the seabed in a relatively good condition, attempts were made to organise an appeal to salvage and raise her to the surface. However, the Irish Government announced in 2009 that she would not be raised, and the Marine Casualty Investigation Board report, released on 27 September 2010, came to the conclusion that the most likely cause of the accident was that the ship collided with a submerged object.

Below: Albert Dock and the Dock Road in 2011.

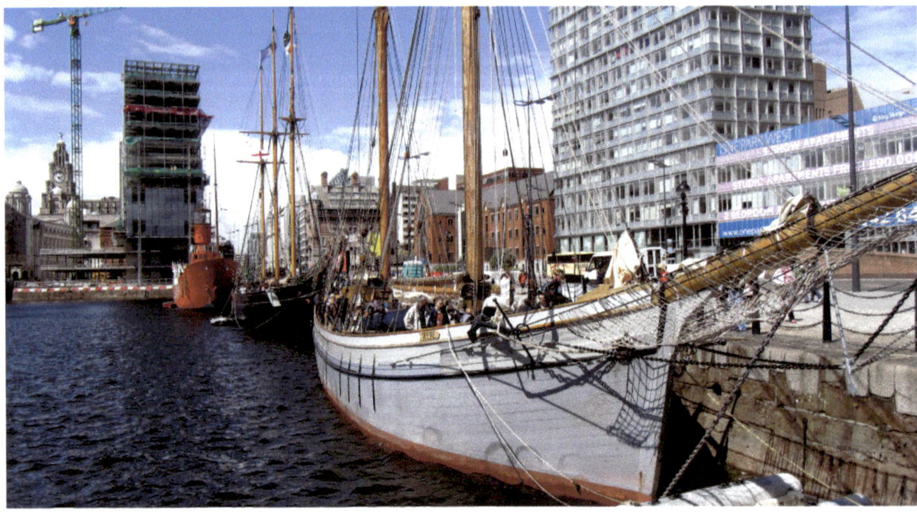

Right: Albert Dock at the beginning of the twentieth century.

Below: The Bar Lightship at Albert Dock. The original offices of the White Star Line can be seen behind the vessel on the photograph. The White Star Line moved their headquarters from 10 Water Street to 30 James Street in Liverpool in 1896. The new building was designed by Richard Norman Shore, who was also responsible for New Scotland Yard, the headquarters of the Metropolitan Police. When the White Star Line was merged with the Cunard Line on 10 May 1934, staff were moved across the road to the Cunard Building and the James Street offices were closed. It later became the headquarters of the Pacific Steam Navigation Company and was renamed Albion House.

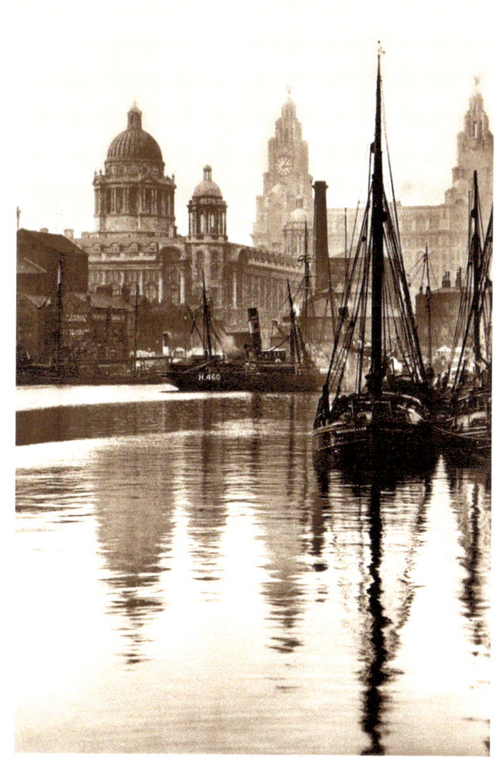

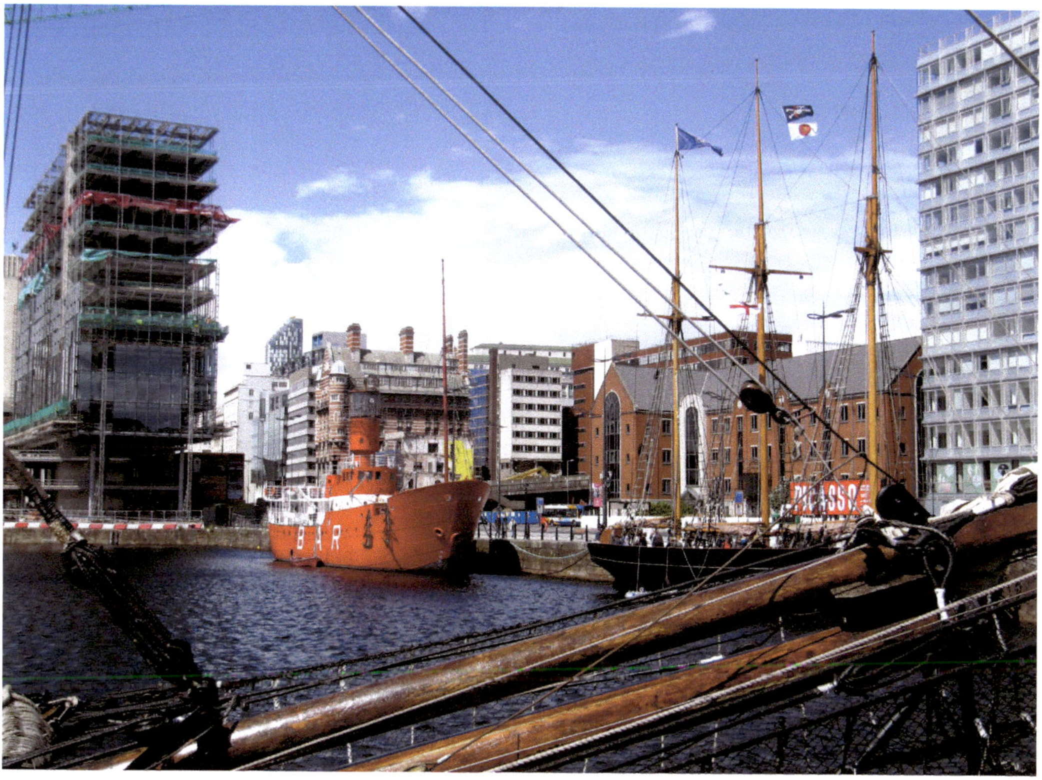

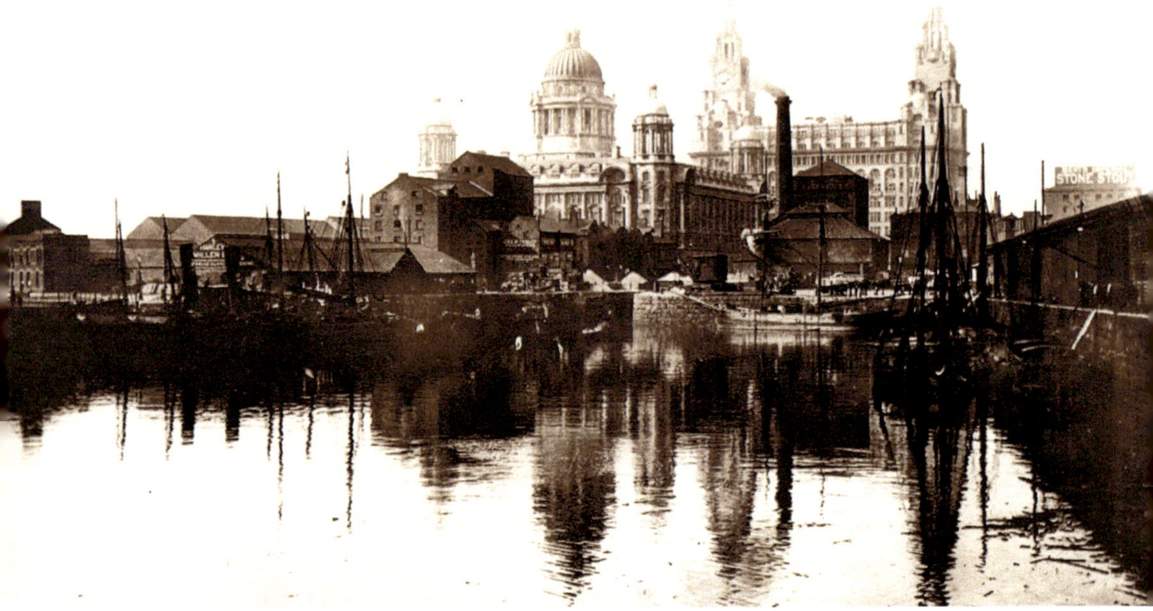

Above and below: The changing face of Albert Dock, with the gradual obscuring of the Three Graces at the Pier Head by the new buildings at Mann Island.

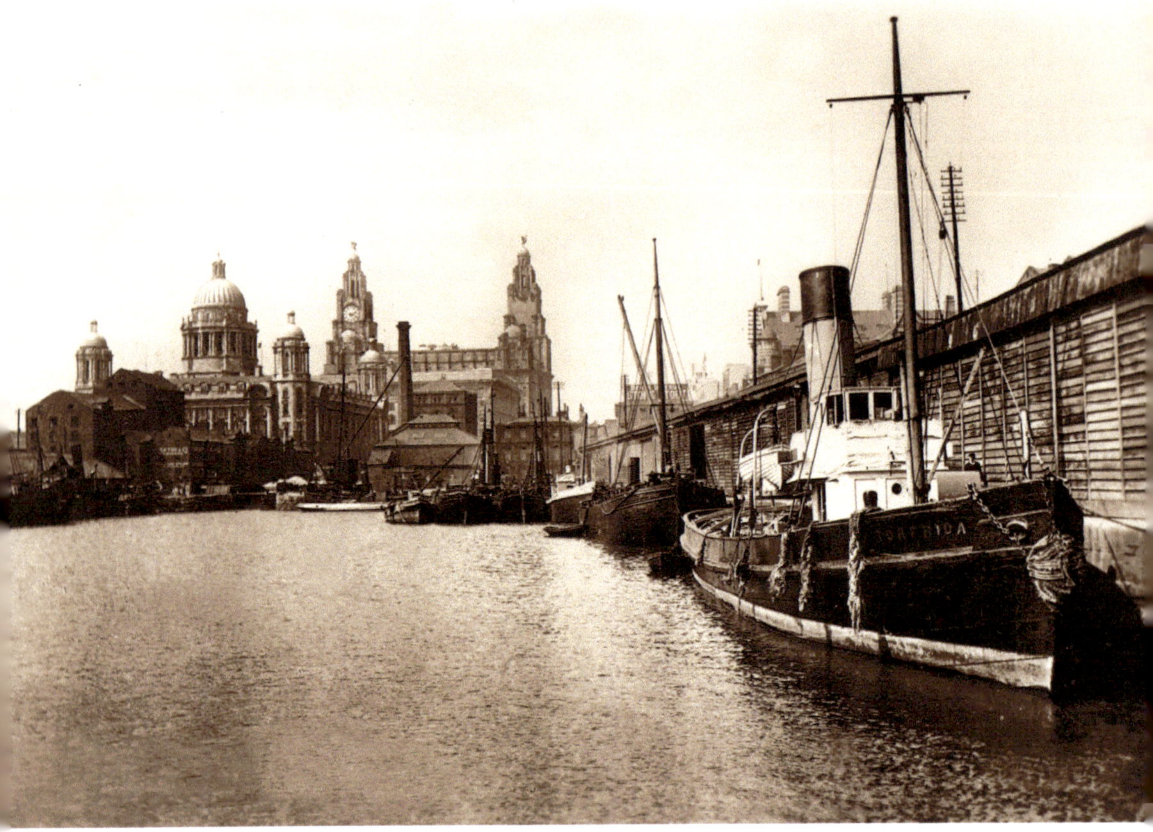

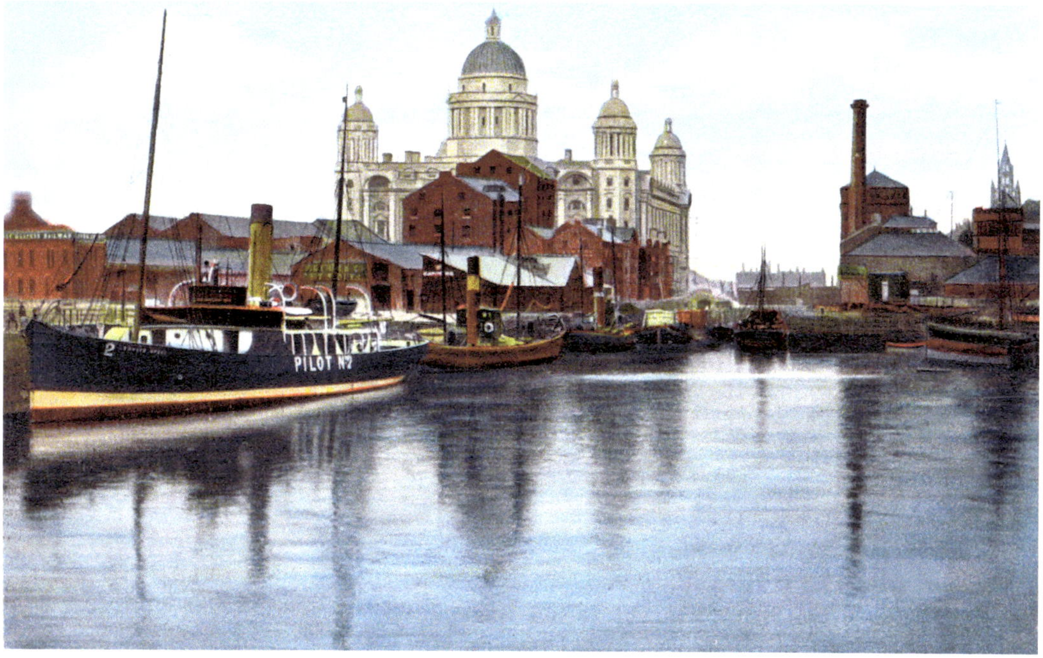

Above and below: Over 100 years at Albert Dock from 1909 to 2009.

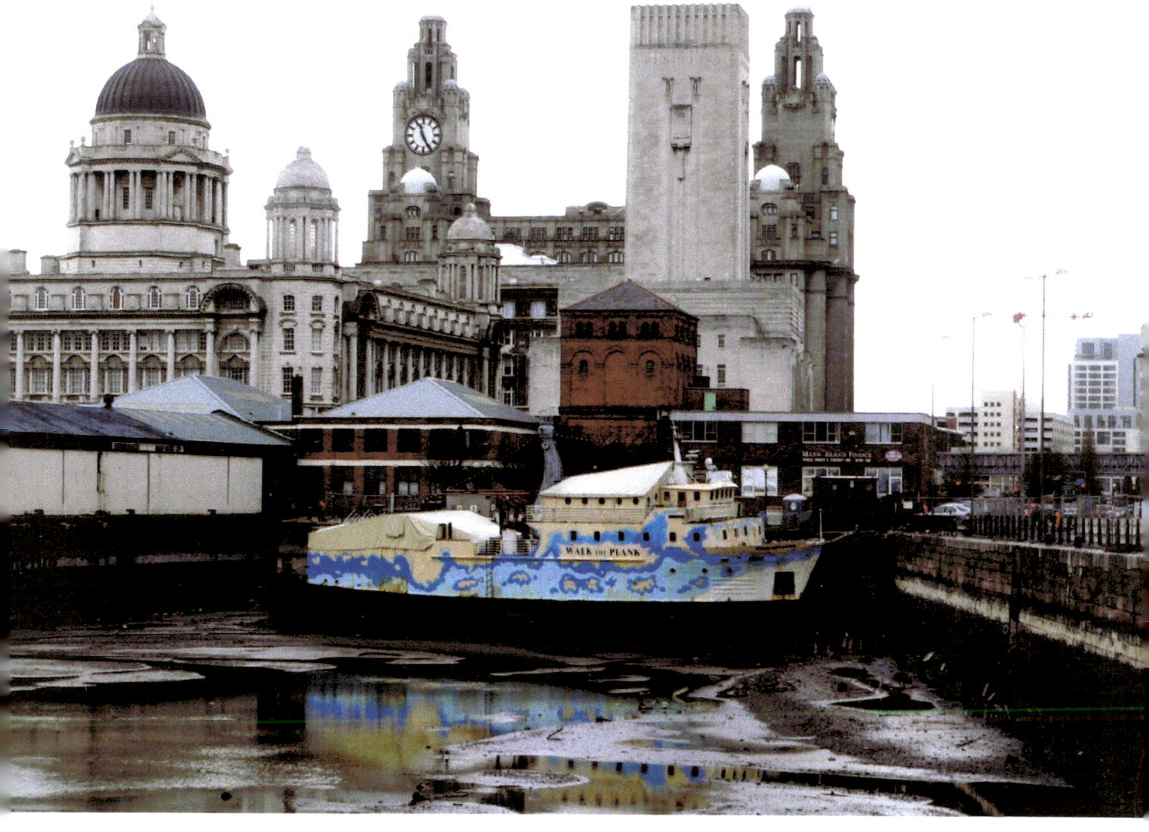

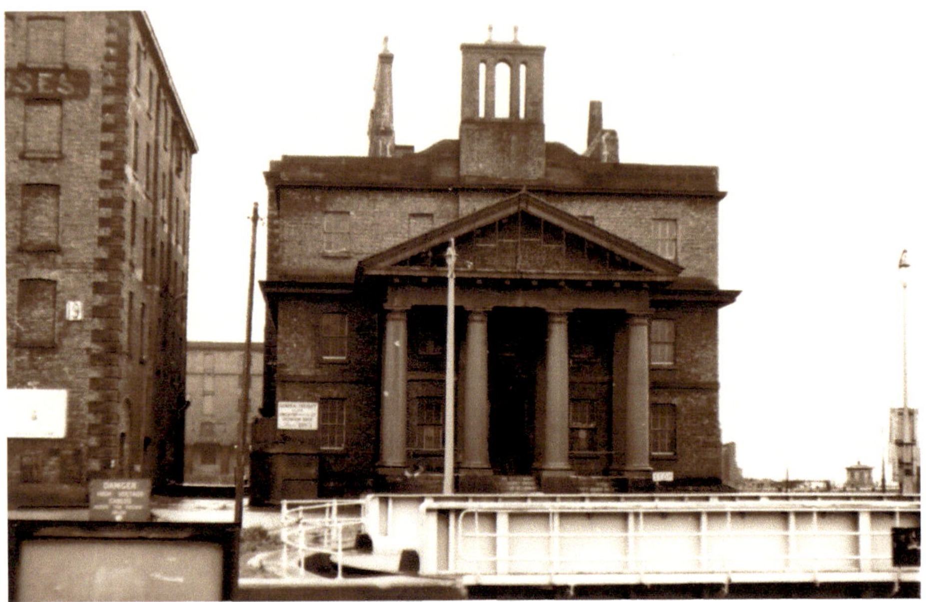

Above and below: The Dock Traffic Office at Albert Dock was built in 1847 and was designed by Philip Hardwick. The top storey of the building was added by Jesse Hartley. It is built of brick with red sandstone dressings and has prominent, battered chimney stacks with connecting arches. There is a cast-iron Tuscan portico and frieze with four columns, which are 3.5 metres high with a diameter of 1 metre at the base and were cast in two halves and brazed together along their length. After many years of neglect the building was restored and was used as television studios for a short time.

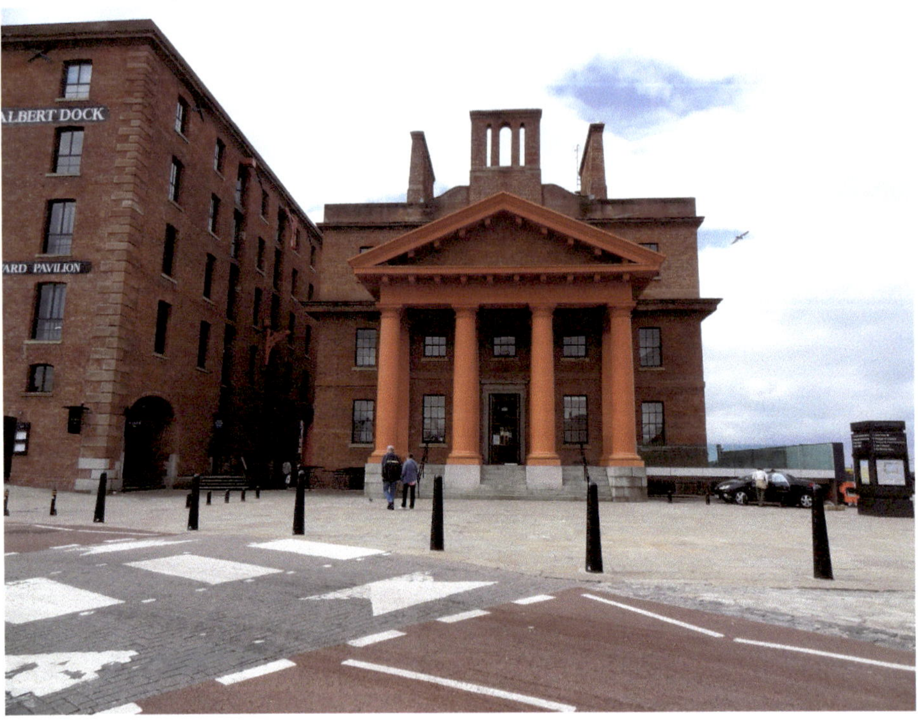

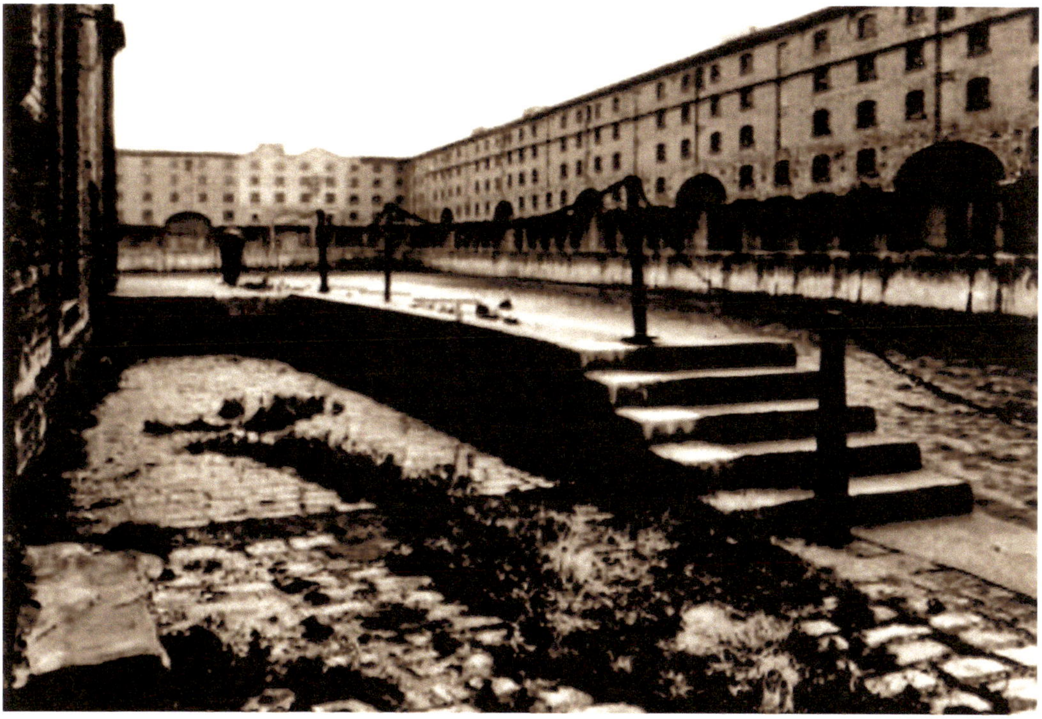

Above and below: The warehouses at Albert Dock.

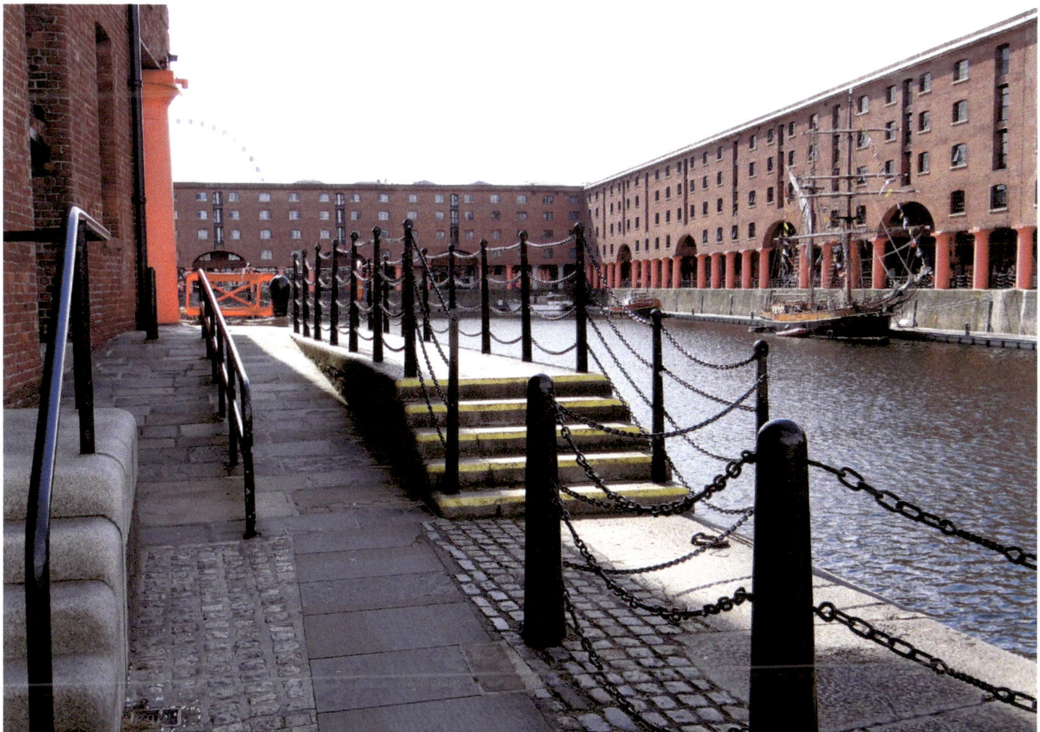

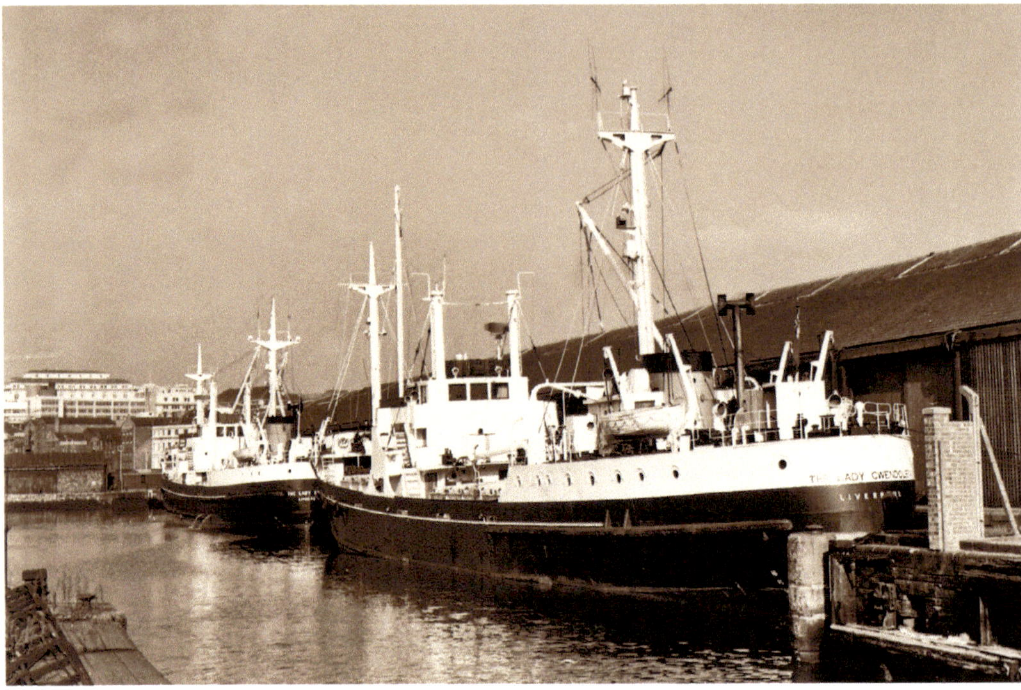

The 'Guinness boats' *The Lady Grania*, *Lady Gwendolen* and *The Lady Patricia* operated between Dublin, and discharged at Salthouse Dock. *The Lady Grania* became *The Lady Scotia* in 1978 and was lost off the Baja Peninsula in 1981. The *Lady Gwendolen* sank in 1979, following a collision, and *The Lady Patricia* was withdrawn in 1993.

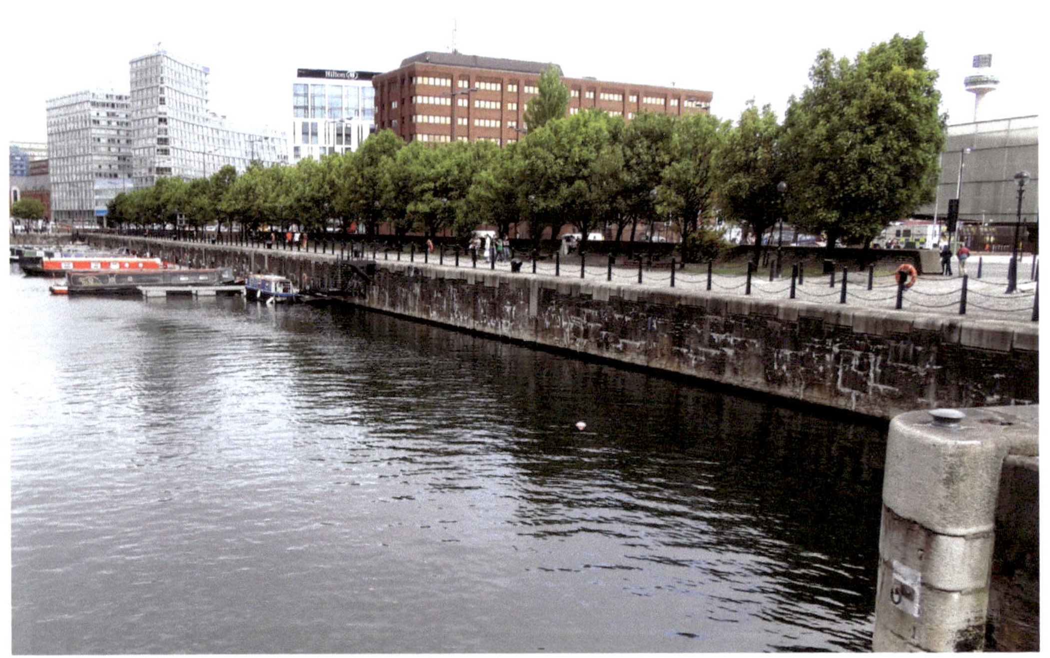

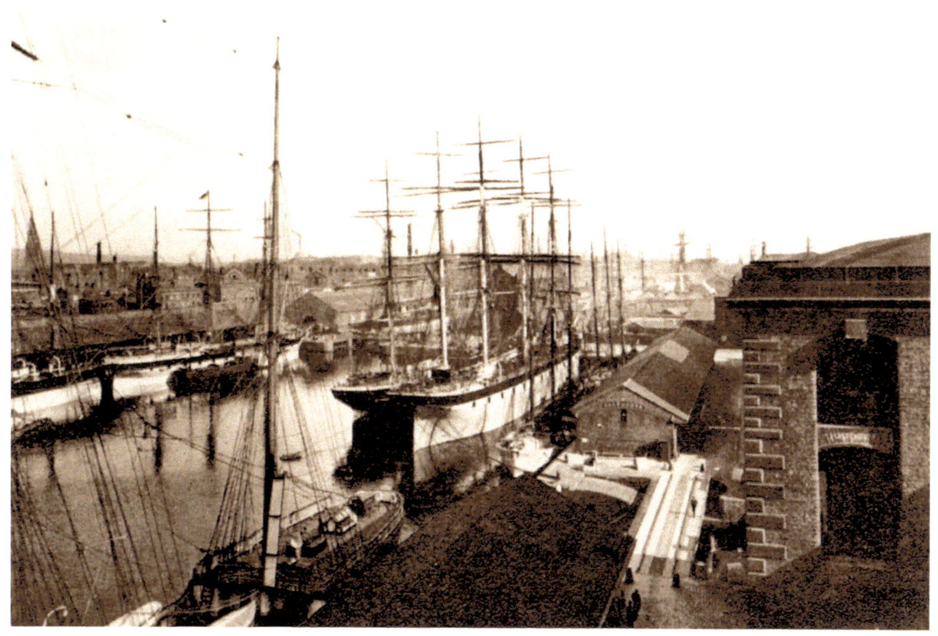

Salthouse Dock in 1907 with the four-masted sailing ship *The Highfields*, built in 1892 for C. W. Kellock & Company of Liverpool. It is connected to Canning Dock to the north, Wapping Dock to the south and Albert Dock to the west. Salthouse Dock was designed by Thomas Steers and was completed after his death by Henry Berry. It was opened in 1753 and the main trade passing through the dock was salt from the Cheshire saltworks. The stone gable and arch is part of a warehouse designed and built by Jesse Hartley.

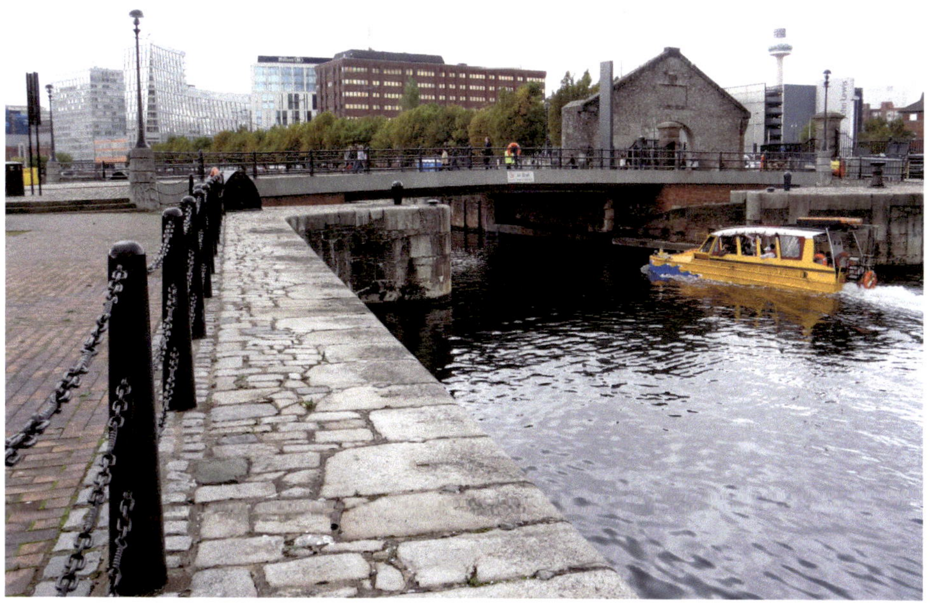

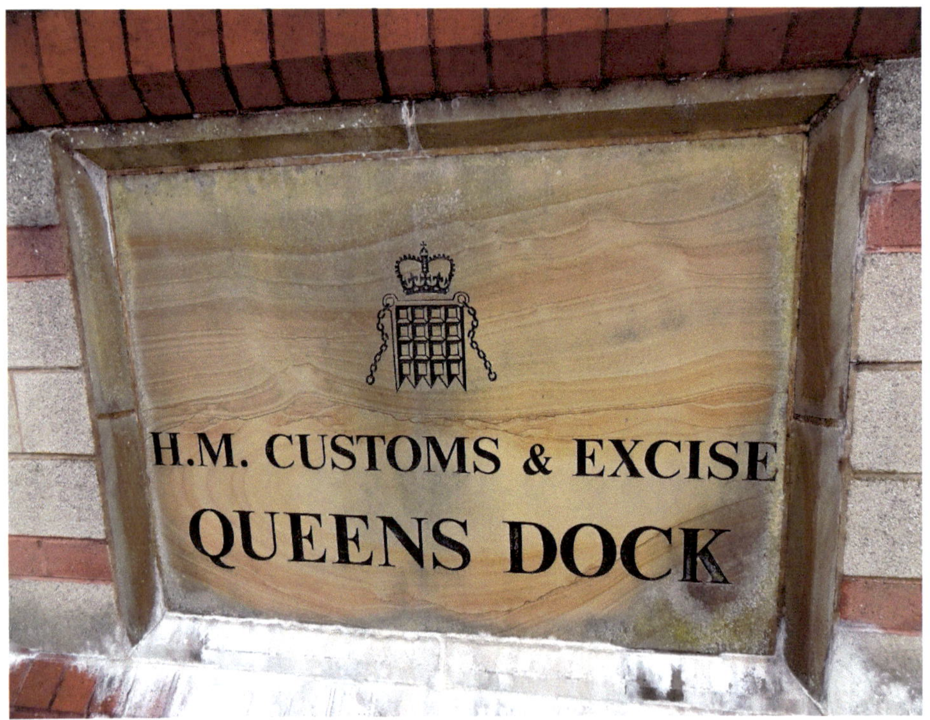

Above and below: Queens Graving Dock is straddled by the HM Customs & Excise building which was constructed over the dock. It was built in 1993 as one of the first new buildings on the south docks site but was threatened with closure in 2011 as part of the government's reorganisation plans of the department.

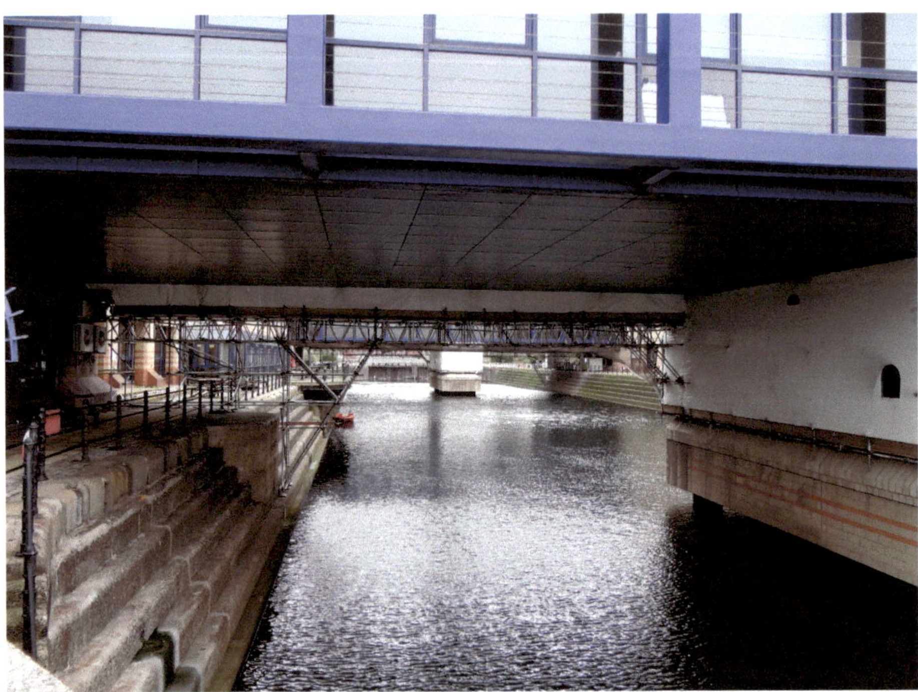

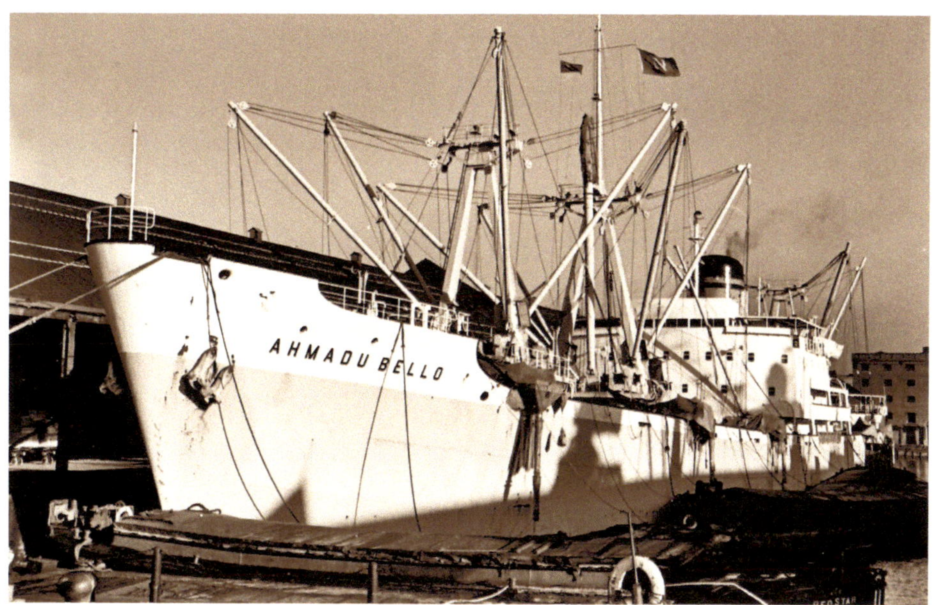

Above: The Nigerian National Shipping Line cargo vessel *Ahmadu Bello* loading cargo in Queen's Dock. She was built by Swan, Hunter & Wigham Richardson at Wallsend-on-Tyne in 1963 and operated on services to West Africa until 1981, when she was sold to Panamanian interests and renamed *Ronson*. She became *Ionian Dream* in 1984 and was sold to shipbreakers at Gadani Beach, where she arrived on 15 May the following year.

Below: Queen's Dock was opened on 17 April 1796 and cost £35,000 to build. It was designed by Henry Barry and extended by John Foster, senior. It consisted of a main basin, two branch docks and a graving dock.

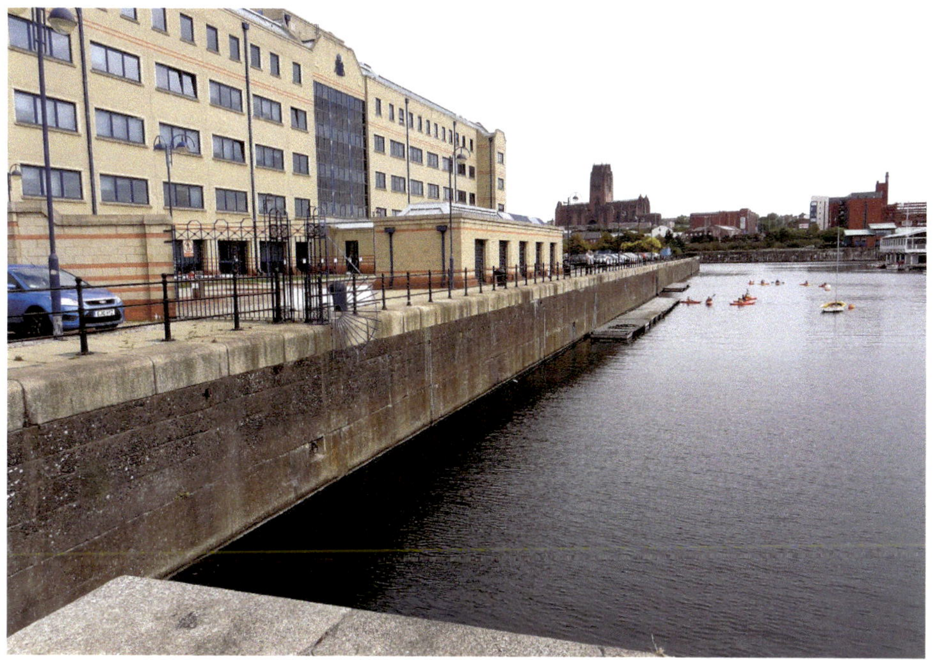

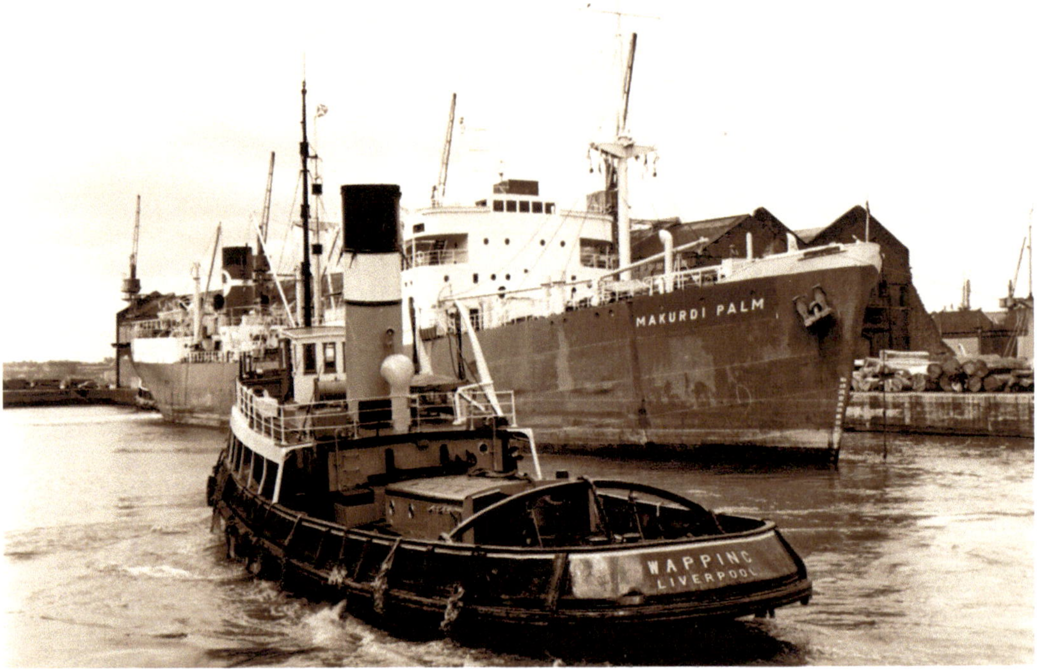

Makurdi Palm was owned by Palm Line and is seen being assisted by the Alexandra tug *Wapping* in Queen's Dock. *Makurdi Palm* was built at Bremerhaven as *Tema Palm* in 1953 and became *Makurdi Palm* in 1960. She was sold to Empresa Naviera Santa of Peru in 1969, renamed *Santamar* and was broken up in 1976.

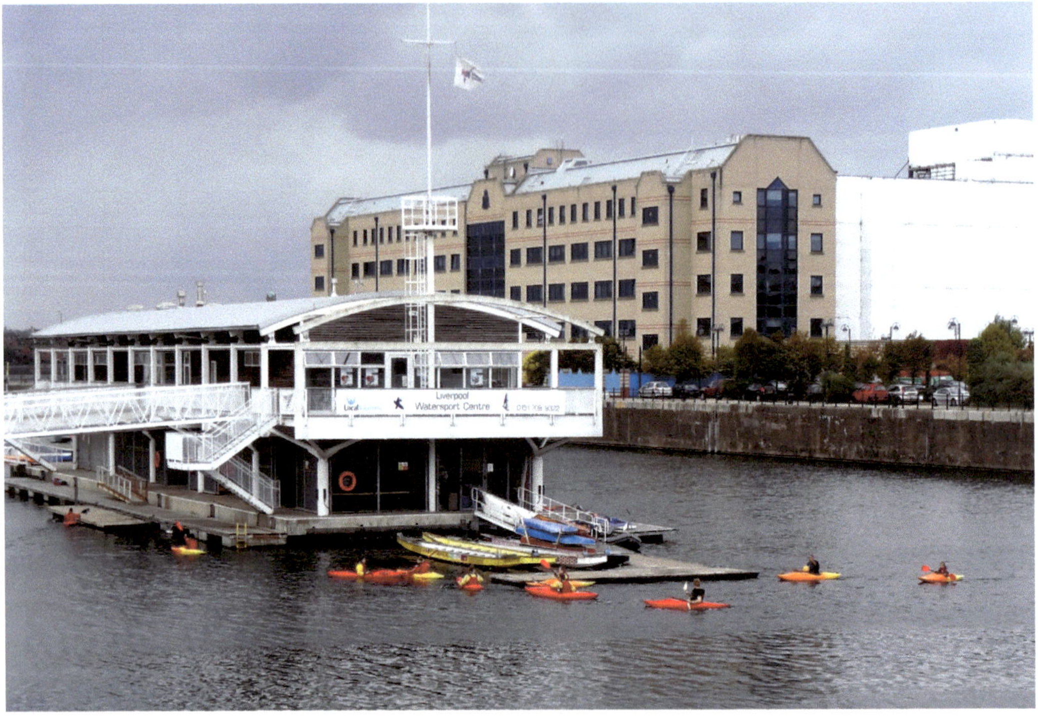

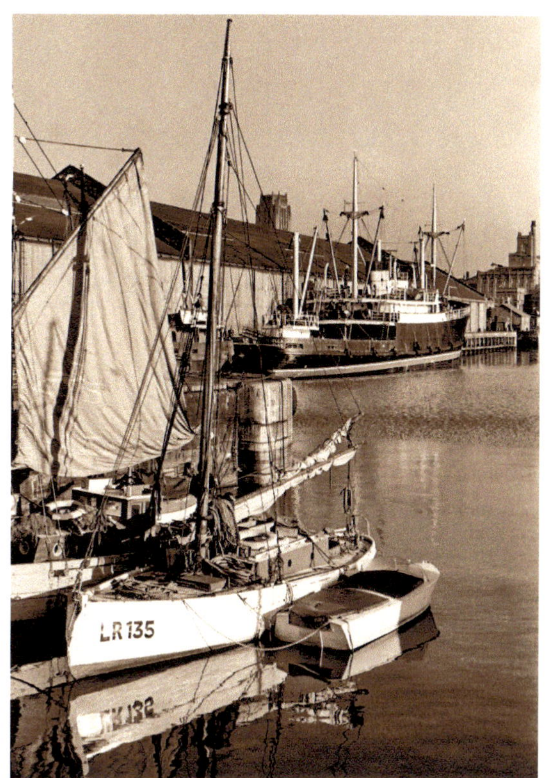

Fenella at the Isle of Man Steam Packet cargo berth in Coburg Dock in 1968. She was built by the Ailsa Shipbuilding Company at Troon in 1951 and was sold in 1973, becoming *Vasso M*, which caught fire and sank in the Mediterranean in May 1978. When opened, Coburg Dock provided direct river access but the passage was eventually in-filled and sealed.

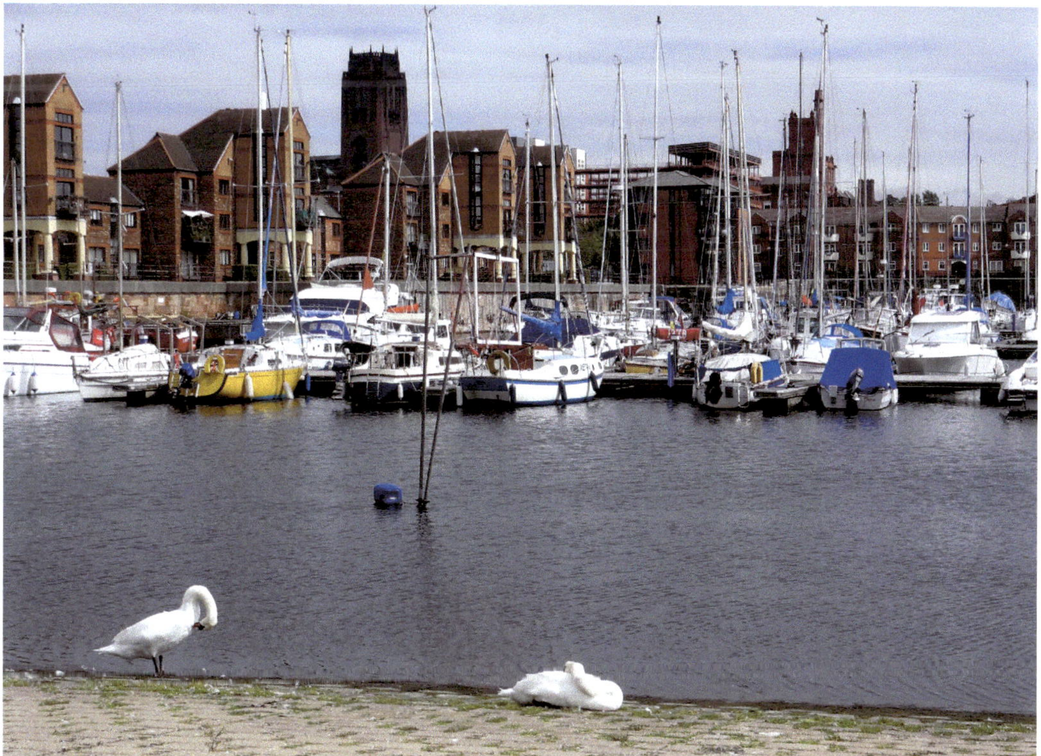

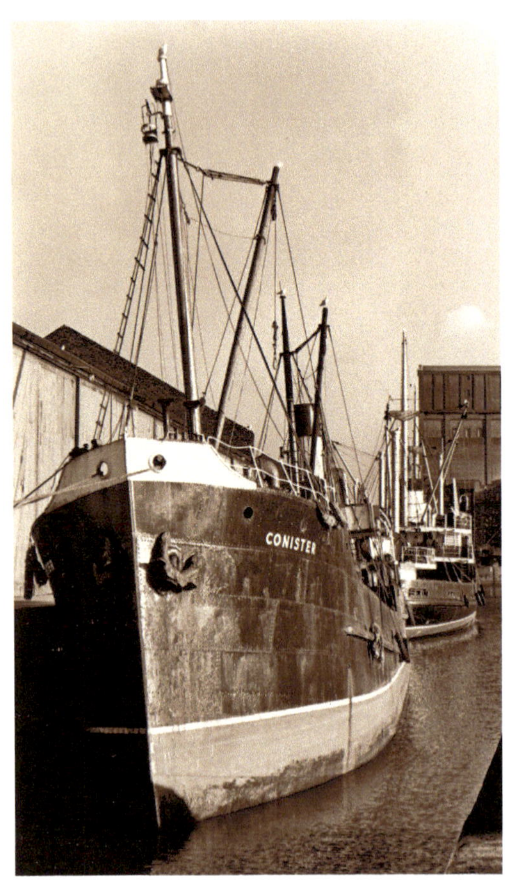

Conister and *Fenella* loading cargo for Douglas, Isle of Man, in Coburg Dock in 1963. *Conister* was built in 1921 as *Abington* for G. T. Gillie & Blair and was acquired by the Isle of Man Steam Packet in 1932, becoming *Conister*. She was broken up at Dalmuir in 1965.

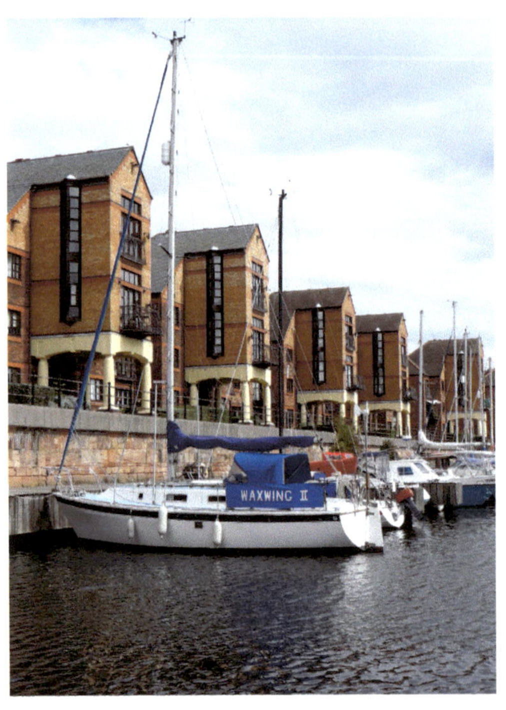

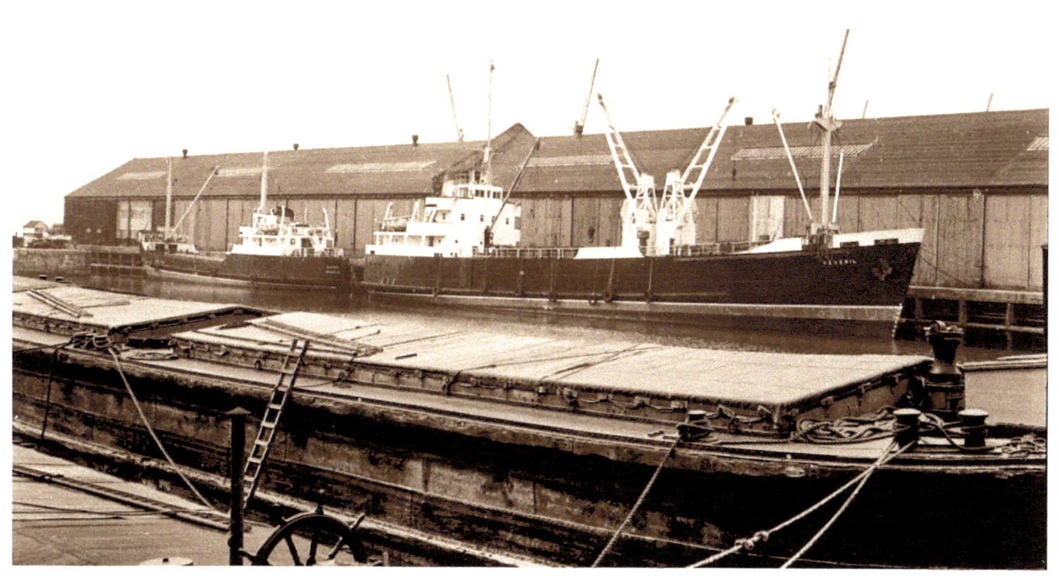

Isle of Man cargo vessels *Ramsey* and *Peveril* loading at Coburg Dock in 1967. *Ramsey* was built in 1964 and became *Hoofort* in 1974, *Boa Entrado* in 1982 and *Arquipelago* in 1990.

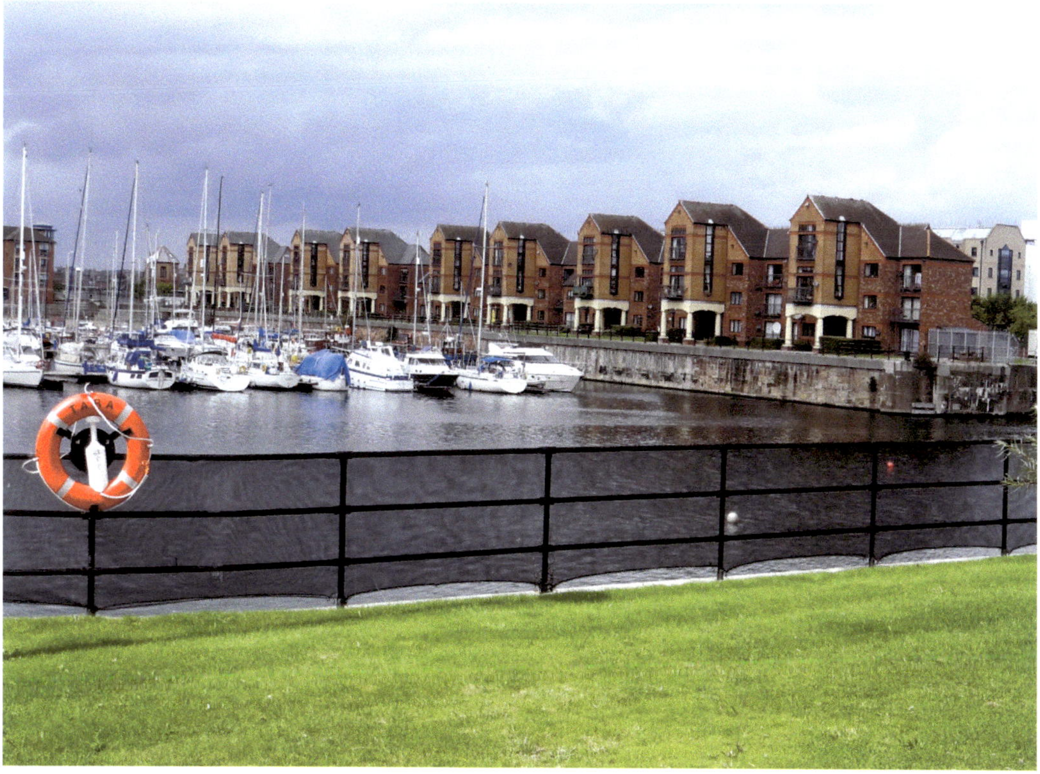

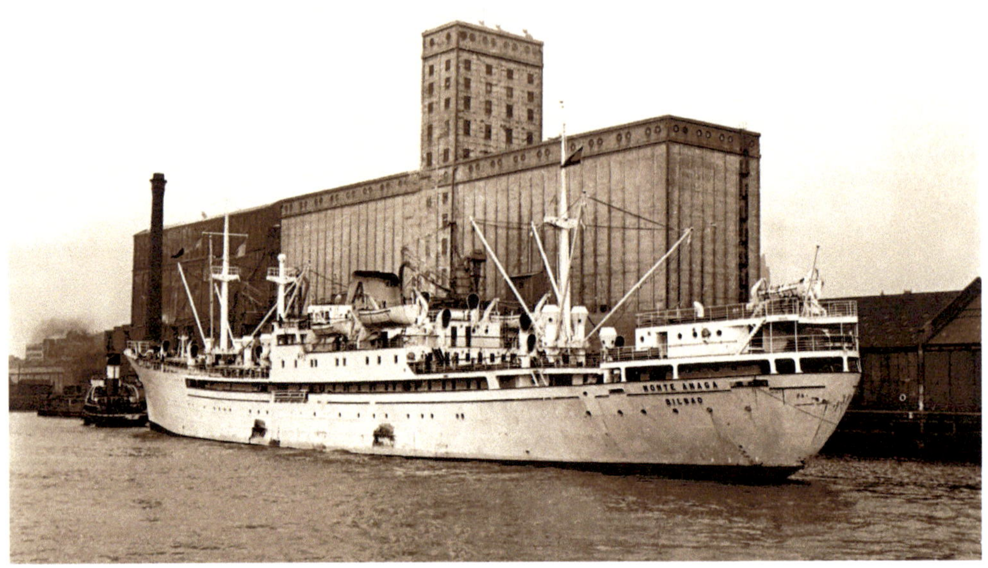

Above: The Aznar Line passenger and cargo liner *Monte Anaga* in Brunswick Dock. She was built in 1959 and operated from Liverpool to the Canary Islands. She was sold in 1975 to the Government of Mexico and used as a training ship, becoming *Primero De Junio.*

Below: Brunswick Dock was designed by Jesse Hartley and was connected to Coburg Dock to the north and Toxteth Dock to the south. It was a base for shipbuilding in the middle of the nineteenth century.

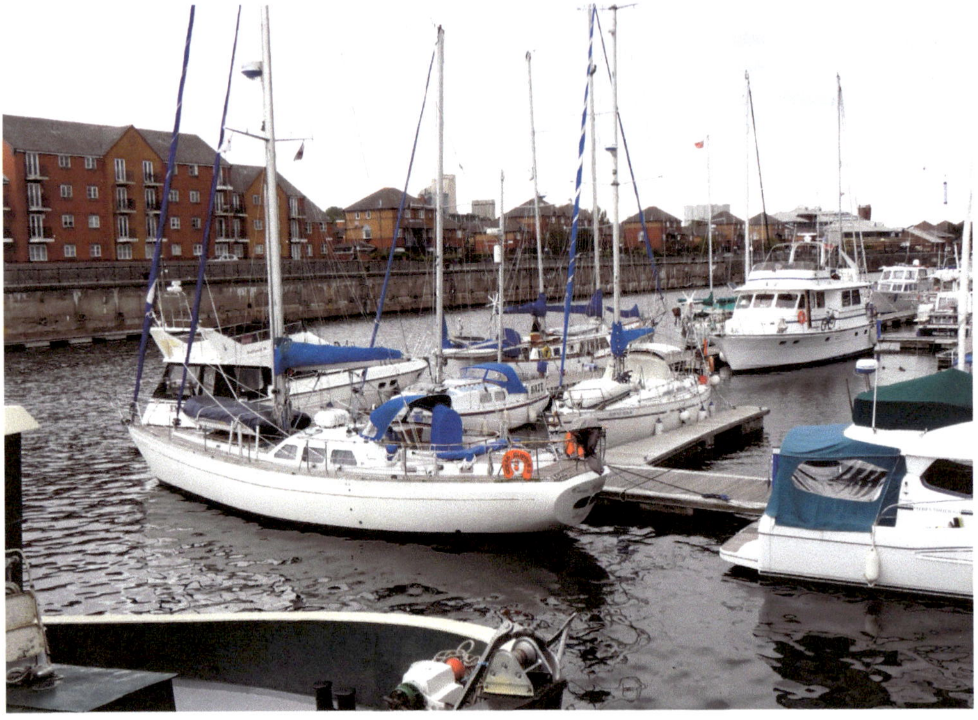

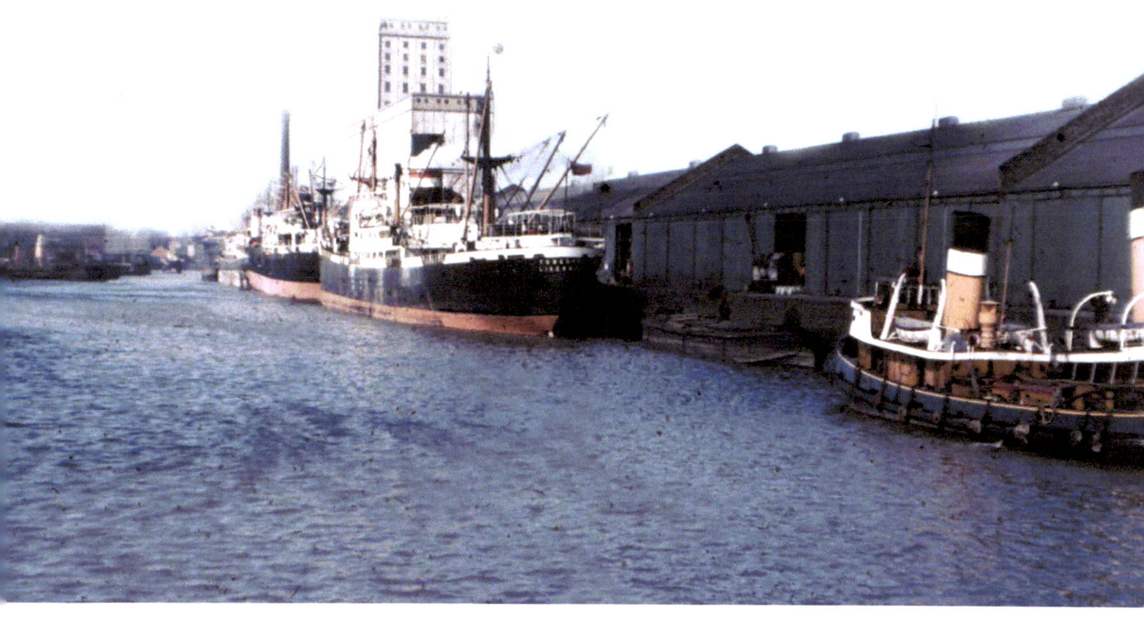

Above: Harrison Line vessels load cargo in Brunswick Dock.

Below: The Alexandra tug *Brocklebank* assists a vessel through the South Docks system.

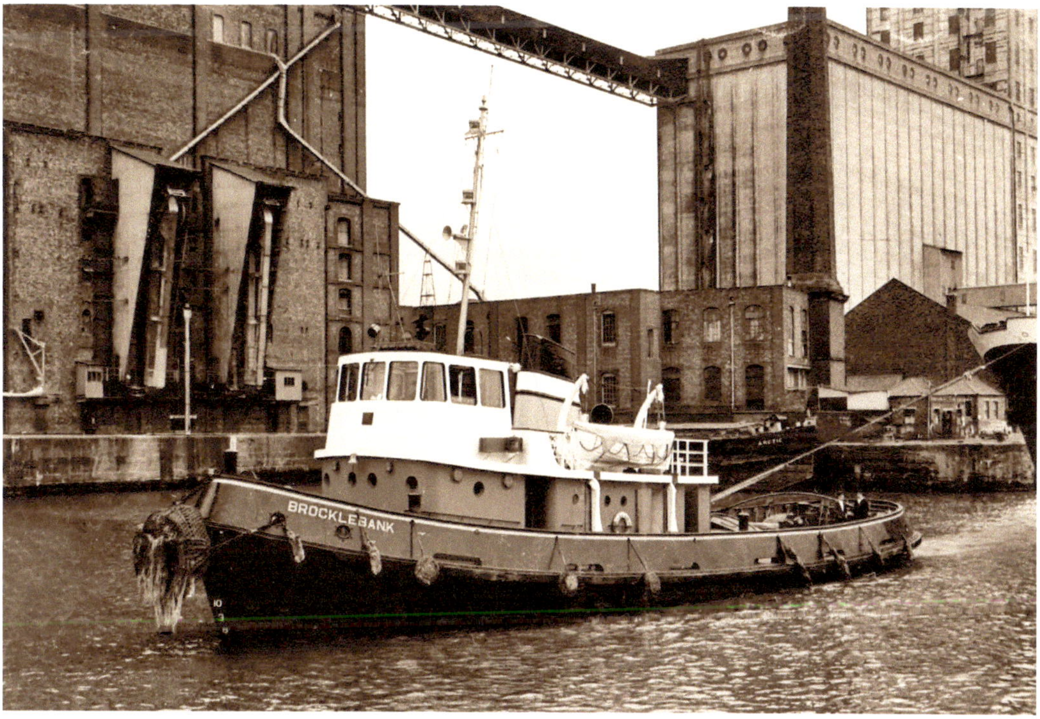

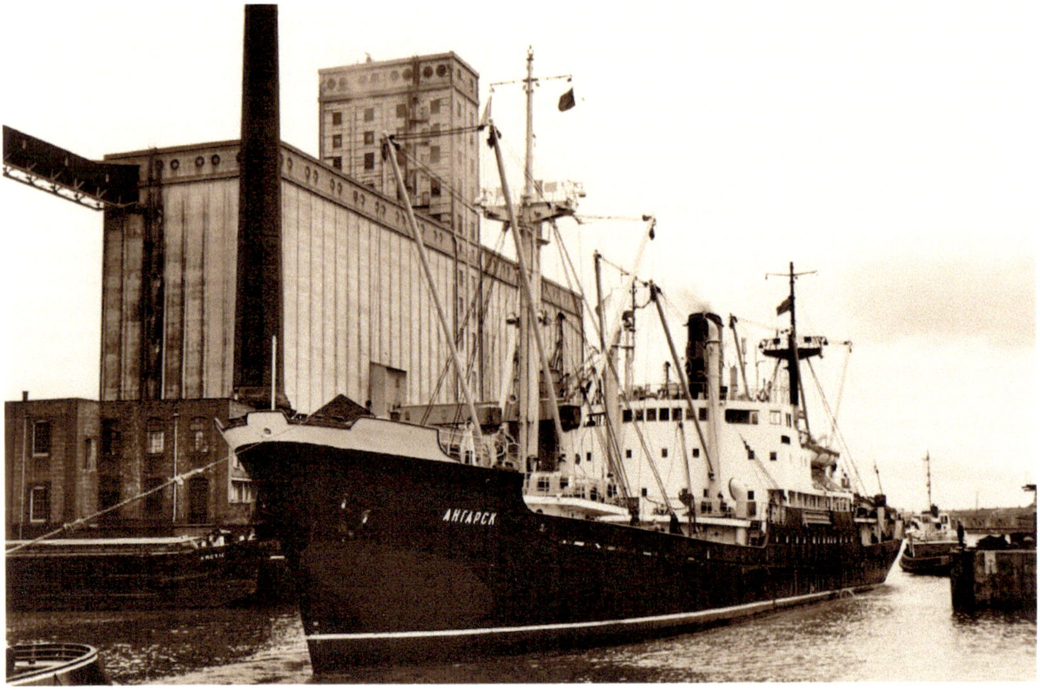

A Russian cargo vessel navigates through the South Docks at Brunswick Dock in 1968.

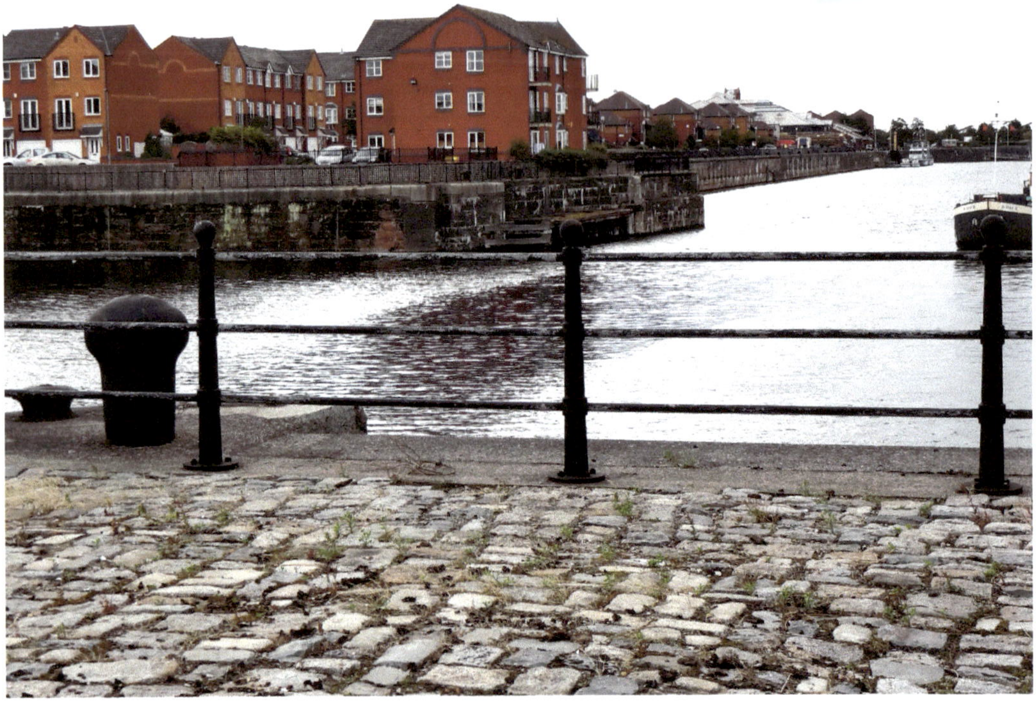

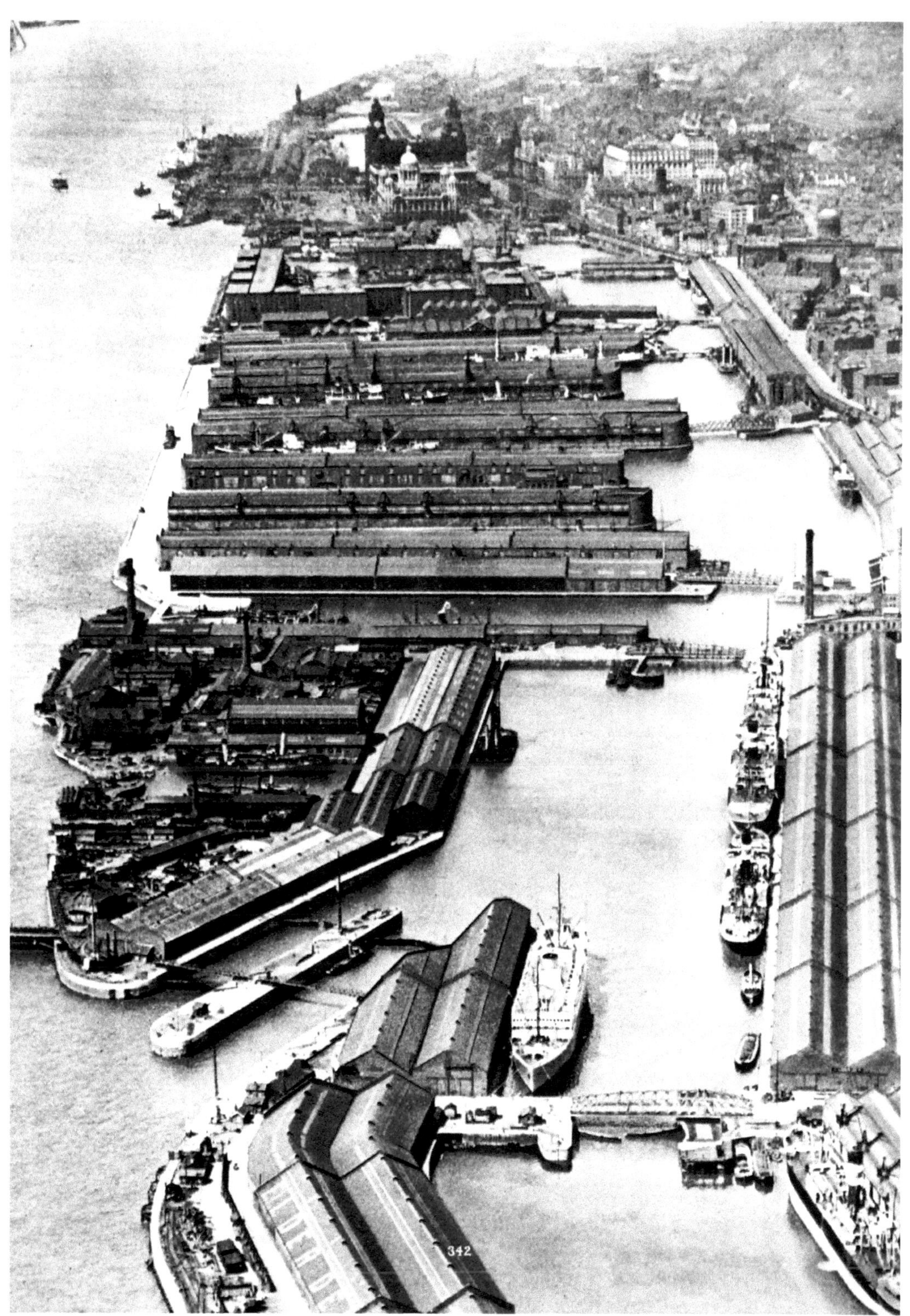

Brunswick Dock.

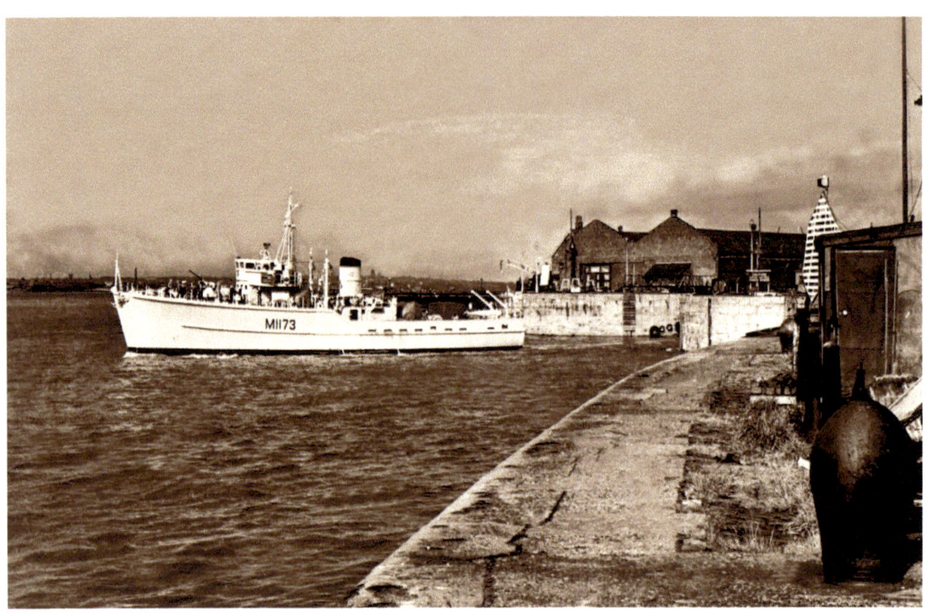

The Ton-class minesweeper HMS *Mersey* sails from Brunswick Dock in the 1960s. She was built by Camper Nicholson as HMS *Pollington* and was launched on 10 October 1957. The class were built to meet the threat of seabed mines laid in shallow coastal waters, rivers, ports and harbours. They were diesel-powered and built of wood and other non-ferromagnetic materials. They were able to navigate in shallow waters and were armed with one Bofors 40 mm gun. The South African members of the class were also equipped with an Oerlikon 20 mm cannon behind the funnel and a M2 Browning machine gun mounted midships. A major reorganisation of the Royal Navy saw her become a base unit for the Royal Naval Reserve at Liverpool and she was renamed HMS *Mersey* in October 1959. She remained in this role until 1975 and was broken up at Cairnryan in 1987. She was the only ship in the Royal Navy named *Pollington*.

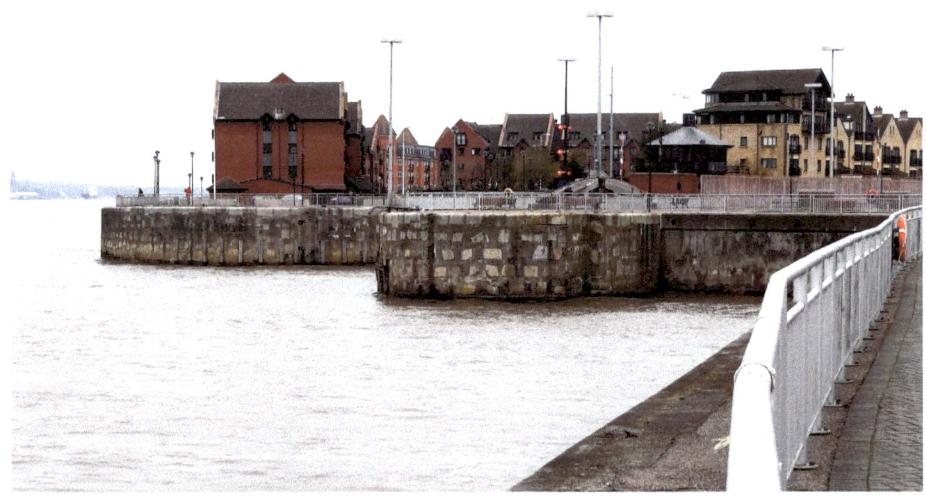

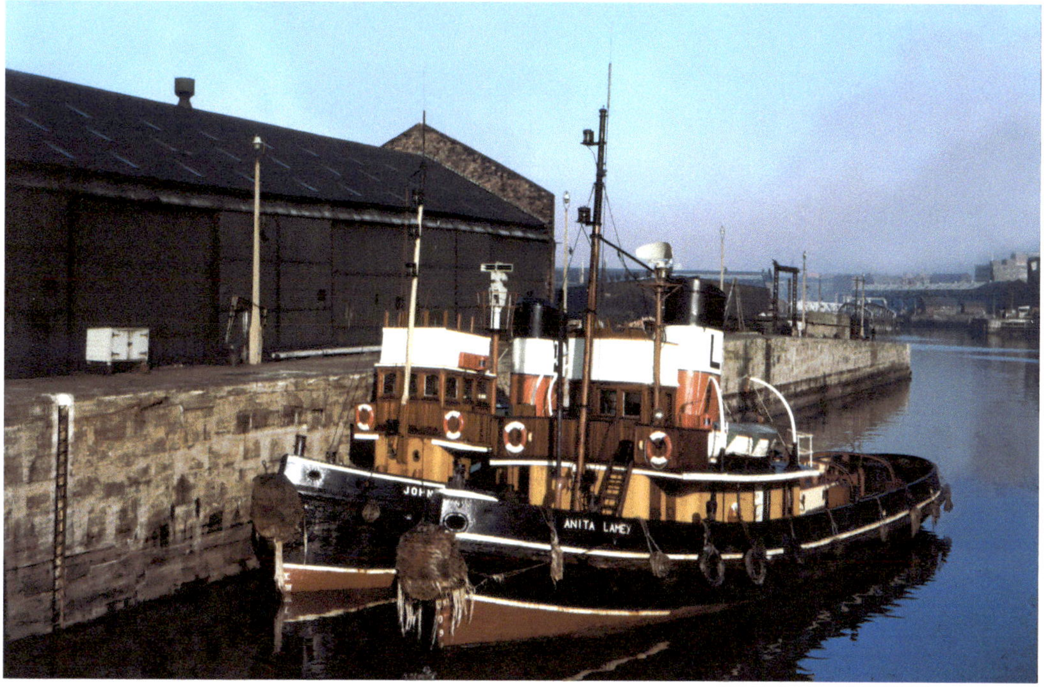

Above: The Lamey tugs *John Lamey* and *Anita Lamey* await orders at Brunswick Dock entrance.

Below: The dock entrance in 2011.

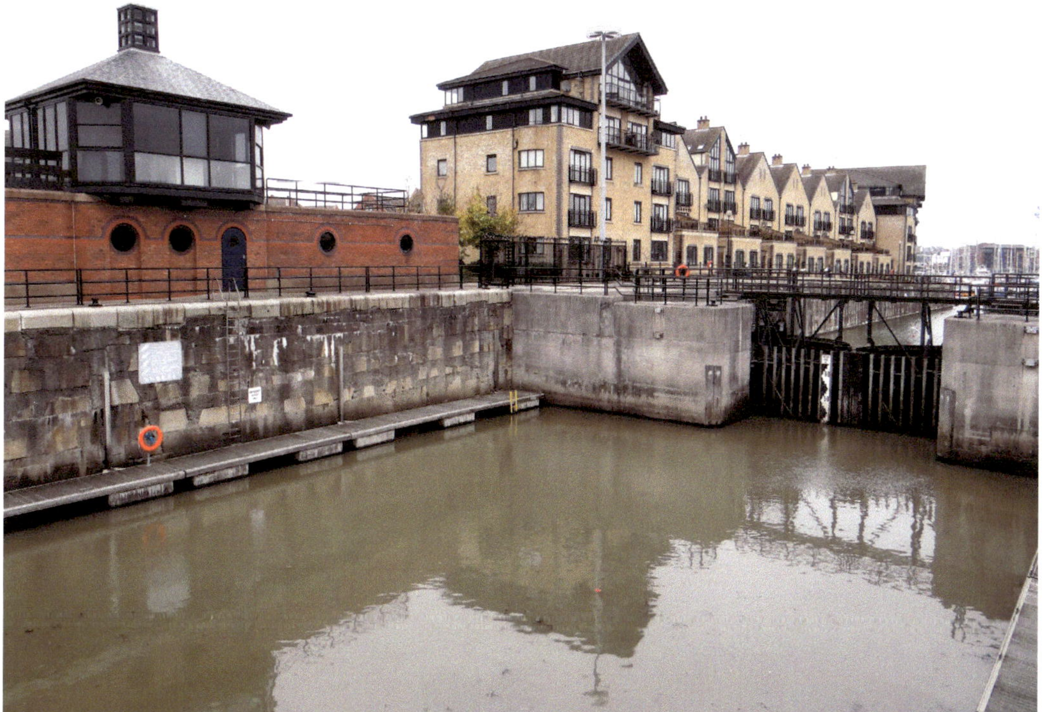

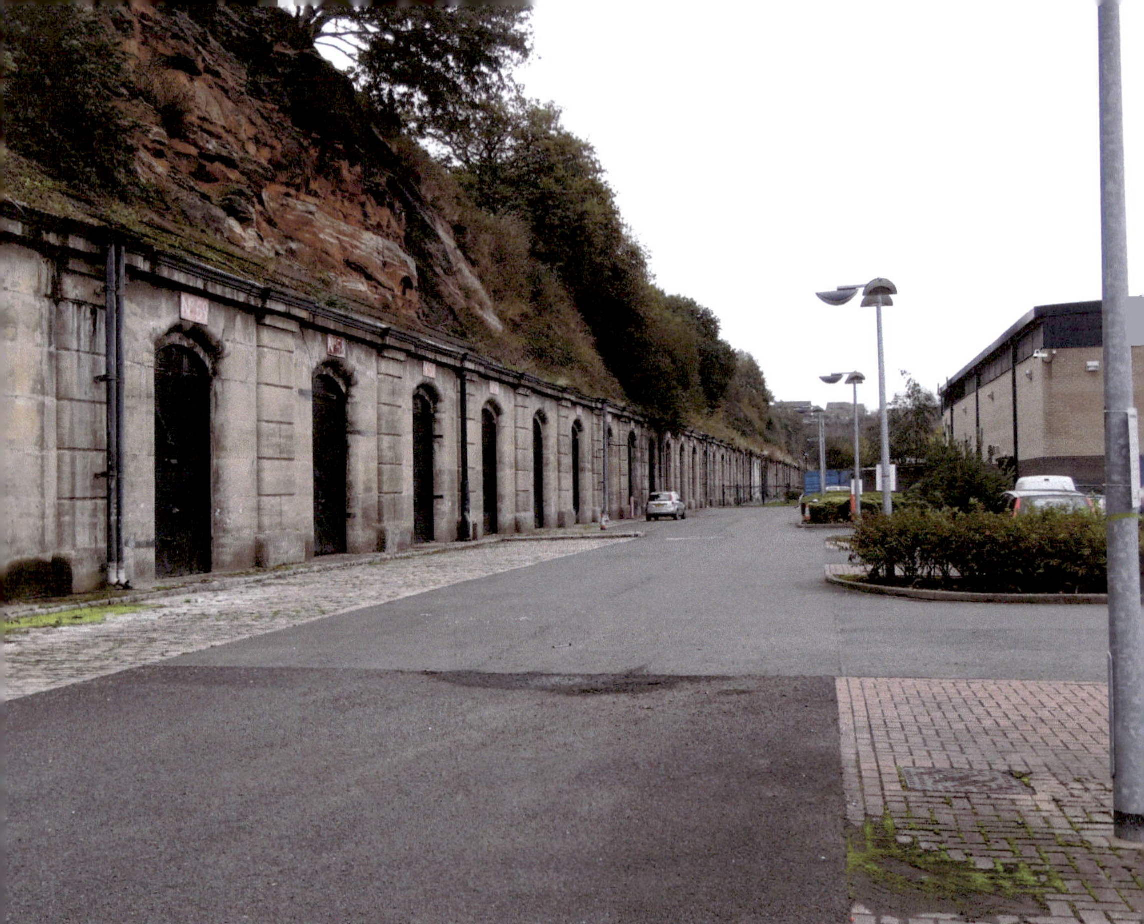

The original storage units at Herculaneum Dock were built into the rock face around the dock.

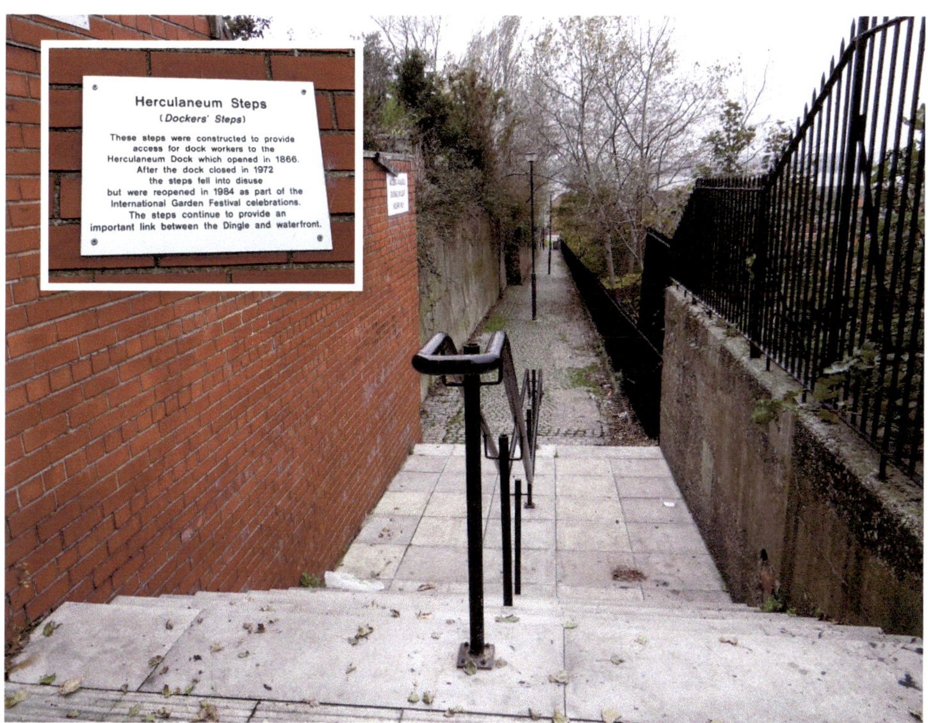

Herculaneum Dock was at the southern end of the Liverpool dock system and was connected to Harrington Dock. It was named after the Herculaneum Pottery Company, which had previously operated from the site. The dock was designed by George Fosbery Lyster and included two graving docks. It was opened in 1866 and a third graving dock was added in 1876. Petroleum was shipped through the dock and in 1878 special casemates were constructed within the sandstone cliffs. Herculaneum Dock was further extended in 1881 and another graving dock was added in 1902. The dock was closed to traffic in 1972 and was filled in during the 1980s and now incorporates a large housing development (*below*).

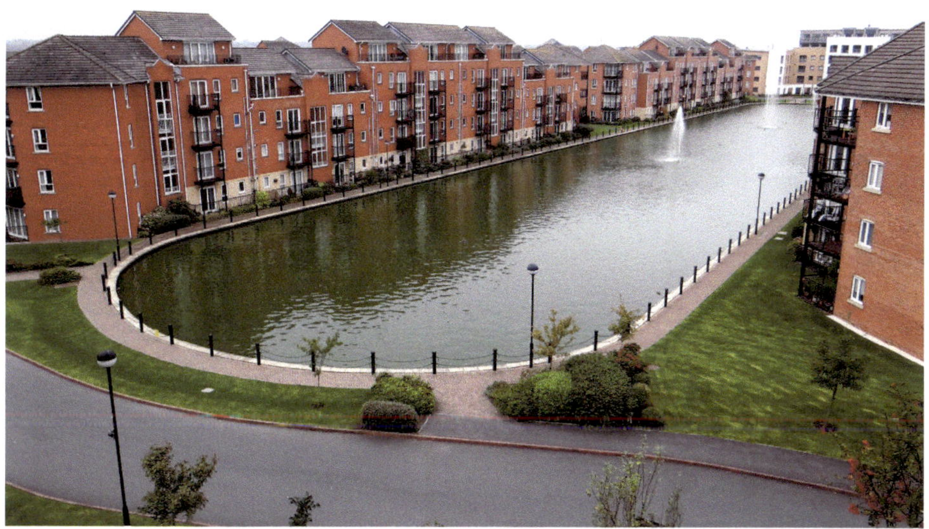

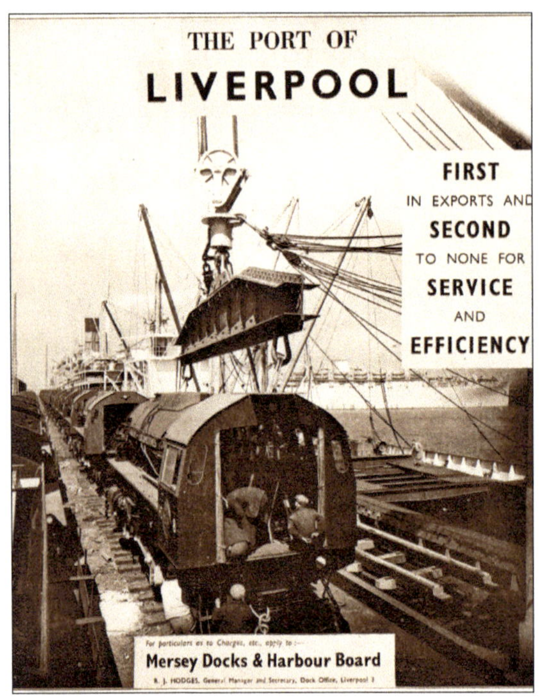

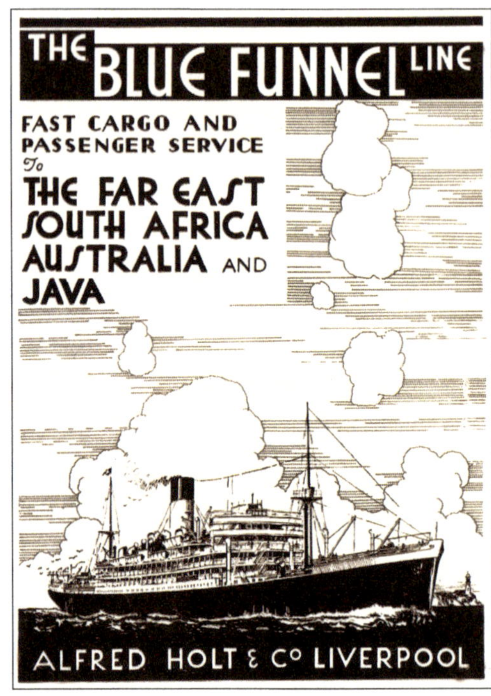

Above left: Port of Liverpool advert, 1949.

Above right: Blue Funnel Line advert.

Left: Rea Towing Company advert.

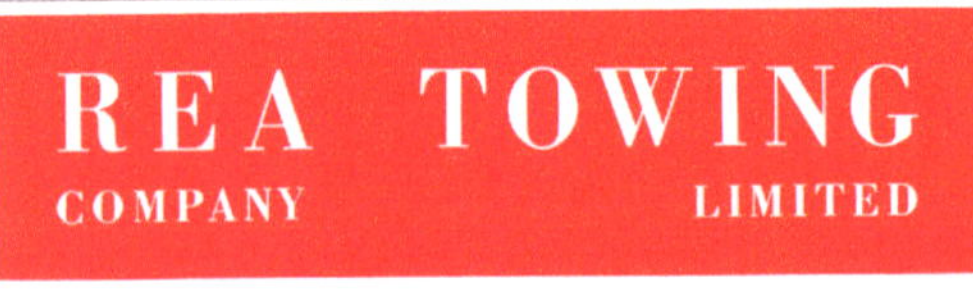

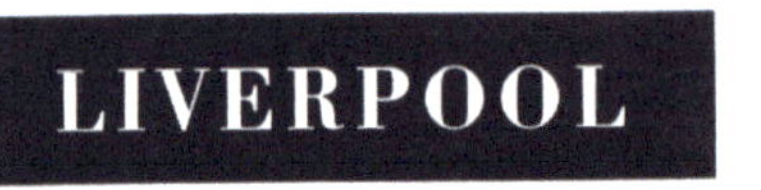

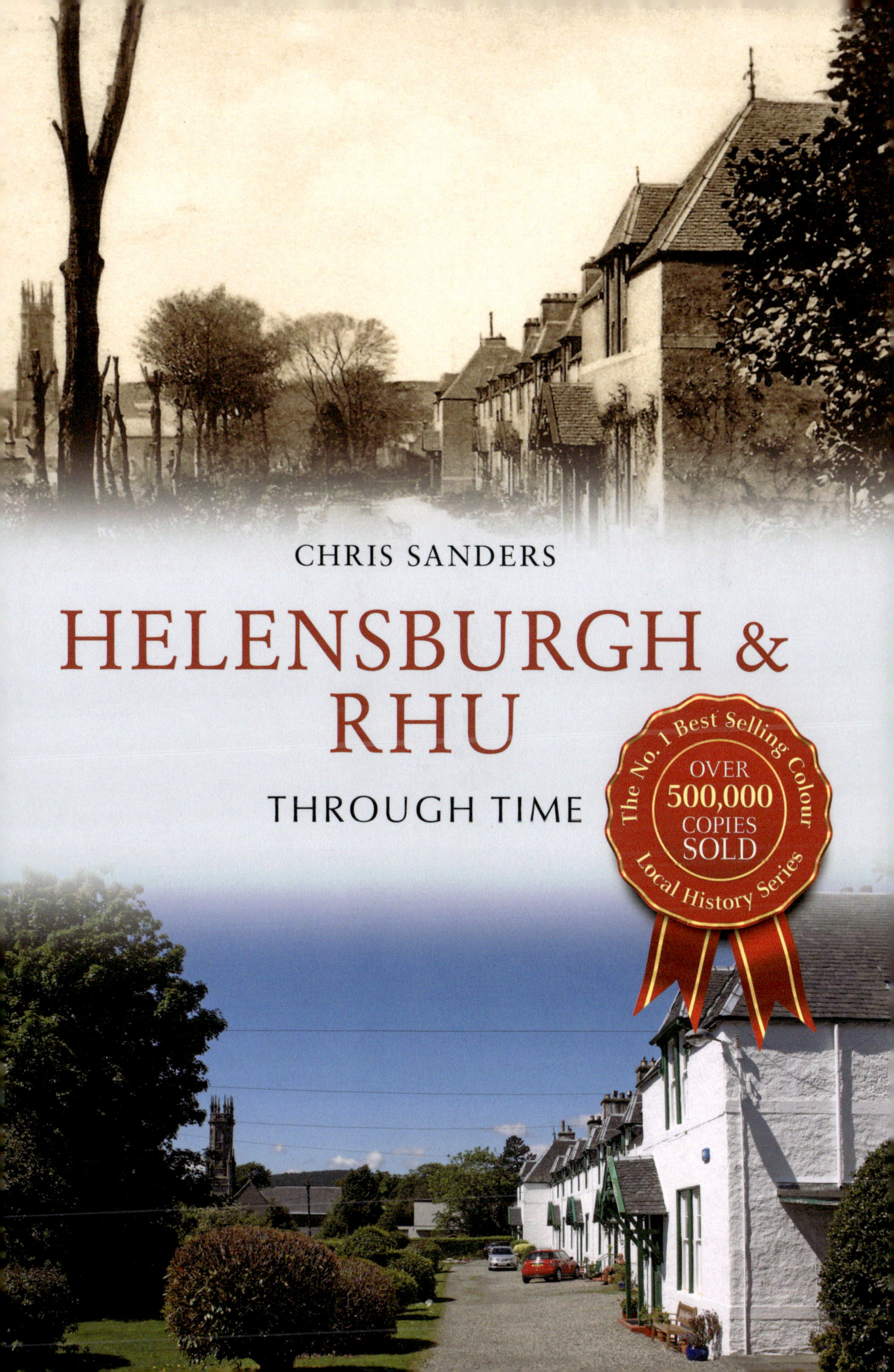

CHRIS SANDERS
HELENSBURGH & RHU
THROUGH TIME
The No. 1 Best Selling Colour
OVER 500,000 COPIES SOLD
Local History Series